JUST
WIN,
BABY

GLENN DICKEY

HARCOURT

BRACE

JOVANOVICH

New York   San Diego   London

JUST WIN, BABY

Al Davis
AND HIS
Raiders

Copyright © 1991 by Glenn Dickey

Requests for permission to make copies of any part of the work should be mailed to:
Permissions Department
Harcourt Brace Jovanovich, Publishers, 8th Floor
Orlando, Florida 32887

Library of Congress Cataloging-in-Publication Data
Dickey, Glenn.
  Just win, baby: Al Davis and his Raiders/Glenn Dickey.
    p.   cm.
  Includes index.
  ISBN 0-15-146580-0
  1. Davis, Al, 1929– . 2. Football—United States—Team owners—
Biography. 3. Football—United States—Coaches—Biography. 4. Los
Angeles Raiders (Football team) I. Title.
GV939.D342D53 1991
796.332′092—dc20 91-20430

Designed by G. B. D. Smith
Printed in the United States of America
First edition
A B C D E

To Nancy and Scott, who give meaning to my life

Contents

An eight-page section of photographs follows page 132.

Acknowledgments

I am grateful to my agent, Mike Hamilburg, who suggested that I write this book, and to my editor, John Radziewicz, who focused my thoughts and writing.

Since Al Davis came to the Raiders in 1963, there have been countless newspaper articles written about him, but I was determined that this book would not be merely a rehash of newspaper clips. Having covered the Raiders for five years and having observed Al Davis then and subsequently, I already had a wealth of material. To further penetrate the mystery of Al Davis, I sought out many people who have witnessed different aspects of the man. It is my pleasant duty here to thank them.

Players, all but one of them retired, were very generous with their time. In alphabetical order, the players I interviewed were Marcus Allen, George Atkinson, Bob Brown, Todd Christensen, Ben Davidson, Lester Hayes, Marv Hubbard, Tom Keating, Jim Otto, Jim Plunkett, Ken Stabler, and Gene Upshaw. The insights of Christensen, Davidson, Hubbard, Keating, Plunkett, and Upshaw were particularly helpful. Former quarterback Lee Grosscup, who served briefly as the club's public relations director, was able to explain clearly and concisely how Davis's offense works.

This book also uses interviews I had previously conducted with players like George Blanda, Clem Daniels, and Daryle Lamonica during their playing careers, as well as interviews with the late Wayne Valley and Don McMahon.

Art Shell, a former player who is now the Raiders head coach, took time from his very busy schedule during the playing season to talk with me. Ollie Spencer, the Raiders offensive line coach and the only assistant Davis retained when he came to the Raiders in 1963, gave me a very informative interview. (Spencer died in April 1991.) Though I was unable to talk to John Madden, I was able to make use of the notes I had from our many conversations during his years as coach of the Raiders.

Three newspaper men who have been very close to Davis— George Ross and Bob Valli in his Oakland years and Mel Durslag in his Los Angeles years—gave me a wealth of information and insight on Davis. The Ross interview spanned an entire afternoon, after which his wife graciously invited me to dinner, though she had to suffer through more talk of Davis during the meal. A face-to-face interview with Durslag was supplemented by telephone conversations; even before I started this book, I had often talked about Davis with Durslag, who remains my journalistic idol. Writer and TV personality Larry Merchant gave me some useful information on Davis from his own research for a book project he had abandoned, and I was also helped by Mark Heisler, who covered the Raiders for the *Los Angeles Times* for five years.

Former coaches Bill Walsh, Sid Gillman, and Hank Stram all contributed their own evaluations of Davis, from both a personal and a professional standpoint. Dr. Robert Albo, a close friend as well as the physician for Davis and his wife, contributed an important look at a side of Davis's personality that is not often seen by the public. Longtime Raiders broadcaster Bill King, who is also close to Davis, gave me another view of Davis's personality.

Bill Robertson, the Los Angeles negotiator, and Bill Cunningham, Robert Nahas, and George Vukasin, who negotiated with Davis from the Oakland side, gave me an idea of what it is like to deal with Davis. Cunningham gave me copies of his own documents related to the 1980 negotiations, some of which were put in testimony at the antitrust trials. Cornell Maier told me the unwritten details of his attempt to make a deal to keep the Raiders in Oakland in 1980, and Joe Bort, then chairman of the Alameda County Board of Supervisors, told me why he opposed that deal.

Jack Brooks gave me precise information about the abortive deal to return the Raiders to Oakland in 1990 and, as a good friend of Davis's, also gave me personal insights about Davis. Dave Dixon provided me with information about an attempt to buy the Raiders and move them to New Orleans in the early 1960s.

Retired judges Leonard S. Dieden and Redmond C. Staats gave me valuable background information on the Warren Wells case and on the legal battle between Valley and Davis, respectively.

I was not able to talk to Davis himself for this book, but in the period during which I covered the Raiders he taught me much of what I know about professional football and also revealed much of himself to me.

Introduction:
Who Is Al Davis?

"I was just a twenty-three-year-old kid wanting to know who was going to negotiate my contract. After all, I'd been talking with Scotty Stirling, the Raiders general manager, before I was traded. I said to Al Davis, 'Who negotiates the contracts?' Davis looked at me and gave me that little rabbit grin. 'Young man, let there be no mistake about this—I do everything here. I hire people and I fire people, and I decide how many wastebaskets we'll have in this office.'"

—FORMER RAIDERS DEFENSIVE TACKLE TOM KEATING,
ON HIS FIRST MEETING WITH AL DAVIS

Al Davis is synonymous with the Raiders, the ultimate outsider directing a team of outlaws. The sinister image he has deliberately cultivated looms over them, whether he is stalking the sidelines at practice in his trademark silver and black or is sitting in his private box high above the field. The Raiders have had different players, different coaches, and different locations over the years, but their style of play and their image remain the same because of one constant—Al Davis.

"It doesn't make any difference who the head coach is," says Hank Stram, the CBS analyst and former Kansas City Chiefs coach. "The Raiders personality is always the same."

There are no more than four significant nonplaying figures in a football franchise: the owner, the general manager, the personnel director, and the head coach. For the Raiders, Davis acts officially in the first two capacities and unofficially in the other two, which makes him unique in the present National Football League. Except for Cincinnati Bengals owner Paul Brown, who was a coach for many years, Davis is the only owner who has *ever* coached.

Davis makes all the important decisions for the team, including where it will play. Art Shell is now the head coach, but he coaches the players Davis has selected and uses the style of play that Davis has developed over the years. Davis has a heavy influence on game plans, as he has had with every Raiders coach but Mike Shanahan, and he still coaches on the practice field. His presence there is felt.

"At Santa Rosa we had two practice fields," Gene Upshaw, the Raiders Hall of Fame guard, remembered, "but Davis would always be there when you were doing a one-on-one drill. You'd look up and he'd be right behind you. You'd never see him leave. Even when I had my back turned, I could tell when Davis had come on the practice field. I didn't have to look. The intensity would change, the coaches would change, *everything* would change when he came in. We used to wish for league meetings, so he wouldn't be there."

Davis is the most talked about personality in football, although he himself talks to only a handful of carefully selected writers around the country, and his rare television appearances seem carefully orchestrated to give him an opportunity to propagandize. The more secretive he becomes, the more others want to penetrate his invisible shield. Using his wits and acting alone, he has beaten the NFL establishment, and that has a great fascination even for those who dislike him.

I'm a Davis watcher. Originally it was by assignment, as the

San Francisco Chronicle's beat writer on the Raiders for five years, but after I became a columnist for the paper in 1971 I was a Davis watcher by choice. He was easily the most fascinating sports figure in an area not wanting in fascinating sports figures (owners like Charles Finley, players like Willie Mays and Rick Barry).

As a result, I've seen Davis from different vantage points, first as a friend and later as an adversary. It has given me an unusual perspective on the man. There have been times when I've defended him vehemently, and even more times when I've wanted to wring his neck. I've seen him evolve from a young man who talked to many people into an older man who has withdrawn into himself and allows only a very few to peek inside; from a man who was always a fierce competitor into one who seems to go out of his way to spite others and to whom humiliation, not just victory, seems the goal.

Whatever my role, I've spent endless time observing Davis and talking about him with others. Some discussions are long-standing, such as the one I've been having for a quarter of a century now with Tom Keating; others begin all the time, whenever people hear about my experiences with Davis. Everybody wants to get inside his mind to figure out why he acts the way he does.

Within his profession, the men at the very top talk to and about him. Bill Walsh, for instance, worked a year as a Raiders assistant in the 1960s before going on to great success and fame as the coach and general manager of the San Francisco 49ers. While I was collaborating with Walsh on a book, never did a working day pass without a phone call to him from Al Davis.

Walsh's methods were quite different from Davis's—everybody's are, after all—but Walsh has great admiration for him. "He's relentless, and as ruthless as he has to be," Walsh said. "He's a tireless worker, though I'm not sure work would be the proper word. I'm sure he doesn't look at it as work because he enjoys it so much. It's his life. He's absolutely the first man you'd choose to be on your side in any kind of competition. Even after he's defied the NFL, if owners thought he could be on their side they'd want him."

Of course, Davis doesn't want to be on any side but his own. Even with a man he respects as much as he does Walsh, he shares little of consequence. His many phone calls are made to pick the brains of others, not to disclose information. Those who have worked with him have been permitted only brief glimpses into the man. "He was never a guy who talked about his goals or himself," said Scotty Stirling, who was the Raiders general manager in the 1960s.

What manner of man is this? He can be shrewd, imitative, generous, vindictive, vain, insecure. Choose your adjective. They all apply at one time or another. He can be respected and despised, shunned and cultivated—often by the same people.

He has devoted his life to the Raiders. "He has nothing else," said one of his former coaches, John Madden. He has a very narrow focus, but in his chosen area he has an amazing ability to analyze tactics, evaluate performance, and almost predict what others will do.

A shy man, he hides behind an image he has carefully constructed over the years, so it's often difficult to tell exactly where image and reality merge. One clue: his accent. When he's trying to make a point in a serious talk, his accent is strongly reminiscent of the Brooklyn in which he spent his childhood. When he's trying to con, it's southern, a legacy from the time he coached in the South. But his conning doesn't mean lying. When I was close to Davis, I observed that he would use the politician's tricks of not quite answering the question or of making a point that would lead someone to the wrong conclusion. He never lied to me, nor did I ever hear him lie to another person. I thought at the time that he had too much pride in his intellect to think he had to lie.

With his friends Davis feels free to be himself, but the public Davis is always concerned with his image, and he will play that image to the hilt.

I collided with that image as far back as 1965, while covering a Raiders game with the Buffalo Bills in Oakland. That day the Raiders outplayed the Bills (who went on to become the AFL champions) before losing on a Buffalo touchdown in the final minute. Only three reporters, including me, were in the Raiders dressing room after the game. Davis was sitting on a stool in the middle of the room, his head in his hands. The three of us walked over to him. None of us wanted to be the first to ask a question, but I finally broke the ice. Davis looked up at me and said, "Who the fuck are you?"

Since I had gone on a Raiders road trip the year before and had talked at great length with Davis, he knew very well who I was. He knew who all the reporters were—there weren't many of them writing about the Raiders in those days—but his answer was supposed to impress on us how crushed he was by the loss.

His theatrics over, Davis proceeded to answer our questions.

A better example of Davis's love of melodrama occurred in the 1967 exhibition season, after the Raiders had lost to the Denver Broncos on a high-school field in North Platte, Nebraska. Davis again sat with his head in his hands, long after the stands had emptied, and a photographer caught his pose. The photograph became a favorite of Davis's, and it hung in the Raiders offices for years.

It was only a pose. Davis has never been very concerned about wins and losses in the exhibition season, only about the team's development. He was disappointed over the loss, but hardly crushed. I know, because we talked about it on the plane trip home.

His love of the melodramatic has not abated. In the spring of 1990, Andy Herrera, a former Raiders limited partner and the father of John Herrera, who still works for the club, died in the Bay Area. Davis arrived at the last moment for the church services, in the inevitable black limousine. Dressed in silver and black, he walked all the way to the front of the church before he sat down. Nobody could miss seeing him.

As part of the image, Davis likes to portray himself as a

man so tough that he doesn't care what others think about him. "Al is the only man I know who likes to make people think he's worse than he actually is," said his Los Angeles newspaper friend Mel Durslag. In my early relationship with Davis he told me many times, "I don't care if people like me. I just want them to respect me, even fear me."

There are many contradictions in Davis's behavior. His friends, for instance, cite his loyalty. "If you're his friend, he can't do enough for you," said Dr. Bob Albo, who is one of those friends. Davis has spent large sums of money on hospital care for his friends and has donated to their favorite charities, without publicity. Another example: when the Raiders played an exhibition game in London in July of 1990, Davis paid the way for several former players and their wives, as well as for other friends, including his first pro coach, Sid Gillman, and Gillman's wife.

Yet he can be Sicilian in his wrath if a friend or associate does something to displease him. Raiders executive Al Lo-Casale is almost embarrassing in his devotion to Davis (once even threatening to punch me because I had criticized Davis in my *Chronicle* column). But when LoCasale made a mess of ticket distribution during the Raiders' first year in Los Angeles, in 1982, Davis cut him dead. LoCasale was removed from any connection with the football operation, and only recently has there been any thaw in Davis's attitude toward him.

Davis has many alliances, from Bill Walsh to attorney Joseph Alioto, men with whom he shares professional interests or goals. His inner circle is much smaller, and his friends pay an exacting price. Davis's friends do not question him—not if they want to remain friends.

Davis's behavior strikes me as remarkably similar to that of Frank Sinatra, which is probably more than coincidence. "What does it mean if rich men use their money to help friends?" one former player said to me. "That's just a statement they like to make about themselves. It doesn't cost them anything important."

One episode that drew respect even from Davis's enemies

came in 1977, when he almost willed his wife back from death after she'd suffered a near-fatal heart attack. It is hard to reconcile that Davis with the one who has spent so little time with his wife in recent years, since she has chosen to remain in their Oakland-area home while he spends most of his time with the team in Los Angeles. Davis can make the dramatic gesture, but day-to-day consideration is beyond him. His one son, Mark, became a ball boy at the Raiders camp to see something of his father. Davis argued that it was the quality of the time he spent with his son that mattered, not the amount. Mark Davis apparently didn't agree. He was estranged from his father for years. They speak now, but are not close.

Davis is known for his confrontations, but in fact he does not like to confront anyone personally. Even his negotiations are usually conducted through another party; for years he used LoCasale as his front man to press his arguments for contract concessions from the Oakland Coliseum.

After five years of writing articles and columns that almost always praised or defended Davis, I criticized him in 1972, when Wayne Valley, one of the Raiders owners, sued Davis for control of the club. Instead of challenging me, Davis simply stopped talking to me and tried to avoid any personal contact. Because I spent so much time around the Raiders, these efforts were often amusing. One time, for instance, he got into the press-box elevator at the Coliseum with Kansas City Chiefs owner Lamar Hunt. Spotting me at the back of the elevator, he turned to the front and spoke over his shoulder to Hunt. At other times, seeing me walking toward him to the dressing-room hallway, he would thrust whoever he was with in my direction so that we couldn't come face to face. Finally Davis had LoCasale tell my managing editor that I couldn't travel on the Raiders team plane any more, because on the previous trip I had sat up front pretending to read a book while trying to overhear a conversation between Davis and John Madden.

"How do you deal with these clowns?" my managing editor asked.

Jack Brooks, a Raiders limited partner who is close to Davis, was his intermediary during negotiations in 1989 and 1990 that attempted to return the club to Oakland from Los Angeles. Brooks claims that Davis has always been straightforward with him. "If Al says he'll do something, he does it," Brooks told me. "He's never been the slightest bit devious with me."

Really? Although it was obvious from the start that the negotiations with Oakland had the purpose of bringing the Raiders back, Davis for months instructed Brooks to pretend that the talks were only general ones about getting an expansion team for Oakland. "That was ridiculous," said George Vukasin, president of the Oakland Coliseum Board. "We all knew what team we were talking about. We'd already had a committee working to get an expansion franchise, so we didn't need to talk to Davis about that. From the beginning, the eleven points we discussed included a Raiders Hall of Fame and a relocation fee for the Raiders. Neither would have been part of an expansion team package."

At times Davis can be surprisingly soft in dealing with an employee who has outlived his usefulness. Lee Grosscup, a former Raiders quarterback, was a public relations director for the club in 1968. Early the next year Davis suggested to Grosscup that he find another job. "But for three months I kept coming to the office and I kept getting my paycheck," Grosscup remembered. "Finally I got a job with ABC-TV and left, but Al never really fired me."

At other times, Davis can be brutal. When he fired Ray Malavasi as an assistant coach, Malavasi left the office to find that his company car had already been removed from the parking lot.

Davis is known as a "players' owner" because of the freedom he gives his players, and even Fred Biletnikoff and George Blanda, who fought him while they were with the team, had Davis as their presenter when they were inducted into the Pro Football Hall of Fame. Yet he has often been very harsh toward players who, knowingly or unknowingly, have displeased him, as have, for example, Marcus Allen, Todd Christensen,

Lester Hayes, and Vann McElroy in just the last few years.

Even his vaunted generosity—some NFL owners openly call him crazy for spending so much money in pursuit of his Super Bowl rings—has its limits, as players from Ben Davidson to Steve Beuerlein have discovered in contract negotiations.

The one constant has been his drive to win, and that he has displayed in the courtroom as well as on the playing field. Davis likes to talk of "dominating" his environment, and to a large extent he *has* dominated it. Whether as coach, commissioner, or owner, he has been able to force his will on others. He fought successfully for control of the Raiders, and, in an epic struggle, he defied the entire National Football League to move the team to Los Angeles, radically changing the face of pro football.

Davis has put his stamp on the Raiders even to the point of selecting the team's colors. "He was very impressed by Army's uniforms," recalled George Ross, the retired sports editor of the *Oakland Tribune,* who was close to Davis in the early days. "He thought those uniforms made the players look bigger than they were, and that's the way it worked with the Raiders. It's been a good color combination for them."

Silver and black is not a subtle combination, and the Raiders are not a subtle operation. Davis prefers propaganda to public relations. He has constantly hammered the media and the public with the same theme: the Raiders' outstanding record over the years. His slogans—"Pride and Poise" and "Commitment to Excellence"—have remained throughout his time with the club. He doesn't care that the most ardent of Raiders fans sometimes tire of his one-note campaigns.

When he appears in public Davis talks chiefly in slogans, to the point of embarrassment. In February 1991, in presenting John Madden for induction into the Bay Area Sports Hall of Fame, he spent twenty minutes—far longer than Madden himself talked—in self-serving praise of the Raiders, dragging out all their statistics and records. As he talked the dinner guests squirmed in their seats. Some made conspicuous exits, others hissed or yelled, "Sit down, Al." Davis didn't upstage Madden, but he had certainly tried.

Recently Davis has been repeating another theme: the Green Bay Packers were the team of the 1960s, the Miami Dolphins and Pittsburgh Steelers the teams of the 1970s, and the San Francisco 49ers the team of the 1980s, but the Raiders are the team for all decades, having been to the Super Bowl in each of those three decades. That slogan looks good for at least another ten years.

The Dallas Cowboys call themselves "America's Team," but the Raiders could perhaps better claim that title. Everywhere across the United States are found those who love the Raiders, and even more who hate them. "I remember one time I was talking to Ted Kwalick," said longtime Raiders announcer Bill King. "Ted had played for the 49ers and in the World Football League, so he'd been around, but he was just amazed at the reaction the Raiders got from fans on the road. 'This team never plays just another game,' he said."

Davis goes his own way, always. The Raiders do not belong to a computer system to evaluate college players, one of only three teams in the NFL (the San Francisco 49ers and the Denver Broncos are the other two) who do not. Davis prefers to rely on his own scouts and an unofficial network of friends and cohorts around the country. The Raiders are the only team that does not belong to NFL Charities. And when Davis decided to move his team from Oakland to Los Angeles, he didn't bother to seek the approval of the other league owners. Fully knowing what it would cost him in time and effort, he defied both the owners and the league commissioner, Pete Rozelle. What would have been a last resort for other owners was the first option for Davis.

"He needs that kind of adversarial relationship with others," Walsh noted. "He thrives on that."

So, it seems, does his team. The Raiders have become known for their ability to pull out games that have seemed lost, and they have thrived in circumstances that would be daunting for any other team. In 1980, when the football world was united against Davis and his team because of the move to Los Angeles, the Raiders won the Super Bowl as a wild-card team.

Although he sets himself apart, Davis manages to draw others to him. "He's a very charismatic man," Walsh said. "Even at the height of his battles with the NFL, at the Shrine East-West practices I'd see scouts crowding around him on the sidelines trying to hear what he had to say. He can be very charming when he wants to be. People go to him like moths to a flame."

When Fred Biletnikoff was near the end of his career with the Raiders, Davis ordered him benched so that one of Davis's favorites, Morris Bradshaw, could play. For years Biletnikoff fumed about the way Davis had treated him, and he would refuse to speak to Davis if they happened to be in the same room. But when Davis decided he needed a receivers coach he called Biletnikoff, who is now a Raiders assistant.

Davis has an intimidating presence. In my quarter of a century of covering pro football, I have privately heard countless critical opinions of Davis and many jokes made at his expense. Back in the late 1960s a magazine article about him was entitled "The Most Hated Man in Football." Yet few are willing to talk critically about him on the record. Davis encourages that attitude with allusions to gangsters and Las Vegas connections. In his early years in Oakland, club employees used to talk behind his back about the "trunk story": after a dispute with someone, Davis would say, "He might wind up in the trunk of a car." Nobody ever did, and when Davis learned that he was being mocked he made no further references to mob hits.

Davis has taught an intimidating, take-no-prisoners style of football, which once led Pittsburgh Steelers coach Chuck Noll to refer to the Raiders as "a criminal element in the NFL." The Raiders often lead the league in penalties, with an unusually high number of personal fouls.

Davis has tolerated, even encouraged, a free-living style for his players, concerned only that they play well on Sunday. "I can't believe that people are concerned because Jose Canseco was arrested for having a gun in his car," Tom Keating told me. "A lot of guys brought guns to training camp with the Raiders. Some guys had two. Nobody thought anything of it." One of the gun carriers was Bob Brown, an intimidating offensive tackle for the Raiders for four years in the 1970s. "I went through a shooting period," Brown said. "I must have brought six or eight types of ordnance to training camp. There were some other guys who brought ordnance up, too. When I would fire, somebody would answer."

Davis played Warren Wells while Wells was awaiting sentencing on a rape charge. He played troubled man-child John Matuszak, who had nearly killed himself while with the Kansas City Chiefs by combining liquor and drugs. He played Dan Pastorini, who once drove his car into a tree and on another occasion threatened to shoot the policemen who arrested him for drunk driving.

Before drugs became prominent in the sports world (and in society) the Raiders were taking uppers and downers. A big basket of pills sat in the locker room at practice, and players would grab handfuls as they walked by. Former offensive line coach Ollie Spencer remembered one of his players taking an extra suitcase with him on the road. "He had every kind of drug imaginable in there," Spencer said. "One time, about half an hour before a game, he told me, 'If you've got anything you want to say to me, better say it now.' I knew what he meant."

"I remember one year when Bernie Jackson (then NFL security chief) was giving the standard antidrug lecture in training camp," said Ben Davidson, one Raider who did not take drugs. "Bob Brown jumped up and said, 'Do you know what it feels like to go out there all alone?' Everybody broke up, and John Madden just kind of shook his head, as if he were saying, 'What are you going to do with these guys?' "

It is part of the mystique surrounding Davis that there is no way to separate the practical and the altruistic in his signing of players who have been rejected by the rest of the league. He often feels genuine sympathy for the players and wants to give them a chance to redeem themselves, but he also realizes that he has tapped into a talent pool that other teams ignore.

Davis has always been able to use players who have been labeled troublemakers by other teams. Brown was one, and he has said, "Guys come to the Raiders and think, 'This is a place where I can be me.' Nobody gives a damn as long as you play on Sunday. Over the years, the Raiders have had a lot of guys who played very hard on Sunday but were head cases—and that includes me—during the week."

Raiders players have had an extraordinary freedom of speech. On the practice field, when Davis tried to give advice to the hot-tempered Biletnikoff, the player would scream, "Shut up, you Jew mother-fucker." Davis would say, "Ah, Freddie doesn't mean it."

The Raiders' way has always been different from the way of the rest of the league, and that has been an important factor in the team's success. "Teams would look over at us in the fourth quarter," Keating remembered, "and Ben Davidson and I would be talking on the bench, and Ben would be twirling his mustache. Blanda would be up in the tunnel smoking a cigarette. They'd think, 'There's no way we're going to beat these guys.' "

Davis has never had any dress codes, or any other unnecessary rules. Even his curfew is a joke. "I maybe snuck out once in my first seven years in the NFL," said quarterback Jim Plunkett. Then, in 1978, he came to the Raiders. "In the Raiders training camp it was almost a daily routine. Even a coach would say, 'I'll meet you at such-and-such a place at eleven-thirty,' which was after curfew." I remember once being able to observe this on a Raider road trip in 1969. I was sitting in a hotel lobby in East Orange, New Jersey, at 11:00 P.M., curfew time. A group of young women came giggling down the outside fire escape and into the lobby, promptly heading for the elevators to go back up.

Another time, I was awakened at home by a 4:00 A.M. phone call from partying fullback Marv Hubbard, who demanded to know how I could write that football players were dumb. At camp the next day coach John Madden told us reporters that Hubbard had missed practice because he had "dysentery."

"Other teams always seemed to have a lot of petty rules," said Hubbard, now a responsible Oakland businessman, "but we didn't. We knew the boundaries. Murder was out, but drinking and carousing definitely were not."

Hubbard learned how different it was with other teams when he went to the Detroit Lions for the last year of his pro career. "They had a binder full of things that could get you fined. With the Raiders, we might have had a page. If you lost your playbook you were fined. If you were late to practice you were fined. That was about it. You always say that the top man in an organization sets a tone for the whole organization, and Al Davis did that for us. On a lot of teams coaches and general managers set themselves up as father figures, but on the Raiders it was more like a business operation. Al Davis and John Madden were both out there on the field, and we were all trying to do what we had to do to win.

"The players policed themselves. There was a lot of peer pressure to do things right, so we'd keep winning."

Hubbard remembered two incidents involving Bob Brown, who was always determined to do things his own way. "The first time was when Bob came out on the practice field one Wednesday without his helmet and announced that veterans shouldn't have to wear their helmets on Wednesdays. On any other team, the coaches would have said, 'You can't do that, we have rules.' Ollie Spencer only said, 'I don't think that's a good idea, Bob,' but let him go. We were running four plays and out. On Brown's first play, Matsuzak grabbed him by his jersey, pulled him in, and gave him a ferocious head butt. Bob didn't say anything, but when his four plays were up he trotted into the locker room and got his helmet, and that was the end of that.

"Another time, we had played an exhibition game and Bob had had a bad day. The guy he was supposed to block was smaller but very fast—like Charles Haley of the 49ers today—and he had beaten Bob a couple of times on pass protection. In the locker room after, Bob was dressing, and he had two guns holstered under each arm. Phil Villapiano said, 'You can't block him so you're going to shoot him?' and everybody laughed. Well, that was the last time Brown brought guns into the locker room. He wanted to be accepted by this tough group of men— he didn't want to be laughed at. So a situation that might have been a nasty one on another club was quickly defused."

Neither Davis nor his players care what the rest of the football world thinks about their methods. Davis does not have a public relations director any more, because he sees no correlation between good public relations and his bottom line, winning.

"I think about the look Davis could give you after a loss," Gene Upshaw said. "That was probably the thing that made us want to win. You knew after a loss that he'd be standing at the locker-room door. There was no getting beyond him. You had to face him. It was the same feeling all week. The only way to erase it was to win."

Davis's need to triumph has led him onto unorthodox paths, and he and his team have provided great entertainment, on and off the field. As a veteran Davis watcher, I've observed and even participated in this carnival, and I'm now able to detail the struggles, the victories, and even the rare setbacks of Davis and his Raiders.

Just win, baby.

· 1 ·

Al Davis Saves the Oakland Franchise

The National Football League's owners form an exclusive club. Had Al Davis chosen to exercise the charm he turns on and off like a light bulb, he would certainly be at the center of that club now. Instead, he has elected to take a different path entirely, one that has led him to a very lonely life. Davis and his Raiders have been outsiders from the start, and that outsider feeling has intensified since Davis defied his fellow owners to move the Raiders to Los Angeles.

Why has he deliberately sought the role of outsider? There are some clues in his early life, but first it's necessary to get rid of the myths that surround the young Davis, most of them propagated by Davis himself.

The first myth is that Davis fought his way up from humble beginnings. "I'm always amused by people who call Al a street fighter from Brooklyn and portray Pete Rozelle as the patrician," said Davis's friend, Los Angeles newspaper columnist Mel Durslag. "If anything, it was the other way around. Pete's family never had any real money. Al's family was much more comfortable."

Davis was born on July 4, 1929, in Brockton, Massachusetts (also the birthplace of onetime heavyweight boxing champion Rocky Marciano), and his family moved to Brooklyn when he was a young boy. He went to Erasmus High School, a large school with a student enrollment of about 7,000, which was considered one of the elite public schools in the city.

Davis's father was in the garment-manufacturing business, and the family lived in an upper-middle-class neighborhood. Don McMahon, the former major league pitcher, went to school with Davis and remained a close friend until McMahon's death a few years ago. I once spoke to McMahon about Davis, and he remembered that Davis was popular in school and lived in a good neighborhood. "Their house was a lot better than ours, for sure," McMahon said. Money was not a problem for Davis, and making money has never been a major goal for him. Although his football success has made him a rich man, he doesn't live extravagantly. "Al isn't a man who lives up to his wealth at all," Durslag said. "You'd never know being around him how much money he has."

After his high-school graduation, Davis went first to Wittenberg College, in Ohio, and then to Syracuse University, majoring in English. Throughout, there was one failure that always nagged at Davis: his inability to make it on the athletic field.

"Al told me one time he would have given his eyeteeth to have the ability that some athletes have," said former *Oakland Tribune* sports editor George Ross. "He could sit in the stands and see what could be done, and he could see that they didn't know how to do it, even though they had the ability he didn't have."

His physical appearance has always been important to Davis. He works out regularly with weights and even takes the weights with him on road trips, renting an extra room for them. While other NFL owners and executives—including many who were athletes in their youth—succumb to middle-aged spread, Davis looks as fit today as he was when he first became the Raiders head coach. Although he's been able to build up his upper body with his work on weights, Davis has always had thin legs.

To disguise them, he used to wear pants with baggy legs early in his career with the Raiders—which only accentuated the defect. He dropped the baggy-pants look after a magazine story ridiculed it. Today he would never be considered a style setter, but when he does not feel the need to wear the Raiders colors, he dresses stylishly, if conservatively.

The importance Davis put on athletic ability is reflected in the information contained in early Raiders press guides, which called Davis a "star athlete" who lettered in baseball and football in college. When journalists investigated and learned that he had not lettered, this was changed, and the entry now says he was a star "while playing football, basketball and baseball." In fact, he wasn't a first-stringer in any sport in high school.

Davis's embellishment of the details of his playing career was done less to add to his status than because he feared that a lack of a strong athletic background would hinder his coaching progress. The fear was legitimate. Traditionally, football coaches are former players, though not necessarily stars; "Bear" Bryant, for instance, was the end opposite Don Hutson, possibly the best receiver in football history, at Alabama, and Bill Walsh was an ordinary wide receiver at San Jose State. Yet no one has ever advanced so far in football with so little playing background as Davis has. "Instead of putting Al down for a lack of football background, I always thought people should give him credit for being so superlative in knowing the game without a background," Ross said.

Davis may also have felt insecure because he grew up in Brooklyn (at the time comedians could get an easy laugh simply by mentioning the borough's name) and because of his religious background: he was a Jew. His concern on the latter count may not have been misplaced. Sid Gillman once told me that he thought being a Jew probably cost *him* an early chance to get a coaching job in the Big Ten. Big-time coaches, college or pro, have tended to be either Protestant or Catholic and, of course, white. This may help explain why Davis is a remarkably unprejudiced man. No racial or religious bias shows in his actions or even in casual jokes or offhand remarks. Davis has always been especially known for his ability to work with blacks; it is fitting that he should be the first NFL owner to hire a black, Art Shell, as a head coach.

Believing himself to be an outsider, Davis pursued tactics that took him even further outside the norm. He intended to show everybody, but every success has pushed him further and further from the NFL mainstream and into his private place.

When he left college Davis became an assistant coach, in both football and baseball, at Adelphi University on Long Island. He attracted attention with coaching-magazine articles on football techniques and strategy. After being inducted into the U.S. Army, Davis got his first head-coaching job at Fort Belvoir, Virginia—where he had his first contact with Pete Rozelle, later to be a memorable foe. It was in 1953 or 1954, Rozelle remembered, when he was doing public relations work for the Los Angeles Rams and one of the owners, Dan Reeves, had everyone working on some part of the draft. "I was involved in service scouting," Rozelle said. "I would call around to coaches on service teams and find out what players they were high on. I called Fort Belvoir, and Al Davis was the coach. But he wanted to be paid for any information. He was the only one who wanted that. Dan Reeves didn't give me any budget, so I didn't get any dope out of him."

Following the army job, Davis worked as a scout for the Baltimore Colts and then as the line coach at The Citadel. From there he became an assistant coach at the University of Southern California, where he was an innovative and effective recruiter. Dick Vertlieb, then a USC basketball assistant coach, whose locker was next to Davis's, remembered when Davis was trying to get Angelo Coia to transfer from The Citadel to USC. "He took Coia out to the L.A. Coliseum at night and had all the lights turned on, one by one. Then he told Coia, 'You're playing your last game for USC against Notre Dame, and a hundred thousand people are cheering for you as you run into the Coliseum.'" Coia did come to USC, and he is now on the Raiders front-office staff.

Those who knew Davis were impressed by his inquisitive mind. Sid Gillman's first meeting with Davis had come at a football clinic in Atlantic City at which Gillman was lecturing. "Al was sitting in the front row and taking notes on everything," Gillman said. "When I was through he came up and asked me a million questions."

In 1959 Gillman was fired as coach of the Los Angeles Rams and was quickly hired as coach of the new American Football League franchise, the Los Angeles Chargers (which moved to San Diego after its first season). Gillman added Davis to a remarkable Chargers staff, which included Chuck Noll, who would coach four Super Bowl champions in Pittsburgh, and Jack Faulkner, later a coach with the Denver Broncos and the general manager of the Los Angeles Rams.

"I was always biased toward college coaches rather than the old pro types who didn't know anything about drilling players," said Gillman, now retired and living beside a golf course near San Diego. "Al was a fine coach, a splendid coach, and he was very good at signing players. Al had that knack of telling people what they wanted to hear. He was very persuasive."

It was Davis who first recommended and then signed Lance Alworth of Arkansas, perhaps the finest wide receiver in pro football history.

"Al was a great judge of talent," Gillman said. "It was hard to tell whether Alworth could catch the ball, because Arkansas didn't throw it. They ran a wing-T, with Alworth as a wingback running the ball. But Al was convinced Alworth was going to be a great receiver. We used to have some fearsome arguments before the draft, because all my coaches had very strong opinions on players. But Al never wavered on Alworth. He was so convincing that we drafted Lance."

The San Francisco 49ers, in the NFL, also drafted Alworth, but Davis won the battle by telling Alworth that the Chargers and the AFL were going to grow and challenging him to be a part of it. In this case everything Davis promised came true: the Chargers became one of the premier teams in the AFL, which eventually became an equal partner with the NFL via a 1966 agreement, while the 49ers were muddling their way through the 1960s.

In 1962, when Davis was in his third year with the Chargers, Wayne Valley, the Oakland Raiders general partner, was looking for someone who could bring his franchise to life. "We needed somebody who wanted to win so badly he would do anything," Valley once said to me. "Everywhere I went, people told me what a son of a bitch Al Davis was, so I figured he must be doing something right.

"I talked to a lot of people about Davis, and they'd tell me, 'You don't want him.' But nobody could tell me exactly what it was that he'd done wrong. I figured a lot of it was jealousy. I know from my own experience that some people don't like you because you're too sharp for them. I didn't care whether he was devious or whether he was likable or not. I wanted a winner, and I thought he would be one. I knew he would work sixteen hours a day to make sure nobody got ahead of him."

One man who did tell Valley that Davis was the right man for the job was Hank Stram, then coaching the Kansas City Chiefs. He had known Davis since the late 1950s, when Stram was interviewed for a job at USC, and he had observed Davis's work with the Chargers. "He's a very good interrogator, and I mean that in a complimentary sense," Stram said. "He was always asking questions. He wanted to know what you did, and why you did it. He's a real student of the game. When Valley asked me what I thought of Al, I told him, 'From a competitive standpoint, I'd hate to see you hire Al, because we've had it pretty easy against the Raiders. But I can't think of anybody who could turn your team around faster.' "

Even within the AFL, the NFL was regarded as the standard for professional football, and some of the Raiders owners thought that Green Bay Packers assistant coach Bill Austin would be the best choice. But Austin was lukewarm about the job, probably reasoning that it would not be a promotion to go from the best-in-football Packers to a 1-and-13 team in a league that might not survive.

So the first and last man interviewed for the job was Al Davis. It was hardly a typical interview. Davis, only thirty-three and virtually unknown, took charge. It was he who decided whether he could work with Valley and Ed McGah, the Raiders' other general partner, not the reverse. Valley and McGah really had no choice: the Raiders were in bad shape and desperate. Without Al Davis, the franchise would not survive in Oakland.

•　•　•

In the beginning, the Raiders weren't the Raiders, and they weren't Oakland, either.

The American Football League began play in 1960, primarily because oilmen and football fanciers Lamar Hunt and Bud Adams had been frozen out of the National Football League and had decided to start their own league.

Originally, one of the AFL franchises was scheduled for Minneapolis, but George Halas, the owner of the Chicago Bears, didn't want competition from a rival league that close to home—and in those days what George Halas wanted, George Halas got. The NFL announced plans to expand to Minneapolis and to Dallas (another city in the AFL's plans) and offered the Minnesota franchise to Max Winter, who had been in line to get the AFL team. Winter took the NFL offer, and the AFL had to look for another city. Barron Hilton, the owner of the Los Angeles Chargers, wanted another team in California, to create a rivalry and cut down on travel costs. After a cursory examination of other possible sites, the AFL chose Oakland for its final team—which was news to almost everyone in Oakland.

"The first we heard of it," remembered George Ross, "was when it came across the Associated Press wire. We immediately started calling guys around town who might be expected to buy into the team, and they had never been approached. But some of them were interested, and eventually a group got together to buy the franchise."

It was an orphan franchise. When the AFL had been

formed, club owners and executives had met to assign players to teams, but while the future of the franchise that eventually landed in Oakland was being determined, other clubs signed the best players originally assigned to the franchise. Quarterback Tom Flores, an unknown out of a small California college, who was later to become the team's head coach, and center Jim Otto were virtually the only good players left—and Otto was an accident. He had played at a weight of only 200 pounds in college and was not highly regarded, but he bulked up to 250 pounds with an intensive weight-lifting program in his rookie year and went on to a Hall of Fame career.

The management couldn't even get the franchise's name right. After an area-wide contest, Chet Soda, the first president of the team, announced the winning name: the Senors. It was supposed to reflect the state's Spanish heritage. But newspaper columnists quickly pointed out that the plural of *señor* is spelled *señores*, and also that Oakland's Latin population was relatively small. The Oakland City Council officially denounced the name. A persistent rumor said it had been chosen because it was the suggestion of Soda's girlfriend. "I don't know about that, but Chet certainly liked the name," Ross said. "He envisioned the cheerleaders on the sidelines wearing big sombreros with balls on them, and serapes."

Neither Soda nor anyone else got a chance to see that. The team's name was quickly changed to the Raiders, another name from the contest, and nobody objected.

Unfortunately, the episode was typical of the team's early management style. "The team was run more like a semipro operation," said Flores, now the president and general manager of the Seattle Seahawks. Several of the original owners, including Soda, dropped out after taking a financial bath the first year. When an impasse developed over control of the club between factions led by Charles Harney (who had built Candlestick Park in San Francisco) and Valley, an East Bay building contractor, Valley suggested flipping a coin. Valley won the coin flip, and Harney swung at him with his cane.

On the field, the Raiders were a respectable 6–8 that first

season of 1960, but they soon deteriorated. Other AFL teams, by contrast, started to build. The Chargers, now in San Diego, got players like Lance Alworth, John Hadl, Tobin Rote, Keith Lincoln, and Paul Lowe, along with their original "Fearsome Foursome" anchored by Ernie Ladd and Earl Faison. Hunt's Dallas Texans eventually moved to Kansas City and built the Chiefs into a strong team. The Boston Patriots and the Buffalo Bills put together teams that could have challenged NFL teams.

At the time, in fact, the AFL was more solid than most fans and the media realized. Many prominent sportswriters were predicting that the NFL would simply pick up the best AFL teams as the league collapsed, much as the NFL had done in 1950 when it picked off the San Francisco 49ers and the Cleveland Browns as the All American Conference collapsed. "One thing the new league did right," George Ross said. "They had a clause in their constitution that any owner attempting to jump out of the league would not only forfeit the franchise but also all the player contracts, which would stay with the league."

The league was able to stay together because its best franchises would not leave, but as other teams were moving ahead the Raiders slipped back. "The early draft choices were terrible," Ross remembered. And the coaches were dreadful. The first, Eddie Erdelatz, was brought in from the U.S. Naval Academy, where he'd been successful, but he was totally unprepared to coach in a pro league. "He had something he called the 'jitterbug defense,' " Ross said. "He had his players jumping around on defense as the ball was snapped. In theory, that was to keep blockers from getting to them, but oftentimes ballcarriers would just go through the holes they were leaving. And when veteran linemen came into camp they'd look at that defense and say, 'What the hell is this?' "

Erdelatz's team started 1961 with 55–0 and 44–0 losses. Erdelatz was fired and was replaced by one of his assistants, Marty Feldman.

Feldman didn't regard his promotion as a lifetime job. While the team was flying to Denver for its final game of the season,

Feldman gathered the players together and told them he would be fired. He was somewhat premature: he stayed on for the first two games of the 1962 season. But then he *was* fired, to be replaced by another assistant, Red Conkright.

Conkright's term would be notable largely for the time he decided to put in an ersatz Statue of Liberty play: quarterback Cotton Davidson was to leap into the air and pretend to throw a pass, meanwhile dropping the ball off to a trailing running back. Scotty Stirling, then the *Oakland Tribune* beat writer, told Conkright, "If you use that play, you'll score a touchdown—and it will make the other team so mad they'll beat you 77–7."

The Raiders went 2–12 in 1961, losing their final six games. Could it get any worse? Yes, because the Raiders had no place to play in Oakland. They played their games, in virtual privacy, at Kezar Stadium and Candlestick Park in San Francisco. Their *total* attendance in 1961 was about 50,000. There was talk of a large stadium to be built at some point in Oakland, but Valley told Oakland city officials that if the Raiders didn't have an Oakland field in time for the 1962 season, they would be moved. He wasn't kidding.

With George Ross prodding him, Oakland's mayor, John Houlihan, came up with a plan to build Frank Youell Field, which would be used by the city schools as well as by the Raiders. Seating was originally just 18,000, though it was later increased to 22,000. It was a cozy field; fans were so close to the sidelines that they sometimes caught passes or punts that sailed out of bounds, and they were enthusiastic, despite the Raiders losses. They were the nucleus of what would become the fan base for a thirteen-year run of sellouts at the Oakland Coliseum.

But it still wasn't certain the franchise would remain in Oakland. Valley, not convinced that plans for the proposed Coliseum would go through, talked with New Orleans entrepreneur Dave Dixon about the possibility of selling the team. Dixon, who was later involved in creating the World Football

League and the United States Football League, remembered it this way:

"In 1962 I had what you might call an option on an option to buy the Raiders and move them to New Orleans. But that would have happened only if they couldn't get a new stadium in Oakland. Don Klosterman would have been our general manager. Right after that I was out in Oakland to talk to Valley, and I went to a game. Even then, at Frank Youell Field, I could feel the support of the Oakland fans for the team, and it made me feel dirty, like soiled laundry, to think I might take the team away. About ten days after that I got a call from Valley, and he told me that Senator William Knowland had thrown his support behind a new stadium, and it looked like it was going to go. As, of course, it eventually did. I was sure we could have put together the financing we needed to buy the team, but that was the end of our deal."

So the Raiders had a temporary field, and a permanent one on the way. What they didn't have was a good team: they lost their first thirteen games in 1962—extending their losing streak to nineteen over two seasons—before winning the last game of the season.

But the savior, a.k.a. "the Genius," was on the horizon.

•   •   •

George Ross is a country squire these days, having retired to the small community of Graeagle, in the Sierra, about fifty miles north of Lake Tahoe. When I visited him there, we sat on his back porch, amid a stand of pines, and he would break off our conversation to point out the various kinds of birds. He is a docent at the nearby state park and frequently conducts nature hikes.

In 1963, though, he was a man with a mission: to give the city of Oakland the respect he thought it deserved. Oakland had long been the poor sister to San Francisco, one of the world's most glamorous cities, and no one resented that more than Ross. "I thought the Raiders would be good for Oakland," he said. "If they prospered, so would we. Nobody in the news-paper's front office told me to push the Raiders, but they didn't discourage me, either, and I thought that was the thing to do."

George Ross had a very special relationship with the Raid-ers from the time he was appointed sports editor of the *Oak-land Tribune* in 1961; he was even head of the Raiders Boosters Club at one time. He was privy to decisions and conversations from which newspapermen would normally be excluded. It seemed natural enough to Ross that he and Scotty Stirling, the *Tribune* beat writer, were in the room when Valley and Ed McGah interviewed Al Davis in a San Diego hotel. It was Jan-uary 1, 1963, and football history was about to be made.

From the start of the interview Davis was contemptuous of both Raiders owners. McGah was a joke, he told Ross, and added that he didn't like the other guy. During their breaks Davis sneered that "they don't even know what questions to ask." "Al was fully prepared," Ross said. "He knew all about the business side, he knew what it took to be a general man-ager. I was really impressed that he seemed to know so much about everything."

The interview session lasted about six hours. The next day Ross got a telephone call from Davis, who wanted to know: (1) Would the Raiders ownership hang in there? (2) Would the *Tribune* support the Raiders? (3) Would a new stadium be built? Ross was able to reassure Davis on every count, the most crit-ical of which was probably the first. "I told Al, 'I know you don't like Wayne, but he's the glue. He'll hold everybody to-gether.'"

Davis took the job, though only after getting a three-year contract—Valley had originally offered two years. And the legend began, much of it fostered by Davis himself.

The press release announcing Davis's hiring revealed much about the man. There was, for instance, a sentence that said he had been voted "the most popular boy" in his senior class in high school. If this is true—and with Davis you can never be sure where image and reality part—what kind of man hangs on, at the age of thirty-three, to something that happened when he was seventeen or eighteen? The same press release claimed that the team Davis had coached at Fort Belvoir had beaten Maryland, the national champion, in a "squad game." What was the relevance? A squad game is simply a glorified practice.

Most significantly, that release originated the term "young coaching genius" to describe Davis. In later years the Raiders media guide would say that *Sports Illustrated* had first called Davis a "young genius," but that first press release proves otherwise. Herman Masin had used the term in *Scholastic* magazine to describe Davis as a high-school coach; Davis had liked it and had it inserted in the release.

The interview session with Davis, Valley, and McGah was the first time Ross had met Davis, and it began a symbiotic relationship between newsman and coach that lasted nearly ten years.

"I wasn't naive," Ross insisted. "I recognized the Machiavellian trait in Al from the start. But this was an unparalleled opportunity for me, to be so close to one of the major newsmakers in the area. I got a chance to sit in on film sessions and coaches' meetings." Most of all, Ross felt that he and Davis were "walking down the same road"—the success of the Raiders would bring Oakland and the *Tribune* the recognition Ross sought.

"Al was always very good at playing up the 'little old Oakland' routine," Ross remembered. "He said to me from the start, 'We can't make it by copying San Francisco. We've got to do it our way.' So he basically ignored the San Francisco media. He felt they were biased in favor of the NFL and the 49ers, and he didn't care about them. He developed his own fan base in the East Bay, and he was enormously successful with that strategy. Once you've got 50,000 people buying season tickets and another 10,000 on the waiting list, you don't have to worry about the other 3 million or more in the area. They may watch the games on television, but they don't have any impact on your gate. You don't need them, and Al realized that." Davis's attitude toward San Francisco may well have come naturally to him because his youthful home of Brooklyn has basically the same relationship with the more glamorous Manhattan that Oakland has with San Francisco.

Ross fostered the feeling with a sports section that told readers everything they wanted to know about the Raiders, and more. "Maybe we had too many stories," he said, "but the readers seemed to love it. They couldn't get too much on the Raiders. We never got any complaints."

Virtually the only early coverage of the Raiders was in the *Tribune*, but when Davis, in his first year, turned the sad-sack Raiders into a 10−4 team that twice beat the Chargers, the AFL champion that year, the Raiders suddenly became big news. While Ross and the *Tribune* emphasized the positive aspects of Davis's behavior, others, who were looking more for a story than for propaganda, began to notice that Davis could be a peculiar man indeed.

There was, for instance, his mania for secrecy. At the time the Raiders practiced at Bushrod Park in Oakland, which was next to a large apartment building. Davis was so certain that spies from other teams were watching the practice that he had his players wear numbers different from their game-uniform numbers, and on occasion he ran plays with twelve players on the offense to totally confuse anyone watching.

The idea that other AFL teams, most of whom had very tight budgets in those early days of the league, would pay someone to watch a Raiders practice seemed absurd. Only a highly trained person can observe anything of value at a practice. Besides, the Raiders of that day were not a team that others were much concerned about.

But Davis never lost the fear that other teams were spying on the Raiders. The practice of having players use different uniform numbers continued. At Santa Rosa, the training-camp field was surrounded by high fences, and only people Davis knew—reporters, his or a coach's friends, Raiders limited partners—were allowed in. Beyond the practice field was a huge expanse of open fields, with hills in the distance, but if Davis spotted a reflection from the hills he would stop practice momentarily. Sometimes he would even send someone out to see whether the reflection was coming from binoculars. A practice site a few miles from the Oakland Airport that the Raiders got from the Port of Oakland had no vantage points for possible spies, but if a small plane flew overhead Davis would order practice stopped until it was gone. I thought Davis feared that others were spying on him because he knew that, given the opportunity, he would spy on them.

Fears and insecurities didn't prevent Davis from turning the Raiders around very quickly. How did he do it? In part, simply by picking up talented players who had been over-looked elsewhere. His defensive ends, Ben Davidson and Ike Lassiter, were both rejects, for instance.

Davidson was a late bloomer. Although news stories later referred to him as an "All American from Washington," in truth he had not even been a full-time starter. He was a huge man, 6 feet 8 inches and 275 pounds, with strength and surprising speed; he had been a hurdler in junior college. He had bounced around the NFL, learning something more with every team, and by the time he got to Oakland in 1964 he was ready to play. Davis used psychology to improve Davidson's play. "Ben is a guy who likes to lead the parade," noted Tom Keating, his former teammate and longtime friend. "Other teams had played him inside, at tackle. That's no good. Al put him out at end, where everybody could see him."

Ike Lassiter, at the other end, came to the Raiders from the Denver Broncos, where he had been the coaches' whipping boy. Thinking the Broncos wanted him to be heavy, Lassiter had bulked up and was in terrible condition at training camp. The coaches ran him through exhausting drills in the high altitude; when he couldn't perform, the Broncos traded him to Oakland. "I know what happened to you in Denver," Davis said. "That doesn't matter. All that's behind you now. I know how well you can play, and I want you to do it here." The relieved Lassiter played his heart out for Davis. "That man gave me back my manhood," Lassiter would say to anyone who would listen.

Davis always seemed to know the right psychological buttons to push. He once told center Jim Otto, "When I was with the Chargers, we always felt that if we could get you out of the game we had the Raiders beat." That was nonsense. In the AFL's first three seasons the Chargers had seldom had any trouble with the Raiders, winning all six of their games (by scores as lopsided as 44 – 0 and 41 – 10), but Otto believed Davis. He became a team leader and played with injuries so often that he has an artificial hip today. Although he has days when he can hardly get out of bed, Jim Otto swears that he'd gladly do it all over again.

"There was a big difference in his approach," Otto said. "He talked to us like men, and he treated us like men. When we went out to the practice field, we knew he was serious about the game because he worked us very hard."

Otto, who now runs a Burger King franchise north of Sacramento, may be a devoted Davis admirer today, but he was skeptical of some of Davis's early moves. "Being a smart old veteran—I was in my fourth year with the Raiders then—I couldn't understand some of the things he was doing," Otto remembered. "Like bringing in Art Powell, who had been trouble with other teams. Or Archie Matsos, who I had blocked so many times when he was with Buffalo. Or guys like Proverb Jacobs and Frank Youso at offensive tackle, who hadn't made it with other teams. But after a while I realized he could recognize guys who could help the Raiders, even if it was only for a year or two, and that was how he built the team. His direction made us a winner. That was fine with me. I wanted to win, and we hadn't done very much of that in my first three years."

Art Powell, in fact, was a real key for the Raiders. Davis had two capable quarterbacks, Tom Flores and Cotton Davidson, but he needed a receiver. So one of the first things he did after being named coach was to fly through a snowstorm to Chicago to meet with Powell.

Powell, a wide receiver, had played for the New York Jets in the AFL and in Canada. He had often been labeled a troublemaker, but that was far less important to Davis than the fact that Powell was tall and fast and had great hands. Davis got the rights to Powell; nobody is quite sure how, but in those days many deals in the AFL were made on the basis of "Can you sign him?"—to keep players away from the NFL.

"I know Al didn't find Powell difficult," Ross said. "Some other players complained that Powell was being stroked. Well, Al did that. He knew some guys needed to be stroked. Art merited that treatment. He didn't practice near as much as some other guys, but when he was pulling down seven balls a game, he didn't need to."

From the start, Davis brought an intensity to the Raiders that had been lacking with their other coaches. Scotty Stirling, who observed Davis as a beat reporter and later as the club's general manager (he moved on to work in the National Basketball Association), thought that the sport itself was partially responsible for Davis's intensity.

"He had a bunker mentality, but you see a lot of that in the NFL because there's only one game a week and that game is so important," Stirling said. "The only basketball coach I've seen who's comparable to Davis is Bobby Knight. Davis was so consumed with winning, so single-minded. He had goals, and he was able to achieve them. I've always thought he was the best I've seen at knowing what players he had to get and knowing how to get them."

The final element was Davis's system, or, more properly, the Sid Gillman system he brought with him to Oakland. He modified it so that it became even more explosive for the Raiders than it had been for the Chargers.

"Sid Gillman has been called the father of the modern passing offense by Bill Walsh," Lee Grosscup, a former Raiders quarterback, said, "because Sid had been able to get five receivers into passing patterns very quickly and really spread the defense. Al took that system and extended it. He deepened the patterns so that Fred Biletnikoff, for instance, would go out eighteen yards on a sideline pattern and then come back for the ball, which was more than enough for a first down."

Ross remembered Davis telling receivers that if they cut their patterns off short, the cornerback could recover in time to prevent a completion; if they took the patterns deeper, the cornerback wouldn't be able to stay with them when they cut back toward the quarterback. "We can win that battle," Davis said, and that comeback pattern became Biletnikoff's trademark in a Hall of Fame career.

There was much more to the Gillman-Davis system. At a time when most NFL clubs were using their running backs as receivers only for "safety valves"—when the quarterback could not find a receiver downfield—Davis used his backs as primary receivers. Grosscup has estimated that the Raiders had at least twenty-nine plays using backs as receivers.

Davis's system made a star out of Clem Daniels, a Negro All-American as a running back for Prairie View A&M. Daniels was signed by the Dallas Texans, soon to become the Kansas City Chiefs, but after one season as a reserve defensive back he was released. Eddie Erdelatz signed him for the Raiders just before Erdelatz was fired. By the time Davis arrived Daniels's abilities were no secret. He had rushed for a season total of 766 yards and had a one-game mark of 187 yards in a game against the Houston Oilers in 1962. What Davis saw was a back with size, power, a speed of 9.8 seconds in the 100-yard dash, and hands capable of catching passes far down the field. Daniels was ideal for the Davis system—the best back the Raiders would have while in Oakland.

Davis had the horse his system needed, and he rode that horse hard, making Daniels the key to the whole offense. With the fullback, Alan Miller, used almost entirely as a blocking back, Daniels carried 215 times for 1,099 yards in 1963, an AFL record at the time, and caught 30 passes for 685 yards. Five of his eight touchdowns came on pass receptions. The package was enough to make him Most Valuable Player in the AFL for 1963. The pass routes Daniels ran were more like flanker routes. He was especially dangerous coming out of what Davis called the "east" formation. Both the split end and the flanker would line up on one side of the field, and Daniels would come out of the backfield and down the sideline. That would force the defense to cover either Daniels or Art Powell one on one with a safety, which was a mismatch. At 220 pounds, Daniels was bigger—and usually faster—than any safety. If the Raiders quarterback, either Tom Flores or Cotton Davidson, had enough time, there was no way a safety could defend against Daniels.

The approach was typical of Davis, who believed in an attacking style of play that emphasized the long pass. When the Raiders got as far as their opponents' 40-yard line, Davis wanted to try three straight passes into the end zone. He didn't worry that all three might fail; just having to defend against them would panic the other team. "The next time we get down there, they won't know what to do," he often said. He scorned the short-pass approach. After a 1968 win over the Houston Oilers, who had thrown 5-yard passes all day, Davis said to me, "They have to be almost perfect, because if they miss one pass in a series they're in a hole."

The quarterback best suited to the Davis system may have been Daryle Lamonica, who arrived in 1967, but in 1963 Flores was also effective throwing long, and the deep passing system was certainly the key to the Raiders success that season.

"My first meeting with Al," Flores remembered, "we were going over his offense, talking football, and I smiled. He wondered what I was laughing at. I said, 'This is going to be fun. I'm going to enjoy this.' I had always liked to throw long, so I just took to this offense like a duck takes to water. It wasn't difficult for me at all. At that time, teams played the same eleven guys on defense, whether it was at midfield or on a goal-line stand, so you didn't have to worry about a lot of different defenses. A lot of AFL teams blitzed like crazy. Boston and Houston used to use a safety blitz all the time. So you prepared to stop that, and the rest was pretty easy."

Davis also had a more sophisticated system of calling audibles than other pro coaches did. The quarterback could change his call at the line of scrimmage to any other play in the offense.

"When I was with the Giants," Grosscup told me, "they might have just three to six audibles a quarterback could use in a given game, and that was pretty much typical of the league at the time. But with the Raiders, a quarterback could call any play. Most teams at that time would use a color to audibilize. A quarterback might come to the line and say 'red . . . 24 . . . set.' The 'red' would tell players he was changing the call. But Al used numbers. Say the play was supposed to be called on 3. If the quarterback wanted to change the call, he'd say something like '3 . . . 89 . . . 9.' The 3 would tell players the call was being changed, the 89 would give the routes to the wide receivers, and the 9 would be the running-back patterns. You could even audibilize to a play-action pass by using the letter K. In that situation, a quarterback might call '3 . . . K . . . 24.' The whole offense was a quarterback's dream because there was so much available. It took more time to learn it because it was so complex, but it was worthwhile."

A dream? Jim Otto called it "a nightmare," at least at first, because there was so much to learn and remember. "I wanted to be perfect," he said. "I'd dream about my plays at night." Now he has a different view. "The AFL, and really pro football as a whole, owes a lot to Al Davis and Sid Gillman," Otto said. "Their passing offenses really opened up the game."

The blocking systems were more complex in the Gillman-Davis system, too. Joe Madro, Gillman's offensive line coach, who is still on the Raiders payroll as a consultant, taught a system of blocking that gave the linemen options, depending on the rush from across the line of scrimmage. Davis's line coach, Ollie Spencer, the only assistant Davis retained when he took over as coach, taught the same system. It made little difference what the defensive linemen did, because the Raiders had a counter for every move.

The Raiders linemen also held. They got called for more holding penalties than any other team in the league, and other teams claimed that the Raiders got away with even more holding that wasn't called. "We always told our linemen, 'If the only way you can protect the quarterback is by holding, then hold,' " Spencer said. "But really, what we did—extending the arms and pulling the guy into you—is what's being taught these days. It's legal now."

"It was much harder to control the defensive players then because we had to keep our arms in against our bodies," Otto said. "But we did it. The lines I played on later, with guys like Gene Upshaw, Art Shell, and Bob Brown, were among the best ever to play the game."

Davis had a clear idea of the type of team he wanted and the players he needed for that team, but in 1963 he didn't have many of them. "He really did it with mirrors that year," Ross said.

When Davis saw weaknesses, he had a way of compensating. Offensive guard Wayne Hawkins was slow, so Davis shortened the route he had to run on sweeps. Middle linebacker Archie Matsos was fast for a linebacker but weighed only 195 pounds, so Davis instructed his defensive linemen to hold up the offensive linemen, giving them no chance to block Matsos. Running free, Matsos could make tackles from sideline to sideline. (Miami Dolphins Coach Don Shula later used much the same system to make a star of Nick Buoniconti.) In 1965 Davis traded Matsos for tight end Hewritt Dixon. "Archie couldn't understand why he'd been traded, because he'd had such great success," Ross said. "He never had that kind of success again."

Davis took the AFL's defensive approach a step further than most teams did. "Much of what was done in the AFL was out of necessity, because the teams didn't have the players the NFL had," Ross said. "At that time in the NFL everybody lined up in the four-three defense. It was a matter of 'our people against your people,' and the team that was stronger physically was the team that won. It was all pretty boring, really. But in the AFL you saw a lot of blitzing and three-man fronts, which now are pretty much standard throughout the NFL."

"We were the first to use the 'over' defense, with a man directly over the center," Otto said. "Pretty soon everybody in our league was using it. I had the advantage of working against it in practice earlier than anybody else."

"The AFL in the 1960s was really a much more exciting league," said Bill King, who became the Raiders announcer in 1966. "There was a willingness to try something new that was really quite refreshing, and the Raiders, especially, were always going for the big play."

. . .

The public saw only what was happening on the field, but for Davis it was important that the whole organization be changed. He brought in many of his own people—like George Glace, the longtime ticket manager—and he constantly worked to upgrade the organization.

It needed upgrading. Ben Davidson still remembers when he joined the Raiders, late in the 1964 training camp. "John Herrera picked me up at the airport and drove me to camp in Santa Rosa. The bed I slept on that night couldn't have been even six feet long, and it was narrow. I'd just come off a long flight, from Washington, D.C., and was already tired; that didn't help. Then, when we broke camp, I stayed for a while in a small motel in Oakland, near Lake Merritt. The Raiders ticket office was just up the street, and it was a real ramshackle affair. I had to wonder how they could sell tickets out of a place like that. Then I drove by Frank Youell Field, which looked like an overgrown high-school field, and I wondered what I was getting into."

The Raiders didn't turn into a sleek operation overnight, but Davis was improving everything. The team offices had been in a dumpy downtown office. Davis got bigger and better quarters nearby, and he later arranged for a permanent new office to be built across the freeway from the Oakland Coliseum.

"I was always impressed by the way Al handled everything," Ross said. "He was very surefooted. He knew how to get things done. He negotiated a deal with the El Rancho Motel in Santa Rosa, for instance, that included a football field built behind the motel, and all for the basic price of the rooms." Davis and Wayne Valley sometimes clashed over the budget.

"Wayne didn't want to open up his pocketbook until he knew what was happening," Ross said. "But Wayne adjusted pretty quickly when he saw the direction the team was going. Al would sometimes call Wayne cheap, but I didn't see that. Our travel, our hotel rooms seemed to be pretty standard to me."

Davis's own way of traveling—by limousine when the team was on the road, by a chauffeur-driven car at home—was more than standard. "Wayne said to me one time, 'The guy dips pretty heavy into personal expenses, but that doesn't bother me. If he wants to create the image of being first class, that's fine,' " Ross remembered.

Davis was already working on his image as a man of mystery. The limousine always had tinted windows, so that Davis could see out but nobody could see in. When he went to his favorite restaurant, Vince's, he would sit at a table in the back, with a telephone. No one bothered him, but the owner made sure that everyone in the restaurant knew who was at the back table.

Davis knew that his image was only as good as his team, and he spent what was necessary to get players. As the war between the AFL and the NFL escalated, the Kansas City Chiefs and Oakland became the only AFL teams willing to spend what they had to to get to the top. The San Diego Chargers, the Boston Patriots, the Buffalo Bills, and the Houston Oilers, which had excellent teams early in the 1960s, gradually fell back because they were no longer signing the best players.

Davis was hardly throwing money around wildly. Players, who, for one reason or another, didn't have negotiating power often got squeezed. Even his stars, Daniels and Powell, felt they were underpaid, and one year they held out together for more money, without success.

"Al Davis wasn't as generous as he became later," Ben Davidson noted. "He ran a tight ship. I was in my fourth year of pro ball, and I had worked my way up from $9,000 in my rookie season to $11,000 with the Redskins, but he told me my salary would be $10,500. When we negotiated in the following years, he would kind of half apologize to me and say, 'We're not making much money,' and he'd mention a figure that was always lower than what I had in mind. It was kind of take or leave it."

When the Raiders were competing with NFL teams for players, though, they paid top dollar. In 1966 defensive back Rodger Bird signed a contract for a total of $379,000, second in the AFL only to the legendary $400,000 contract (actually, $389,000) of the New York Jets' Joe Namath.

Usually it wasn't money that made the difference when the Raiders went after players. Davis had a system and a method of persuasion that worked very well, as Spencer remembered:

"Al got his coaches from all sections of the country. I was from the midwest, Kansas-Missouri area, John Rauch was from the southeast, Charley Sumner was from the east, Tom Dahms was from California. We all recruited from our specific areas. At that time, AFL teams thought money was the answer, especially teams like Kansas City, with Lamar Hunt, and Houston, with Bud Adams. But most of the best college players wanted to play in the NFL, so they'd take an offer from an AFL team and then go to the NFL team that drafted them and get what they wanted. Al never talked money. We were told to tell players that they could get what they wanted and then sell them on playing for Oakland. We used anything we could. I was able to get defensive back Kent McCloughan from Kansas and linebacker Gus Otto from Missouri because they wanted to play in a warm-weather city."

Those were crazy times, as teams from both leagues bribed and cajoled college coaches into helping them get players and hired "baby-sitters" for top prospects until they could be signed. The rules meant nothing. For example, Pete Rozelle, later to become the NFL commissioner, signed Heisman Trophy winner Billy Cannon from Louisiana State to a Los Angeles Rams contract, but when the Houston Oilers also signed Cannon, the case went to court. The Oilers won.

Davis's most bizarre signing was probably that of offensive tackle Harry Schuh, a number-one draft pick in 1965. Following the draft, Schuh was spirited away from his home in Memphis, and the Rams, who had also drafted him, tried to get his parents to swear out a kidnapping complaint. Schuh was taken to Las Vegas by Ron Wolf, then a Raiders scout, but Davis was fearful the Rams would get to him, because the hotel in Las Vegas was swarming with NFL scouts. Maury Schleicher, a longtime Davis friend and an occasional scout for the Raiders, was sent to Las Vegas. As soon as he entered the hotel lobby, he had all the NFL scouts he saw paged, and while they were answering the pages he whisked Schuh out. Schleicher first took Schuh to southern California, to a hotel from which they could see the Rams offices, and finally to Hawaii. Somewhere along the way Schuh agreed to contract terms.

Davis almost always got a player he wanted, although Bob Valli, now the sports editor of the *Oakland Tribune* but a *Tribune* beat writer in the 1960s, remembered one big exception. "He drafted Tony Lorick, a running back from Arizona State, number one in 1964, but Baltimore signed Lorick. Davis went into a rage. He vowed that he would never again lose a number one, and he never did."

Davis also vowed revenge on the Arizona State coach, Frank Kush. The next year he signed Arizona State running back Larry Todd, who had a year of college eligibility left. (Todd showed flashes of brilliance, both as a running back and later as a receiver, but he never developed into the star it seemed he could be.)

Davis's insecurities showed over the drafting of Cal quarterback Craig Morton in 1964. Morton was drafted number one by the Dallas Cowboys of the NFL. Davis drafted him tenth, because he feared that the Cowboys might trade Morton's rights to the San Francisco 49ers—and if the 49ers signed him after the Raiders had picked him first, it would make the Raiders seem second-rate in their own Bay Area. That fear evaporated when the Cowboys made Morton an offer, but Davis was still reluctant. "He used George Ross as his go-between," Valli remembered, "and told Morton to wait until he got an offer from the Raiders. But Davis never made an offer. He was afraid he'd be under pressure to play Morton and that Morton wouldn't be good enough."

There were some amusing moments along with the drama. Valli remembered the time Davis had assistant Charley Sumner hiding a player in a hotel in the east. "Davis called Charley and told him, 'Don't even answer the door or the phone.' Then, a little later, he had something he wanted to ask Charley, so he called him. The hotel operator told him, 'I've been told not to put calls through to him.' Well, Al just about went up the wall. He said, 'Young lady, do you know who this is? This is Al Davis of the Oakland Raiders, and I want to talk to my coach.' But she wouldn't put him through. I had all I could do to keep from laughing, because I knew Al had set it all up, and now he couldn't get through himself."

• • •

In 1963, all that was in the future. Davis wanted to win now, with the players he had, and the training camp in Santa Rosa was charged with excitement.

"Al was really close to the players in those early years," Spencer remembered. "He'd be right with them, talking to them, coaching them."

"It was so impressive when Al went on the field and showed the assistant coaches all the techniques," said Ross, who also remembered John Rauch's first meeting with Davis. "Here was a guy who'd been an All-American quarterback at Georgia, but when Al went to the blackboard and showed him an offense with five wide receivers, John was jumping up and down. He'd never seen anything like it."

The Raiders won their first two games in 1963, lost the next four, and then won eight straight. How? By deception, from play to play and game to game. "The opponent would see the game film from last week, but by the next week the offense and defense wouldn't be the same," Ross said. "Especially on defense. They didn't have enough good guys, so Al had to keep changing."

The offense was explosive. Seven times the Raiders scored more than 30 points; twice they scored more than 40; once they scored more than 50. "The way his pass offense was set up, the Raiders might go for a time without a score and then hit three touchdowns in a quarter," Ross said. He remembered most vividly the season finale against the Houston Oilers. "The Raiders trailed by three touchdowns, and people started leaving the game, but they were listening on their car radios. As the Raiders rallied they started to come back to the game, and many of them were back in the stands by the time the game ended." With the Raiders on top, 52–49.

Their most memorable games were against Davis's former team, the San Diego Chargers: the Chargers won the AFL championship that season, but they lost both games to the Raiders, 34–33 at San Diego and 41–27 at Oakland. The Raiders won mainly by neutralizing the great pass rush of the Chargers. "Davis had taught a system of blocking he called 'storm blocking,'" Ross said. "One blocker would hold up a man and the other would chop at his legs. Well, the one thing linemen don't like is somebody blocking their legs, but that technique—clipping anywhere else on the field—is legal on the line of scrimmage. Earl Faison of the Chargers became so enraged at one point that he took off his helmet and swung it at a Raiders player. That blocking technique took all the steam out of the Chargers pass rushers. Their 'Fearsome Foursome' totally intimidated people in those days, but they didn't do much against the Raiders."

Even with their two wins over the Chargers, the Raiders finished the 1963 season a game back, but their fans were delirious at the rapid turnabout Davis had fashioned. At thirty-three, Davis was chosen Coach of the Year in the AFL and Young Man of the Year in Oakland, the first sports figure to get that honor. He was on top of the world.

But he wouldn't stay there.

· 2 ·

The Commissioner Returns

Bob Valli was in his first season on the Raiders beat for the *Oakland Tribune* in 1964. After an exhibition-game loss he and George Ross were invited to have dinner with Al Davis and his wife, Carol.

"We were sitting at the table," Valli remembered, "and Al said he was driving back to training camp in Santa Rosa that night. His wife said, 'No, you're not. You're staying home with your wife tonight and taking care of my needs.' Well, Davis just went wild. He said, 'Can you imagine a woman talking that way? We've just lost a football game. I've got to get back to camp.' Carol said, 'No, you don't. I don't care if you drive up in the middle of the night, but you're coming home with me.' They went back and forth like that for a long time. I just wanted to crawl under the table, I was so embarrassed. It's bad enough to be in the middle of something like that when you know the people, but that was the first time I'd even met his wife.

"Al finally stomped out of the restaurant and drove back to Santa Rosa, and his wife went home by herself. I don't even know why he had to go back there that night. That was in the days before videotape, when teams would have to wait a day or two to get the films, so there was nothing for him to look at.

"But that was Davis. He had incredible tunnel vision. He'd talk about other things, but the subject always came back to football. I never saw him drink. Maybe he'd order a drink, but he'd just hold it. I never knew him to chase women. He told me one time, out of the blue, 'You know, I have to do this'— he meant football. 'If I didn't, I'd be chasing waitresses all the time.' But other than that, I never heard him even mention women."

When I was on the Raiders beat, I had many conversations with Davis, and he always controlled the subject matter. It quickly became obvious that, with rare exceptions, he was interested in talking only about football. There was no light chatting about the weather, no retelling of the latest jokes, no discussion of women. It was just football.

That was true in larger groups as well as one on one. After the Kansas City Chiefs beat the Minnesota Vikings in the fourth Super Bowl, Davis entertained a small group in a New Orleans restaurant; I was invited, along with several Raiders employees and some of his friends. Davis was a gracious host, and countless bottles of champagne were consumed that night. (Davis's glass, however, remained untouched.) Those at the table talked about the game, but also about the good food and ambience of New Orleans. Davis talked nothing but football.

Why this obsession? One reason, I have always thought, is that he always wants to be in control of the conversation; he can do that with football, but not necessarily with other subjects. Certainly he is uncomfortable with lighthearted conversation, because he has an underdeveloped sense of humor. If someone laughs unexpectedly in his presence, he'll stop immediately and ask, "What are you laughing at?"—apparently fearful that it might be him.

Occasionally he will discuss other topics, though he often relates them to football. With me, for instance, he would sometimes talk politics and power. I remember in particular his explanation of why the Soviet Union would never allow the 1968 revolution in Czechoslovakia to occur. Power and powerful men have always intrigued him.

With Valli he was more relaxed. "He'd say crazy things to me sometimes. One time he asked me how much money it would take to make me happy. I said, 'Well, Al, I've never needed a lot of money. I think if I had $350,000, I could put that in a bank at 10 percent and draw out $35,000 a year, and that would make me happy.' Remember, that was in 1964, and $35,000 was a lot of money. I was probably making less than $200 a week at the time. But Al couldn't believe it. He said, 'How could you live on $35,000 a year?' But he always came back to football. He couldn't understand anybody who didn't feel the same way. He accused me one time of being 'against us.' I said, 'Al, I'm not against you. I want you to win because I know the players. But if you win or lose, I still sleep nights.' He said, 'That's what I mean. You're not with us.' "

Because Valli worked for George Ross, Davis could be confident that nothing he said would get in the newspaper unless he wanted it there. So he often said things to Valli that he would not have said to any other newspaperman, giving Valli an insight into Davis's plans for the future.

"In training camp, we'd go out to dinner," Valli recalled. "Sometimes he'd draw up a list of, say, tight ends and say, 'Our guy is the eighth best tight end in the league. We've got to have the third best tight end to be the kind of team we want to be.' That's how he worked to improve his team—he compared his players to those on other teams.

"He was trying to educate me in football, I think. I had been out of sports"—Valli had been running a public relations firm that, among other things, promoted the World's Fair in Seattle—"and I didn't know any of the players on the team. I wouldn't have known Tom Flores from Art Powell when I first came there. But Davis was also using me as a sounding board, thinking out loud. He needed somebody to bounce his ideas off. I remember one time much later when he asked me, 'What

would you think if I traded Gene Upshaw for Bubba Smith?'
I told him, 'You'd be crazy.' He agreed but said, 'But we're
going to get Bubba.' " Davis did finally get Bubba Smith, in a
1973 trade for Raymond Chester.

Information has always been vital to Davis. He talked to
everyone. Tom Keating remembered their contract talks. "We
were supposed to be talking money, but he'd always ask me
about players. 'What do you think of number 50? Is he doing
the job?' " Then, as he does now, he spent countless hours on
the telephone talking to people around the league. "Al has
always wanted to talk to successful people," Ollie Spencer said.
"He always feels he can learn something from somebody who's
successful. Maybe the other guy is doing something he hadn't
thought of."

"He always knew who the good players were around the
league," Valli said. "He told me one time, 'There's a cornerback in Denver, Willie Brown, who's the best defensive player
in the league. It isn't even close. I'm going to get him somehow.' " That was probably Davis's most lopsided trade. He got
Brown—the best cornerback I ever saw, and now in the Pro
Football Hall of Fame—for a reserve quarterback, Mickey
Slaughter.

"He told me in 1965 that he'd made a trade with Buffalo
for a defensive lineman named Tom Keating," Valli added. "I
didn't even know who Keating was—he wasn't on the Buffalo
roster. Davis told me, 'He's injured now, but you watch, he's
going to be a great one.' And when Keating came to camp the
next year, I saw what Davis meant. Tom was so quick, he was
almost beating the center snap to the quarterback into the
backfield."

Ross remembered the time in Denver in 1965 when Davis
told him to keep an eye on a Broncos tight end named Hewritt
Dixon. Then Davis asked Ross what he thought. Ross replied
that he thought Dixon was one of the best tight ends in the
league. "He's also the best fullback in the league, but Denver
doesn't know it," said Davis, who had already agreed to trade
middle linebacker Archie Matsos for Dixon. With Oakland,

Dixon did become the league's best fullback, as Davis had predicted.

Those were the years during which Davis was able to make excellent trades by taking advantage of club officials with less football knowledge—which basically meant the rest of the AFL. But he made a basic mistake: he gloated.

"Al always liked to rub it in," Ross said. "If he pulled off a trade, he'd let everybody know he'd hoodwinked the other guy. There weren't many guys he respected." That attitude would eventually hurt him, because teams became reluctant to trade with the Raiders. But in the 1960s Davis got his players every way he could: through the draft, through free agency, through trades. Once he had them, he knew what to do with them, even—maybe especially—if it went against conventional wisdom.

Dixon, for instance, had been a fullback in college, where he had acquired the nickname "Hewie the Freight" because he was said to lack speed. Yes, Dixon was the slowest man in the Florida A&M backfield, but that was because the backfield included three sprinters, one of whom was the Olympics 100-meter champion Bob Hayes. In that company Dixon seemed slow, but in fact he had been timed at 9.9 seconds in the 100-yard dash. Al Davis was not misled by Dixon's nickname. Davis wanted Dixon at fullback because he planned to use him as both a receiver and a runner. Other teams had had problems defending against Clem Daniels as a receiver, and those problems were compounded with Dixon. The Raiders would send Dixon deep to the corner—when no one else had thought of using a fullback in that fashion. In 1967 Dixon caught fifty-nine passes for the Raiders.

With Billy Cannon, Davis reversed the role switch. Cannon, who had a sprinter's speed, had been a Heisman Trophy winner at Louisiana State as a running back. His most dramatic feat had been a punt-return touchdown to beat Ole Miss in a game on Halloween night. Cannon ran through virtually the entire Mississippi team, and the run was so exciting that an LSU radio station replayed the play-by-play account of it for years on the eve of the LSU-Mississippi game.

Cannon played well early in his pro career, earning All-AFL honors with the Houston Oilers, but then he hurt his back. He began running timidly, without the explosiveness he had shown in his prime. He was booed out of Houston and was picked up on the rebound by the Raiders during the 1964 season. His running style didn't change with the Raiders. Sometimes he almost backed into the line of scrimmage. At the end of the season the always direct Cannon said to Davis, "I fucked up, didn't I?" "Yes, you did," Davis agreed, "but don't worry about it. I want you to go home and put on twenty-five pounds. I'm going to put you out at tight end."

Again it was speed that intrigued Davis. His idea was to put speed at positions where it wasn't expected. Tight ends were traditionally selected for their blocking, not their receiving—they had to be big enough and tough enough to block linebackers in order to make the running game work. But Davis wanted a receiver in that position.

The safeties who had to cover Daniels, Dixon, and now Cannon were overmatched. On the 1967 Super Bowl team, Cannon became more of a deep threat than either of the wide receivers, Fred Biletnikoff and Bill Miller, and he caught ten touchdown passes.

Tom Keating was another player who didn't seem to fit the mold, even Davis's. Davis wanted mammoth linemen, because he knew that to win in the AFL he had to beat the San Diego Chargers and the Kansas City Chiefs, which were big teams. Yet he traded for Keating, who was small for a defensive lineman (6 feet 2, 245 pounds). He realized that Keating's explosiveness and quickness made him a special player.

Keating had a simple defensive philosophy: Go for the quarterback. He would make a quick initial burst into the backfield, which left him vulnerable to trap blocking, but it was a gamble he was willing to take. At first Davis questioned that style (through Tom Dahms, his defensive line coach), but when he saw that it worked he said nothing more to Keating about it.

"What Al saw," Keating said, "was that if somebody was different but had a special talent, you could change the way you did things. He never said anything to me except, 'Get the fucking passer.' He was one of the first to realize that if you put the quarterback on the ground enough times, you're going to win the game. At Buffalo I didn't have that kind of leeway. If the guards pulled on a running play, I'd have to follow the play down the line, because Lou Saban wouldn't let me go through the hole. I was getting killed. If I'd stayed in Buffalo I'd never have been more than an average player."

As Davis worked to upgrade his team, the Raiders were changing from a team with a few stars to a team on its way to becoming a dynasty. But that didn't show immediately; the Raiders' record dropped dramatically in the 1964 season, to five wins, seven losses, and two ties. Other teams were catching on to Davis's method of play, and he could no longer sneak up on teams as he had the year before. In fact, the Raiders lost their first five games that season.

In those years the Raiders traditionally made one swing through the east to play the Boston Patriots, the Buffalo Bills, and the New York Jets, staying away an entire two weeks to cut down on travel expenses. In 1964 the Raiders were already 0–3 when they began their eastern trip. It was, Valli remembered, a nightmare.

"Al had the idea of staying in the Catskills, because he thought it would be an idyllic setting and well isolated from the bright lights of New York. But the hotel we were staying at wouldn't allow the black players to eat in the dining room, so they had to eat in their rooms. I really had to wonder if Al would make it. We'd go walking after dinner, and he was ranting and raving. I remember calling George Ross one time and saying, 'I don't think the guy's going to last.'

"The first game of the trip was a loss to Buffalo, and then we went in to New York. Al desperately wanted to look good in New York because he'd grown up there and wanted to show everybody that he'd made good. The Jets were struggling, too, at that time, so he thought he could win the game. But his team lost, 35–13. I don't think I've ever seen anybody so down."

The Raiders finished the year strong, with five wins and a tie in their last eight games, and they had a decent season the next year, 8–5–1, second to the San Diego Chargers in the AFL's Western Division. But 1965 was far from the delirious success of Davis's first season, and his insecurities were beginning to show.

"Al had always talked about how he'd been the first to recognize Lance Alworth's ability," Ross remembered. "When he drafted Fred Biletnikoff in 1965, he knew that Freddie's abilities were not the same as Alworth's, and he didn't even play Freddie the first seven games of that season. It wasn't that he thought Freddie wasn't ready—he just didn't want to look bad. He didn't want people comparing Alworth and Biletnikoff. But Freddie finally played, and caught something like seven balls in that first game, so that was the end of that."

The insecurities were beginning to show off the field, too. "I always thought Al was a very effective public speaker," Ross said, "but after that first year he was very hesitant, almost diffident, when he was asked to speak. It was like he had no confidence in himself."

One reason was that Wayne Valley continued to treat Davis disparagingly. Valley referred to Davis sarcastically as "the Genius" and made ethnic jokes about Jews in his presence. Curiously, Valley was not a prejudiced man, nor an unsophisticated one, but for some reason he liked to affect a rough, boorish attitude. It was two years after I first met him before I was able to penetrate that disguise, and I found him to be an honest, likable man. Valley would also put Davis down in public. "When Al was asked to speak somewhere," Ross remembered, "he would always ask if Wayne would be the one to introduce him. And Wayne always would say things like, 'He's doing a great job, and if he doesn't keep doing it he'll be on his way,' reminding people that Al was working for him."

Davis never forgets a slight, and he eventually made Valley

pay for those early insults. Until then, however, he kept Valley at arm's length. In fact, Ross believed that one reason he was often invited to eat with Davis while on the road was to give Davis an excuse not to be with Valley. "Al always set up strata," Ross said. "He didn't associate with assistant coaches, but he didn't associate with the team owners, either. Wayne always had his drinking buddies along on the trips, and Al had nothing to do with any of them."

There was never any question that Davis was running the team, nor any question that he would continue to do so. Valley once told me, "I've been successful by finding good men who can run my operations, and that's what I did with the Raiders." All he wanted was to have Davis call him occasionally and tell him what was happening, but Davis wouldn't do that. "Al told me many times that he didn't have the time to waste," Ross said. " 'He wants me to give him the fucking game plan,' Al said one time."

While the feud simmered, the Raiders were putting on another good finish, winning three straight before losing the 1965 season finale to the Chargers in San Diego, 24 – 14. It would be the last game Al Davis ever coached—at least from the sideline.

•   •   •

Although the results on the field were disappointing, Davis was finally getting close to having the stadium he felt was essential for the success of the franchise.

In 1960, when Oakland got its AFL franchise, Robert Nahas headed the Oakland Chamber of Commerce. It was obvious that the franchise would need a modern stadium to play in, but it was equally obvious that it would be risky to take a plan to the voters, who had twice turned down proposals to build a stadium. Nahas, who had made his money in land development, devised another plan, the creation of a nonprofit corporation that would issue revenue bonds to pay for a stadium and an arena.

He was the perfect man to organize such a project. Even today, in his seventies, Nahas is a man of high energy and vitality. He runs land-development companies in Castro Valley (near Oakland) and Idaho, and shuttles around by private plane to his homes in Piedmont, Palm Desert, and Lake Tahoe.

Nahas set up a four-man board consisting of himself; former Senator William Knowland, then the editor-publisher of the *Oakland Tribune*; Edgar Kaiser, owner of the construction company bearing his name; and George Loorz, owner of the giant Stolte Construction Company. The men were of such stature that local politicians would hesitate to question what they did. To avoid any hint of conflict of interest, neither Kaiser nor Loorz bid on the construction contracts for the Coliseum, although both men had their company engineers thoroughly examine each phase of the construction. No sports stadium was ever more carefully scrutinized.

Nahas wasn't able to sell the revenue bonds in the Bay Area, largely because of the San Francisco press's ridicule of the project. The late Charles McCabe, a *San Francisco Chronicle* columnist—a brilliant essayist, who seldom let facts get in his way when he was writing about sports—regularly wrote columns denouncing the project and calling Nahas "a greedy land developer." Nahas wasn't surprised at the San Francisco reaction. "You know, San Franciscans have always been very provincial," he said. "It has to be in their backyard or it doesn't mean anything."

But elsewhere, the fact that Davis had turned the Raiders into a viable team with a respectable future impressed potential backers. Nahas sold the bonds in Chicago, and the Coliseum was finished in time for the 1966 football season. It added a baseball client in 1968, when the A's moved to Oakland from Kansas City. Later an arena was built, inducing the basketball Warriors to move from San Francisco; then an exhibition hall. Nowadays the complex hosts everything from rock concerts to home shows. Meanwhile, San Francisco, which likes to bill itself as "The City That Knows How," has lost hockey and basketball teams for lack of a suitable arena and soon may lose the baseball Giants because of its inability to build them a new stadium.

• • •

The war between the AFL and the NFL was reaching a crisis stage, with owners in both leagues spending much more money on players than they'd have preferred. Things were especially critical within the AFL, because its teams usually had to outbid the established NFL teams to get players. Something had to be done, and by early 1966 it was obvious that Joe Foss, the AFL commissioner, wasn't the man to do it.

Wayne Valley might have made slighting remarks about "the Genius," but he was well aware of Al Davis's special talents. When the AFL owners said they needed someone who could fight in the trenches, Valley said, "Hell, you need my guy. He'll do whatever it takes to win." There was some debate—Davis was not loved in the league even then—but the other owners finally agreed to make Davis the league commissioner, succeeding Foss. "Wayne sent Al off to New York with his blessings," Ross noted. "It may have been the only thing they agreed on in the final few years."

Before Davis left to assume the post, on April 8, 1966, he appointed John Rauch his successor as coach and Scotty Stirling as general manager. Those close to the Raiders scene had their doubts. "I didn't think Rauch could handle the job of head coach," Ross said. "He was an excellent assistant, but he just didn't have the overall vision to be a head coach."

In New York, Davis prepared to meet the press by having Jack Horrigan, then the AFL public relations director, fire questions at him for two hours the night before. "I'm not sure he needed that," Horrigan told me once. "I have never seen Al in better form than he was that day. The press conference lasted for a couple of hours, and he was brilliant." Davis also read Horrigan's press release before it went out and asked him to make just two changes, inserting "dynamic" and "young genius." Despite Valley's contemptuous use of the word, Davis hadn't tired of the genius label.

Davis's strategy as AFL commissioner was simple: he went after the NFL's quarterbacks, reasoning that they were both the most important players and the ones with the highest public recognition. In two months, he had persuaded seven NFL quarterbacks to sign with AFL teams.

Al Davis has often been accused of using others to get what he wants, but in this case he was the one being used. He thought he had been hired to win the war with the NFL. In fact, the AFL owners only wanted to force a peace. They were quietly negotiating a merger while Davis was fighting a war.

"I went to Dallas and stayed at Cowboys president Tex Schramm's home for over a week," Pete Rozelle, by now the NFL commissioner, told me. "Tex and I would talk around the clock there, and he had arranged some clandestine meetings with Kansas City Chiefs owner Lamar Hunt. We felt that was the best way to approach it because everybody had respect for Lamar. Tex and I would talk, he'd meet with Lamar and exchange ideas, and then get back to me. That was my involvement. I didn't want to get directly involved in case it fell through. And that was the way the league owners wanted it."

On June 8, 1966, a merger agreement was announced. Davis was bitter, especially since the agreement required the New York Jets and the Raiders to pay indemnities to the NFL clubs whose territories they had "invaded," the New York Giants and the San Francisco 49ers. "We had them on the run," Davis said to me later.

Meanwhile, in Oakland, John Rauch had turned from an assistant coach whom everyone liked into a head coach who couldn't get along with anyone. The pressure was too much for Rauch, who called Davis during a minicamp and begged him to come back. "It's your team, Al, everybody knows that," he said, with Scotty Stirling sitting uncomfortably in the same room.

"Scotty would tell me, 'This thing's falling apart. Rauch can't take charge, he won't take charge,' " Ross said. "When Rauch called Al, I know Al told him, 'Jesus Christ, John, you've got the chance of a lifetime. Ease up and you'll find you can do it.' But if you have to talk to a professional coach in those terms . . . well, it didn't inspire a lot of confidence in me."

"Rauch was an excellent technician," said Bill Walsh, who was an assistant with the Raiders in 1966, "and he knew Davis's system very well. Al obviously had confidence in him, because he'd made him his top assistant and then named him as head coach."

But coaching is more than technical knowledge. Davis had the ability that all great coaches have, to get the most out of his players. His players absolutely believed in him. Rauch was never that kind of coach. He couldn't verbalize his thoughts, and he seemed to compensate by working the team even harder than Davis had. The players accepted that—this was an era when players did not question their coaches—but they resented it. Although Rauch was a successful coach with the Raiders, it was almost in spite of himself; the players neither liked nor respected him.

"We worked so hard in training camp and in practice," Ben Davidson said. "It was tough because I liked to work up a real animosity to an opponent to make me play harder. But you couldn't do that against your teammates. We'd beat on each other day after day, but I couldn't work up that viciousness I needed for the game. It was much better when Rauch left. John Madden was a breath of fresh air."

Davis did come back to the Raiders soon, but not as head coach and not until undergoing one more disappointment. He thought he had outdueled NFL commissioner Pete Rozelle and would be named commissioner of the new league. But Valley pointed out the arithmetic—the NFL had twelve clubs at the time, the AFL only eight—and added, "Hell, Al, you couldn't even get the votes of *our* owners." "Davis didn't understand that the guerrilla fighter is never the one who's named commissioner," Bob Valli commented.

Davis was still the AFL commissioner, but the job was now

devoid of meaning for him. No one who knew him thought that he would stay in New York. Valley made him an offer to return as general manager and coach. Davis turned it down. "Wayne kept saying, 'I thought he wanted to come back,'" Ross remembered. "Of course he did, but on his own terms. He was always very surefooted. He knew exactly where he was going."

For sure, it wouldn't be back to coaching. He wanted to move up, into ownership. Valley finally agreed to bring Davis back as the managing general partner, with a 10 percent share of the club. To make the deal sweeter, Valley set the book value of the Raiders at $185,000—though the merger certainly made the team worth far more—so that Davis could buy his share for $18,500. That 10 percent would be worth $10 million to $15 million today.

While he was putting in a carrot, Valley also put in a stick: Davis would have to forfeit his ownership if he left the club before seven years. Rumors were prevalent at the time that Davis wanted to return to his native area, probably with the New York Jets, and Valley thought this provision was a way of keeping Davis.

In retrospect, it seems to be another time when Valley simply did not understand Davis's motivations. Davis may have grown up in Brooklyn, but no one who has known him well over the years thinks that he has ever wanted to return to New York. The city only reminds him of the insecurities of his youth. It is probably significant that Davis, who has had some big-time supporters among national sports columnists—Mel Durslag, Jim Murray, Will McDonough—has not numbered an important New York sportswriter among his friends. Dave Anderson, the Pulitzer Prize–winning sports columnist for the *New York Times*, has been a consistent critic.

When I observed Davis on trips to New York, he always seemed on edge. He was determined to prove to his old friends—and, more important, to his detractors—that he had made it, but his team suffered some crushing defeats by the Jets in New York: his first two games in New York as a coach, the 1967 defeat that was the only Raiders loss of the year, the

1968 AFL championship game. On one trip to New York the Raiders plane was put in a holding pattern over Kennedy Airport. That's hardly unusual, but it enraged Davis. He said to Bob Bestor, then the club's public relations director, "Tell them it's the Raiders up here, and Al Davis." Bestor passed the word along, but it did no good. To me the episode seemed symbolic of Davis's relationship with the area.

• • •

The story of Davis's return to the Raiders, on July 25, 1966, was broken by Mike Berger in the *San Francisco Chronicle*, which was notable as an indication of the change in the way the San Francisco media perceived the Raiders.

In the early years the Raiders had been a joke, and the San Francisco papers, the *Chronicle* and the *Examiner*, had treated them that way. The two papers were locked in a circulation war, and the 49ers were the team that meant extra newsstand sales, not the Raiders. The *Examiner* once sent its fish-and-game writer on a Raiders road trip. The *Chronicle* wasn't quite so cavalier, but it did tend to assign whoever wasn't needed on a more important story to cover the Raiders.

By 1966 the *Chronicle*'s coverage of the Raiders was expanding greatly, and Berger, an excellent reporter who moved to Japan after the season, gave readers a view of the Raiders no *Chronicle* readers had known before. He also gained the confidence of Davis, who respected him more than he had ever respected any other reporter from a San Francisco newspaper. For the first time the Raiders were a serious story to the *Chronicle*, and Berger's story of Davis's return as managing general partner was the lead in the sports section that day.

Davis returned to a team that was only a year away from a championship but that was also a team in turmoil. If Rauch had felt pressure when Davis left, he felt twice as much when Davis returned. Rauch had been Davis's closest assistant, but a gulf had grown between them. "I sensed that John had lost his affection for Davis even before he was named head coach,"

Ross said. "Maybe Davis had jumped on him as an assistant, and now there was a barrier there."

The problem went to the very heart of the matter. Rauch had inherited Davis's offense and his players, and he also had to take Davis's assistants. Rauch had been on the mark in his telephone conversation: it was indeed Davis's team. Rauch was allowed to name just one assistant, and his choice was a curious one—a short, rotund twenty-three-year-old named Bugsy Engleberg, who was supposed to be the kicking coach. Engleberg soon learned the limits of his authority. When he approached kicker George Blanda with some advice, Blanda told him to shut up or he'd be kicked over the goalposts.

Even on the practice field Rauch seemed the lesser figure. Davis was everywhere, coaching specific skills and patterns to the receivers and quarterbacks, overseeing drills elsewhere. Reporters again went to Davis for the definitive word on players. Behind closed doors there were one-on-one confrontations, and even in public the air crackled with tension when the two were in the same room. Desperate to show that he had some authority, Rauch insisted on drawing up his own game plans. That didn't stop Davis. He simply had Ollie Spencer and John Madden plant his ideas with the unsuspecting Rauch at coaches' meetings.

Davis was coaching by proxy, and yet he was able to publicly distance himself from any mistakes. "Al wasn't above second-guessing," Ross noted. Davis would normally sit in the main press box at games, where his second-guessing could be heard easily by nearby writers. He would sometimes be interviewed immediately after games, and even after a Raiders win his criticism could be strong.

What probably hurt Rauch most was that he knew Davis was right. Davis was quick and innovative; Rauch was a plodder. He had been a good assistant because somebody else made the big decisions. As a head coach, he was slow to make decisions and still slower to correct mistakes.

Probably the best example came in 1968, in a strange game

in Kansas City. Because of injuries to his wide receivers, the Chiefs coach, Hank Stram, was using a tight-T offense, with three running backs and with two tight ends as blockers. The Chiefs shredded the Raiders' four-man front with their running attack in the first half; in the game, quarterback Len Dawson threw only three passes, completing two. Early in the second quarter Davis sent down a note to Rauch advising him to switch to a five-man defensive front to stop the run. Rauch didn't even look at the note. From the press box, the writers clearly saw him crumple the paper in his hand and throw it to the ground. At halftime Rauch finally made the adjustment— too late. The Chiefs won the game, 24 – 10.

Most coaches dream of having the kind of team Rauch had inherited, a team that went 13 – 1 and 12 – 2 in his second and third seasons, but Rauch was miserable and looking for a way out. Although he lasted three seasons, there were constant rumors that he would leave.

Davis told George Ross that Rauch was negotiating with the San Francisco 49ers, even on the eve of the Raiders' first Super Bowl appearance, after the 1967 season, but Lou Spadia, then the 49ers president, has firmly denied that. "I never talked to Rauch at all," Spadia told me. "Jack Christiansen was our coach, and I wasn't talking to other coaches at that time. When I did feel I had to make a change, I talked to one college coach and then to Dick Nolan, whom I hired. But Rauch? Never."

Rauch finally went to the Buffalo Bills after the 1968 season, moving from the best team in the league to one of the worst. That was the measure of his desperation.

The Raiders would have been better served at that point if Davis had gone back to coaching the team. "There's something missing," the former star running back, Clem Daniels, noted, about the frustrating period from 1967 to 1976 when the Raiders could not get back to the Super Bowl. "This is Al Davis's team, but he's not coaching it."

Wayne Valley knew why Davis wouldn't come back to coaching. "He doesn't have the guts to stay on the sideline," Valley told me at the time. "The great ones, like George Halas and Vince Lombardi, have gone out there year after year and let people take their shots. 'The Genius' can't do that."

Valley was, of course, speaking out of bitterness, because he had been unable to convince Davis to return to coaching, but I think he was closer to the truth than Davis himself was when he talked about his decision. In 1968, in a training-camp conversation, Davis told me, "I had made a vow to myself— and I'm a guy who sticks to things when I promise myself— that when I became commissioner I was through with coaching. I hadn't done all the things I'd wanted to do, like winning a championship, but I'd done enough. I don't care what others think, as long as I satisfy myself."

Like so many of Davis's statements, that is very self-serving. He could have coached the team and still made all the important personnel decisions, as Bill Walsh did for the 49ers, as Vince Lombardi did for the Green Bay Packers, as Paul Brown did for the Cleveland Browns and the Cincinnati Bengals, as George Halas did for the Chicago Bears. Valley was right: Davis didn't want to take the criticism a coach takes when he isn't successful.

If he had returned to coaching, how successful would Davis have been? Hank Stram, who coached the Chiefs against him, thinks that Davis would have ranked at the very top. "He had good vision," Stram told me. "He has always had a clear idea of what he wanted, and he believes in it strongly.

"For instance, there are basically two methods of attacking a defense. Some coaches like to use a lot of motion, as I did, because you can get the defense moving that way. Al believes in putting out four receivers because you force the defense to cover you in a specific way; why confuse the quarterback? Al is not a guy who succumbs to trends. A lot of guys will just go for something that's worked for somebody else. They don't think it through and realize that it won't work for them. Al is just the opposite. You won't see Al going for the run-and-shoot, for instance. He sticks with what he believes in."

The rivalry between the Raiders and the Chiefs in the 1960s, when Davis was coach and afterward, is a fascinating story. "Al always geared his season to beating the Chiefs and the Chargers," Tom Keating said. "When he beat either of those teams he was really happy. I remember, in my first season with the team, we beat the Chargers in an exhibition game, and he just went nuts. An exhibition game!"

The Chargers were the AFL's best team early on, but as their top players faded the Chiefs became the team Davis had to beat. And, though his team was not the physical equal of the Chiefs in Davis's three coaching years, the Raiders split their six games against Kansas City.

Davis and Stram looked for the same kind of player—size in the line, speed everywhere else—and even coveted some of the same players. "Al always wanted to trade with the Chiefs for Otis Taylor because he thought Otis would be perfect in his system," Bob Valli remembered. "The Chiefs couldn't take full advantage of him because Lenny Dawson didn't have the same kind of arm that Daryle Lamonica had. But Stram was too smart to let him go."

By the time he came back as general partner, Davis knew he had to build a team that could beat Kansas City if the Raiders were to win a championship. "He drafted Gene Upshaw to block Buck Buchanan," Stram noted. "Because we always had great kickers, Jan Stenerud and Jerry Wilson, he upgraded his kicking game by drafting Ray Guy as a punter. In fact, I almost drafted Guy just to keep him away from the Raiders."

Davis and Stram had competed on the sidelines, too, and Stram recalled one particular trait—or tactic. "He'd always spend more time talking to my players than his own before a game. He'd ask them how they were, how they felt." For information, or for psychological purposes? Probably both.

"He had a great capacity for using players," Stram said. "They believed in him. And he was always very good at utilizing players in particular roles. He told me one time that he'd picked up a guy who could only play fifteen plays a game, but they'd be fifteen good plays. He was talking about what we now call situation substitution. Another time, he told me he'd traded for an offensive tackle because this guy could block a defensive end they'd be seeing in the play-offs. Now, who else would be thinking ahead like that?"

We can only speculate on what Davis might have accomplished in a long coaching career, but, to be sure, his greatest success came after he left the sidelines. Stram's Chiefs were the AFL's representative in the first Super Bowl, in 1967. With Al Davis watching from the owners' box, the Raiders were the next.

·3·

The Raiders'
First Super Bowl

Two weeks before training camp was to begin in 1967, my editor told me that I would be covering the Raiders. I met with Al Davis in the Raiders offices, then in downtown Oakland, and after a few moments he gestured to the filing cabinets near his desk. "This has information on every one of our players, and every player around the league. If we learn that we can trust you, I'll let you see these files."

I never did see those files (which may be an indication that Davis never fully trusted me), but the incident illustrated rather dramatically Davis's feeling that it was strictly Us against Them.

Those who have dealt with Davis over the years have diametrically opposing views of him, but there is one aspect of his behavior on which everyone agrees: he is the best friend and the worst enemy a person can have. "At least, you always know where you stand with Al," laughed Hank Stram, who is in the "friends" column. "He decides on his own terms who his friends are," Bill Walsh said. "But if you're his friend, he can't do enough for you."

Even though Davis might not have trusted me in the sense

that he trusted George Ross or my predecessor, Mike Berger, we had many confidential conversations in the year that I covered the Raiders. Most of those conversations were at training camp, usually in the coffee shop of the El Rancho Motel, but there were also many in his office at the Raiders headquarters, opposite the Oakland Coliseum. Our talks at training camp were informal. In his office, we were separated by a desk and an attitude. There was never a time during a talk with Davis in his office that he did not take at least one phone call. He was a busy executive, of course, but other busy executives have their secretaries hold their calls when they are meeting with someone. By not doing so, Davis seemed to be telling me that I was not the only one vying for his time and attention.

It didn't bother me because, like Bob Valli before me, Davis was giving me a football education. I knew relatively little about the sport then because I had not played it as a youth; I didn't like hitting people, and I was even less fond of people hitting me. Not until I met Bill Walsh many years later did I find someone who could tell me as much about the way the game worked.

It wasn't just the basics, which I knew. Davis talked about offensive formations and strategy, about player evaluation, about teams around the league. In retrospect, there was more to our relationship than I understood at the time. Davis is most comfortable around those who do not challenge him. At the time, though he was less than seven years older than I was, he was definitely the mentor and I the pupil—and, of course, we were on his turf.

One thing I clearly understood: John Rauch was the coach of the team, but Davis was the one making the important decisions. I talked to Rauch only to get the routine quotes I needed to satisfy my editor. For the real information I talked to Davis. Much of that information was off the record. I knew the limits, and I did not write about what was clearly intended to be background material. That didn't bother me. I wanted to be able to write authoritatively about the games, and, thanks to Davis, I could.

When I went into the *Chronicle* offices, I would be besieged by questions about Davis. What was he really like? What made him tick? My answers surprised those who thought of Davis as something evil, for that was not at all the way I viewed him. He was cautious, even abrupt to the point of rudeness, with those writers and broadcasters who were not with the team regularly, but to the regulars he could be a great source of information.

Davis had one idiosyncrasy: He would not release the standard information on waived players. During training camp, there were specified dates on which clubs had to cut their squads. To do this, teams would put players on waivers, which meant the players could be claimed by another team. If they were not claimed, the players could be kept on an inactive list by their original team or released. If they were claimed, their original team could either pull them back from the waiver list or let them go.

Other clubs routinely gave out lists of players they had put on waivers. The Raiders did not, so reporters had to check to see which players were still at practice to know who was missing. When Billy Cannon was released on a Thursday in 1970, no reporters were at camp, so no one knew about it until the lineup cards were passed out before the Sunday game and Cannon's name wasn't there.

Davis played games with the waiver lists, using his superior mind and his natural inclination toward deception. Mostly he did it to hold on to younger players who he thought could develop in time.

Davis would sometimes put veteran stars on waivers—Jim Otto and George Blanda, for example, at different times— hoping that other teams would be drawn to them and would overlook younger players he wanted to sneak through. Of course, Davis didn't want any of the veterans to know their names were on the list, even though it meant nothing. (Blanda, in fact, did learn about it from a reporter who had gotten the Raiders waivers from an executive of another NFL team. Blanda was enraged—which only reinforced Davis's point.)

Davis played the waiver game masterfully. One time, for instance, he had a promising rookie receiver named Drew Buie whom he wanted to keep on the practice squad but not on the regular roster. So he called around the league asking about receivers who might be available in a trade, and the word spread that Davis thought he needed a receiver. When Buie's name appeared on the waiver list, every team passed on him.

Another time, Davis wanted to keep a rookie center, Warren Koegel, but he had no room for him on the active squad. He arranged for the New England Patriots, the worst team in the conference and thus the team with the first call on waived players, to claim Koegel and then trade him back to the Raiders in exchange for a draft choice the next year. Koegel, of course, was told nothing about this, only that he would be inactive for at least the first game. He sat in the stands on game day cheering for the Raiders, blissfully unaware that he was, temporarily, the property of the Patriots.

Because it was policy, no Raiders official would release names, even when it made no difference, but one man could always make an exception to the rule. When I kidded Davis once about not making his waivers public, he said, "You want to know who was waived? These are the guys." He named the waived players—all of them players he had no intention of bringing back—and I wrote the story. The next day an irate John Madden, the head coach, screamed at me, "Who gave you those names?" Madden's rage quickly subsided when I told him.

The waiver situation was only a minor irritant to reporters. It was far more important to us that Davis didn't restrict our access to the players. Beat reporters could go into the locker room after practice, they could go into players' rooms during training camp, and they had a list of telephone numbers they could call during the season. The list did not include any bars, but it was easy enough to find those. The bar at the Airport Hilton, near the training facility, was a favorite, as was the Cactus bar in downtown Oakland. At dinnertime any number of Raiders could be found at the Grotto in Jack London Square.

On trips, though writers and players were segregated in their hotel rooms and at meals, we sat together on the planes and buses. That had its disadvantages—I still remember the flight on which I sat between Jim Otto and Bob Kruse, both more than 250 pounds and overflowing their seats—but it also meant that we writers were physically and psychologically close to the players.

In training camp I regularly stopped by Tom Keating's room, in the upper corner of the El Rancho Motel in Santa Rosa. Some players slept after practice, but not in Keating's room. It was a large room, so five or six players always roomed there and many more came in to talk. They would talk freely, because they understood that I would not write anything unless I told them it was an interview. As a result, I learned more about the team than I ever could have from strictly formal interviews.

Of course, Davis knew what he was doing. It was impossible for a beat writer to retain much objectivity about the Raiders. I loved those guys, and I thought Al Davis was smarter than anyone I had ever known. All that showed in my writing, but I never got any complaints, from editors or readers.

Players and writers kidded back and forth in a way that was uncommon even then and would be unheard of now. One time, for instance, when I wore a lime-green T-shirt to training camp, linebacker Bill Laskey said I looked like a bearded avocado, and for weeks after that, players called me "avocado."

Even today, when I see former Raiders players at functions in the Bay Area, there is an affection that is not the norm for writers and athletes. Keating has been a close friend for years. At a recent Bay Area Sports Hall of Fame dinner, George Blanda came over to say hello "to my favorite sportswriter"— though we'd certainly had our differences when he was playing and I was on the beat.

My respect for Davis at the time bordered on idolatry. I had never known anyone quite like him, and I regularly praised him for his accomplishments and defended him against his enemies, a group that was already large.

I recognized that what made the Raiders a fascinating team was Davis's suspension of the normal rules that made so many teams of the era faceless. There was a wealth of stories to be written about the characters on the team—characters like George Blanda, Fred Biletnikoff, Dan Birdwell, Ben Davidson, and others.

George Blanda, a fiery competitor, was already on his third football career, but he remained as intense as ever. When I criticized his kicking during one dry spell, he roared at me, "I ought to kick you over the goalposts." I was far enough away to retaliate bravely, "The way you've been kicking, I'd be wide to the right."

Blanda, a kicker and a quarterback, had played with the Chicago Bears and retired. A year later, when the AFL was formed, he joined the Houston Oilers, but his career seemed over when Davis traded for him before the 1967 season. Davis, knowing that Blanda could be a divisive element, talked very directly to him when he joined the team. "I don't want you fucking up my team, George," Davis said. "Do you understand me? You're here to kick and take some snaps in case Daryle Lamonica gets hurt, but that's all." So, though Blanda ached to continue playing quarterback, he kept his mouth shut.

At thirty-nine, Blanda was older than all the other players and most of the coaches, and everyone treated him with some deference. He set his own training schedule, and after practice he'd often sit in a lawn chair outside his room smoking a cigarette and lost in his thoughts.

Once, during an interview session, a very young writer asked him about curfew, toward which the Raiders had a very casual attitude. Blanda said it was eleven o'clock. The writer, trying to appear worldly, said, "It must be tough to get laid before eleven." Blanda looked at him for a moment and replied, "Not really."

Fred Biletnikoff went on to become a Hall of Fame player, but he was as insecure an athlete as I've ever known. On the way to an exhibition game in 1967, seated next to me in the plane, he confided that he was certain he would be cut after the game. I was astounded, because he was—and still is—the best pass catcher I've ever seen, but he was serious. Until the end of his career, he was always sure the next game would be his last.

Tom Keating tells a story about his first game with the Raiders, when he thought he heard someone in the bathroom grunting, "Earl, Earl." It was Biletnikoff vomiting, as he did before every game of his career.

He was so profane that radio interviewers gave up trying to get him on tape—every other word was a variation of the f-word—but he was a joy to watch. He wasn't as fast as most receivers, but he could catch balls that seemed uncatchable, and he always knew exactly how far he had to go for a first down, or how close he was to the sideline or the end line, and would carefully tiptoe to keep his feet in bounds.

He worked long hours after practice. He caught balls from any quarterback who would stay late with him and then moved to a light punching bag outside the practice field, drilling away on that to improve his hand-eye coordination. It worked. I saw him in every game he played as a Raider, and I cannot remember his ever dropping a pass.

Defensive tackle Dan Birdwell, a rangy Texan, was a constant source of humorous stories. Amazingly, all of them were true.

One time, for instance, a badly hung-over Birdwell vomited all over the ball. The startled center snapped it early and was called for illegal motion. Another time, as the Raiders were preparing to fly home, Birdwell got on the wrong plane. It was completely empty. When a search party finally found him, he said, "I figured I got on the plane. It was up to the rest of you to find it."

Scotty Stirling, the general manager when the Raiders went to the Super Bowl in January 1968, measured the players for Super Bowl rings beforehand, using an adjustable band. When Birdwell slipped on the band he said, "That's a pretty chicken-shit ring for a Super Bowl."

For years Birdwell thought that limited partner Arnie Boscacci was a writer. Boscacci, a liquor-store owner who believed in testing the products he sold, always came on the team plane with a briefcase filled with bottles. Birdwell thought the briefcase contained a typewriter. He would pat the case and say, "Write a good story, pal."

His personal habits were bizarre. He never brought a toothbrush on trips; he would simply borrow his roommate's.

He was born in rural Texas, and he retained in the abstract the prejudices with which he was born, but he never applied them to his own teammates—and he never saw the contradiction in that.

"One time Birdie was looking through the game program before we played Kansas City," Ben Davidson remembered. "I'd hear him grunting and mumbling to himself from time to time, and I suddenly realized he was counting the number of Chiefs players who were black. The Chiefs were far ahead of most teams at that time in the number of blacks they played, and I could see that they had exceeded Birdwell's idea of what the quota should be. John Madden gathered us all together before the game, as he always did, and then we jumped up together, clapped hands, and started out on the field. At just that moment Birdwell shouted, 'Let's beat them niggers!' " Ike Lassiter, who is black, was standing next to Birdwell and looking dumbstruck. "After all," Davidson continued, "he'd been playing next to Birdwell on the line for years. Birdie just looked over at him and said, 'Don't worry, Ike, you're not a nigger. Let's go play.' "

Yet, though everyone regarded Birdwell as a buffoon, he did his job on the field. "He knew all the plays," Keating said. "Not only the defensive plays but the offensive ones. He knew what everybody was expected to do. And when we switched defenses he always picked up the new defense right away. We'd change around sometimes, with Birdie going to the outside and Ike coming inside, or maybe I'd go outside and Ben would come in inside. I was never any good on the outside, so they stopped that, but Birdwell played very well outside. He did the job wherever they put him."

Then there was Ben Davidson. "I always loved Ben because he put the whole world on," said Bill King, the Raiders announcer.

Yes, he did. A delightful, articulate man away from the field, Davidson deliberately encouraged his reputation as a villain, complete with a handlebar mustache that could easily have been worn by the bad guy in an old melodrama.

"After my first season," Ben remembered, "I got a job working on a pipeline for a construction company—those were the years when you needed an off-season job to keep going. I just quit shaving, so when I came to training camp I had a full beard and mustache. Well, those were the days of the free-speech movement at Cal and that kind of thing, and anyone who wore a beard was considered a Communist. Al Davis came up to me and said, 'You are going to shave that beard, aren't you, Ben?' I didn't, and every couple of days he'd come up and ask me about it again. He never actually said I had to shave it, but I didn't have any doubt about his sentiments. Finally I shaved it. Al was so relieved that he never said anything about my mustache."

•   •   •

Davis had made two trades in the off-season that would be the key for both the 1967 season and the years to come. The one that pleased him most sent reserve quarterback Mickey Slaughter to the Denver Broncos for cornerback Willie Brown, but the one that had everyone buzzing was quarterback Tom Flores and wide receiver Art Powell to the Buffalo Bills for quarterback Daryle Lamonica and wide receiver Glenn Bass.

Flores couldn't believe the news when he heard it. "I had just come off my best year," he remembered. "I was just devastated. I was in shock. I heard that it was really John Rauch who fought for it, but Al could have stopped it if he'd wanted to. I knew we were very close to being a very good team." Recalling that the Raiders had beaten Kansas City, the 1966 AFL champion, in their second game that year, Flores added,

"I thought we had a good chance of winning in 1967. And then I was gone."

Lamonica had been a backup to Jack Kemp at Buffalo and, in his limited appearances, had never completed even 50 percent of his passes in a season. He had an ability to throw long that seemed perfectly suited to Davis's style of offense, but his inconsistency worried Davis, who was understandably concerned that his new quarterback would not be able to absorb the Raiders system.

"Al tried to back off from the Lamonica trade," Bob Valli remembered. When asked what he thought, Valli told Davis it sounded like a good trade, since he would still have Cotton Davidson, who was about as good a quarterback as Flores, and Art Powell, while a good receiver, had always been a complainer and a lot of trouble. "Lamonica had a good name," Valli said, "and it looked like he could be a good quarterback, but Davis told me, 'You know, Scotty made that trade.' Well, who was Scotty to make the trade? Davis had all the authority, and we knew it. But he didn't want to be blamed if the trade turned sour."

The trade was essentially two for one, because Bass didn't make it out of training camp with the Raiders, and it was the move that eventually put the Raiders over the top. Still, it rankled Davis that so few took notice of the Willie Brown trade.

Football fans knew little about Brown, who had been poorly used by the hapless Broncos, but there were some around the league who realized how good a cornerback he could be. "I really wanted to trade for him," said Hank Stram, the Kansas City coach, "but we beat Denver so regularly, they just wouldn't trade with us. So Al got him."

In training camp, Davis asked me, "If you put up Lamonica on one side and the cornerbacks on the other side, who would be more valuable?" The implication was that it would be the cornerbacks, Brown and Ken McCloughan. Technically Davis was probably right, because good cornerbacks were the key to his defense. As he explained it to me, he needed cornerbacks who could play tight man-to-man coverage to take away the quick, short pass. He wanted to get a push up the middle, tight coverage from his corners, and a free safety who stayed in the middle, thus taking away the easy reads for the opposing quarterback. That defense would enable the Raiders to beat the San Francisco 49ers two times in three games in the 1980s—a decade in which the 49ers won four Super Bowls. Those 49ers killed teams that tried to pressure Joe Montana, because the 49er receivers would shake loose on crossing patterns across the middle, but the Raider corners couldn't be shaken and a safety was always there to break up or intercept a pass across the middle. And in 1967, when the Raiders did not have to face any team with the talent or offensive sophistication of those 49ers, Brown and McCloughan were an especially devastating combination.

But writers and fans always look at the quarterback. Lamonica was the golden boy, a handsome young man with a musical name, a strong right arm, and unflagging optimism. Between wives when he came to the Raiders, he fit the team's image of playing hard on and off the field, though his partying tended to be one on one. "I get laid as much as Joe Namath," he told me once. "I just don't tell the world about it."

Incompletions and even interceptions didn't faze Lamonica. He always thought his next pass would go for a touchdown, and he was often right. He threw for thirty touchdowns in his first season with the Raiders, twenty-five his second, and thirty-four his third. He might throw five or six straight incomplete passes to start a game and then complete his next five. Against Denver, late in the 1967 season, the Raiders trailed, 17–14, in the fourth quarter, and Lamonica had not completed a pass in the second half; he then threw three third-down passes for first downs as the Raiders drove to the winning touchdown.

His game had many flaws. He had no touch on short passes, and he couldn't throw a screen pass, which requires both deceptive ball handling and acting ability, neither of which was his forte. The Raiders simply dropped that play from their offense as long as he was the quarterback.

But his ability to make the big play more than compensated for his weaknesses. Lamonica was as accurate a long passer as I've seen (the only ones comparable in my experience were Norm Van Brocklin and Joe Namath), and he never conceded anything. That spirit helped carry the Raiders to championships in his first four years with the team. He didn't do it alone— the Raiders had great talent everywhere—but he was the offensive ingredient that had been missing. Lamonica won two Most Valuable Player awards in his first three years in Oakland.

Like so many athletes, Lamonica's strength was also his weakness. He prospered in the AFL because its teams then played man-to-man defenses almost exclusively, and there were very few defensive backs who could cover Fred Biletnikoff, Warren Wells, or Billy Cannon. Every time one of his receivers leaped up with a defensive back to battle for the ball, Lamonica could be confident that the pass was more likely to be a completion than an interception. But when the AFL teams were absorbed into the NFL in 1970 and interlocking schedules were adopted, Lamonica began to see zone coverage for almost the first time, and he never adjusted to it. He kept throwing into the teeth of the zone, instead of backing off, and his production gradually declined, until he lost the quarterback job to Ken Stabler during the 1973 season.

It wasn't just Lamonica. Davis was also slow to adapt to the changing defenses—it was always attack, attack, attack with the long bomb. "Daryle was called 'the Mad Bomber,'" George Ross said, "but really, he was only doing what Al wanted him to do." Nor did Davis want his own team to play zone defense, which added to Lamonica's difficulties, because he never got the chance to work against the zone in practice.

The fans neither knew nor cared about the reasons for Lamonica's failures—they just teed off on him. He deserved better, because he played well under some very adverse conditions.

One game in San Diego against the Chargers in 1969 showed the type of competitor he was. Eight hours before the game he was in a San Diego hospital, a tube pumping glucose into a body racked by gastrointestinal flu and a 103-degree temperature. He hadn't been able to eat anything since early morning, when the fever hit, and had lost eight pounds the hard way. When game time arrived, however, he threw three touchdown passes, and the Raiders beat the Chargers, 24–12.

For some reason the fans turned on Lamonica after his first year. Unlike fans in other cities (especially in the east), Raiders fans in Oakland did not usually boo the players—except for Lamonica. From 1968 on, Davis had the defensive starters introduced at home games to spare Lamonica the booing. If the boos bothered him, he never let it show. He didn't knock the fans, nor did he ever react to criticism in the media. Even at the end of his career, when the bad notices overwhelmed the good ones, Lamonica's only comment to writers was "You've got your job to do."

Lamonica struggled early in the 1967 season, as he slowly became familiar with the Raiders system, but Davis's other big acquisition, Willie Brown, had no such problems. Brown was a great player for the Raiders from the start. "Willie had a great knack for closing on a receiver," noted Raiders announcer Bill King. "He'd lay off a receiver and then, when the quarterback released the ball, he'd quickly move in. A lot of his interceptions came that way."

There were misconceptions about Brown around the league. "The rap on him at the time," King remembered, "was that he wasn't very physical. I don't know where that came from, because I've seen him put some tremendous hits on people." In fact, one of the reasons Davis liked him was that Brown, who played at more than 200 pounds, was big enough to come up and support well against the run. (Raiders defensive backs, even the free safety, were expected to play the run as well as the pass.)

Brown's size also made him effective in the Raiders bump-and-run defense, in which cornerbacks would knock receivers off balance as they came off the line of scrimmage, although that defense was really devised to help the other cornerback, McCloughan. "Kent had great speed but not much quickness," Scotty Stirling noted, "so Al put in this system to help him." McCloughan, now a scout for the Raiders, became a great coverage man.

McCloughan's career came to a premature end because of a knee injury in 1968; he played two more seasons but was never the defender he had been before. In 1967, however, he and Brown were as good as any two corners who ever played on the same team. Dave Grayson, a good cornerback converted to an equally good free safety, and Rodger Bird, a competent though unspectacular strong safety, completed the defensive backfield.

Like the offense, the Raiders defense was geared to making the big play. Davis believed that sacking the quarterback and intercepting passes were the keys to a defense. The Raiders led the AFL in sacks for three straight years, 1966 through 1968. In 1967 they set a league record of sixty-seven sacks, a record that lasted until the 1985 Chicago Bears, playing two more games than the 1967 Raiders had, got seventy-two. The Raiders nailed opposing quarterbacks for 666 yards lost in 1967, and that is still a record.

"Every week Al would tell us, 'We've got to have the push up the middle,'" Tom Keating remembered. "He wanted us to force the quarterback to leave the pocket. When I would get a rest during practice, I used to sit behind the quarterbacks, and I would hear him tell them to step up in the pocket, step up in the pocket. He'd tell them that if they stepped back, the end coming from the outside would come by and swipe at them. Ben Davidson made a living that way for years."

The Raiders defensive line didn't have a catchy nickname like "Fearsome Foursome"—though Bob Valli called the entire defensive unit "the Eleven Angry Men" or, sometimes, just "the Angries"—but it was well balanced and effective. Keating, the quickest defensive lineman in the league at the time, put the inside pressure on the quarterback that Davis felt was critical. Dan Birdwell held his own, protecting first against the run and then going for the quarterback if he saw a pass play developing. On the outside, Ike Lassiter was surprisingly quick for someone of his bulk, using his agility to get past his man and put pressure on the quarterback. Davidson was strong, often overpowering his man, and he came hard throughout the game, on every down. That unrelenting pressure made him most effective late in the game. Even if a blocker had been able to stop him early, he'd wear down his man as the game progressed. The fourth quarter belonged to Davidson.

"The thing I remember most about that season," Davidson said, "is that we just ran over offensive linemen. We were getting so many sacks on the quarterback, we got a little cocky. We were making up calls and stunts. Keating and I might call something in the defensive huddle and then change it at the line of scrimmage. We really weren't paying any attention to what coach Tom Dahms told us to do. What we were doing was working so well, we stuck with it."

The Raiders defense was definitely at the championship level, with no significant weaknesses. The offense wasn't as solid. For one thing, with Fred Biletnikoff and Bill Miller as the wide receivers, the Raiders lacked speed on the outside.

Davis had drafted Gene Upshaw out of Texas A&I on the first round, and Upshaw fit the Davis prototype for an offensive lineman, at 265 pounds and a speed of 4.8 in the 40-yard dash, both far above average for an offensive guard in that era. But the overachieving Wayne Hawkins remained at the other guard, and Davis wouldn't be satisfied until he got a bigger, faster man, George Buehler, in 1969.

Upshaw was, and is, an intriguing man, a player who originally didn't even want to play pro ball but went on to play so well that he was elected to the Pro Football Hall of Fame. Upshaw has remained close to the game as executive director of the Players Association.

"I was upset when I was drafted by the Raiders," Upshaw remembered. "They hadn't even sent me a questionnaire, and here they drafted me. It was crazy. And I'd heard vaguely that they had some problems with Art Powell. I don't know exactly what it was. News travels slowly in Texas. But it was the best thing that ever happened to me. When I first came to the Raiders, they benched Jim Harvey to make room for me, and I had never even played guard. In college I was a tackle and center. But all the time I was learning the position, I got nothing but help from Wayne Hawkins and Jim Otto and Harvey. They felt if I was good enough to play I should be in there, for the good of the team. And Ollie Spencer was a great line coach for a young guy because he was patient and would take the time to let me get through the mistakes. The other thing I remember is that we were really close. We ate together, we drank together, we played golf together."

Still, Upshaw thought his pro career would be a short one, maybe five years. "I hated football. I hated the violence of the game." What changed his mind? "I didn't want to go back to Texas. My options were to play football or teach school in Texas."

On the practice field he improved dramatically. "Keating was the guy who helped me the most. He was the guy who had the most quickness. After going up against Keating in practice every stinking day, when I got up against guys in a game they seemed slow to me. I'd get in a game and I'd say, 'Hey, this guy isn't as quick as Keating. I can block him.'"

Upshaw quickly learned what it was like to play for an Al Davis team. "Even when you won, there were some things he saw that he would remind you of. I remember one game in Oakland when we were talking about a play, and I said I had done it right, but he said, 'No, you missed the block.' I said I didn't, but he showed me the film, and he was right. I don't know how the hell he remembered. It happened to me, and I had forgotten about it."

Upshaw had been drafted to block Kansas City's Buck Buchanan because Upshaw had the size and quickness to stay with Buchanan. But it didn't seem that way in Upshaw's first game, an exhibition in Portland, Oregon, in which the Chiefs destroyed the Raiders, 48–0.

"I never will forget that game," Upshaw said. "I flew in from the College All-Star game and had a couple of days of practice, and then we flew up to Portland for the game. Buchanan absolutely killed me. I just couldn't block him. In my two days at camp I had often heard about players the Raiders had drafted in the past who hadn't panned out, and I didn't want to be one of those mistakes. But after that first game I said to myself, 'I'm one of those mistakes.' It was an awful game."

Davis said nothing to Upshaw that night, but after the team got back to Santa Rosa Davis told him, "One thing about playing this guy, you have to get to him early. You can't mess around with him, because if he beats you in the first quarter, he's going to kill you in the fourth quarter." Upshaw learned from his experience and from Davis's advice, and he played well against the Chiefs that season and later, but he never took anything for granted. "Buchanan was a force. He was the only guy I ever played against who made it awfully difficult to sleep the night before, because I knew he could dominate the game if I didn't play really well."

The entire team played poorly that night in Portland, because the Raiders had left their game on the practice field.

"That was the most brutal of all the camps I was in," Davidson remembered. "We had worked in two full practices the day before the game. It was a very hot night—about 90 degrees—in Portland, and we were exhausted. We just wanted to get the game over. For some reason Rauch kept the starters in the game until the fourth quarter. But there was one light moment. In the fourth quarter we were standing on the sideline, and Dan Birdwell comes up and says, 'C'mon, guys, just seven quick scores and we've got these guys!' "

I wandered morosely into the dressing room after the game. I had thought I was covering a good team, and I was shocked. Some of this must have shown on my face, because Ollie Spencer said, "Don't worry, Glenn, it's not the end of the world."

Despite that horrendous loss and two more exhibition defeats, one of them by 21 – 17 to the Denver Broncos, the Raiders *were* improving. Two weeks after the exhibition loss to Denver, the Raiders opened their 1967 season in Oakland against the Broncos. The score this time: Oakland 51, Denver 0. The Raiders had arrived.

• • •

That year the Raiders won their first three games for the first time in their short history. More important, the third win came over the defending AFL champion, the Kansas City Chiefs, 23 – 21 in Oakland. It definitely looked like it would be the Raiders' year.

One big obstacle loomed—the eastern road trip. On their seven swings previously through the east, the Raiders were a dismal 5 – 13 – 2.

The first game of the trip was in New York against the Jets, a team on the rise behind their "$400,000 quarterback," Joe Namath—who was known as much for his mouth as for his arm. The week before the game Namath told newspapermen covering the Jets that the Raiders were a "dirty" team— not the last time that accusation would be leveled.

"The officials get into town early enough before a game to read the newspapers," Ben Davidson noted, "so every time we got close to Namath in that game, they were yelling, 'Don't hit him, you can't hit him.' Well, that's not the way the rules read, and that's not the way the game should be played. Joe got the idea he could just sit back there with impunity, and he picked us apart." Meanwhile, Daryle Lamonica, still learning the Raiders offense, threw four interceptions. The Jets won, 27 – 14.

Had the Raiders' bubble burst? The next Sunday, in Buffalo, was a critical game. The Bills had won four straight division titles, and twice, in 1964 and 1965, they had been the AFL champion. It was also a homecoming for Lamonica, who had been a favorite of the fans in Buffalo but had not been treated kindly in the newspapers. The Buffalo writers had suggested that Lamonica was traded because he sulked and did not work hard in practice. They also wrote that he hadn't understood the Buffalo offense.

For sure, Lamonica didn't yet know the *Raiders* offense: he threw another four interceptions against the Bills. But this time it didn't matter, because the defense sacked Bills quarterback Jack Kemp eleven times, for losses totaling 96 yards, in a 24 – 20 Raiders win.

That game—and that day—was the turning point for the Raiders. Kansas City lost to San Diego, and the Raiders eventually ended the season four games ahead of the Chiefs. The game was also Lamonica's coming of age. He had obviously felt great pressure coming back to Buffalo and had played poorly there, but he played magnificently the rest of the way. With Lamonica executing the big-play offense in great style, the Raiders scored 51 points against San Diego, 48 against the Boston Patriots, 44 against Kansas City, 41 in a rematch with San Diego, and 38 against the New York Jets in Oakland. They were rolling.

After the clinching of the division title, only one major matter remained to be settled: to get even for the Raiders' one loss when the Jets came to Oakland for the next-to-last game of the season. The Raiders won, 38 – 29.

"I don't recall anybody saying anything about the way the officials had protected Namath in the first game," Davidson said. "But when the Jets came to Oakland, we were all determined to give Namath a bad time. Ike Lassiter hit him with a real shot early in the game, shattering his cheekbone with a right elbow and knocking him down. Late in the game I hit Namath and knocked his helmet off." Russ Reed, an *Oakland Tribune* photographer, got a shot of that hit, and the picture hung on a wall in the Raiders offices for years. "It was a spectacular shot," Davidson continued, "and somehow the visual image transformed the fact of Ike breaking Namath's cheekbone into me breaking his jaw." Lassiter, who felt he never got enough credit (probably correctly) because so much attention was focused on Davidson, was especially upset that everyone thought it was Davidson who had damaged Namath. "I've always denied that," Davidson said, "but it doesn't seem to make any difference. Maybe if Ike had gotten the publicity for that, he'd be the one doing Miller Lite commercials today."

The Raiders dominated the AFL that year, outscoring their opponents by a two-to-one margin, 468–233, and routing the Houston Oilers, 40–7, in the AFC championship game, at the Oakland Coliseum on the last day of 1967.

That earned them what most pro football observers thought was the dubious honor of facing the NFL champion, the Green Bay Packers, in the second Super Bowl. The Packers had dominated the NFL throughout the 1960s, winning five league and six conference titles. They had beaten the Kansas City Chiefs in the first Super Bowl, 35–10, in a game that was all but officially over by halftime.

In an article in *Sports Illustrated* comparing the Packers and the Raiders position by position, pro football writer Tex Maule gave the Raiders a tie at fullback between Hewritt Dixon and Green Bay's Chuck Mercein. At the other twenty-one positions he gave the Packers the edge. Maule's NFL bias was more pronounced than that of most other writers, but his opinions were an indication of the low esteem in which the AFL was held. In fact, the real difference between the NFL and the AFL at the time was probably just the Packers, who were head and shoulders above everyone. In the wake of the Packers' decline, the AFL won the next two Super Bowls. When the NFL was reorganized into two conferences, the National Football Conference and the American Football Conference, the AFC won nine of the next ten Super Bowls.

The Packers' great players had grown old together, and they were to finish under .500 the next year, but they had one last big effort left. And the Raiders had their problems. Tom Keating had a bad leg; his Achilles tendon would snap in the AFL All-Star game. Billy Cannon didn't show up until two days before the Super Bowl because of a dispute with the club about whether his wife would be flown to the game. Most important, the Raiders did not have Clem Daniels, who had broken a bone in his ankle in the ninth game of the season;

this sidelined him for the rest of the year and, in effect, ended his career.

"I always felt the Raiders could have won that game with Clem," George Ross said, "but when he went out, it took an important dimension from their offense. Now the defenses could key on Hewritt Dixon, instead of having to worry about Dixon and Daniels both, as runners or as pass receivers. That made all the difference in the Super Bowl."

Even without Daniels, the Raiders were in the game until a key sequence late in the first half. Holding a 13 – 7 lead, the Packers were kicking from deep in their territory. The Raiders seemed certain to get the ball in good field position, with time to score at least a field goal and possibly a touchdown. But Rodger Bird fumbled the punt, the Packers recovered, and Don Chandler kicked one of his four field goals, to give Green Bay a 16 – 7 lead. In effect, the game was over. The Packers won, 33 – 14, with Herb Adderly sealing the victory by a 60-yard interception return for a touchdown. Quarterback Bart Starr was the game's Most Valuable Player, completing 13 of 24 passes for 202 yards.

Davis was livid about the game. He said to me and others that the coaches had blown it by not realizing that the Green Bay punter, Donny Anderson, was left-footed. This gave the ball a different spin, he said, and caused Bird to fumble the punt. Years later, Mel Durslag said, "Al really thinks he could have won that Super Bowl. It's the only one he's lost, and that really bugs him. But he's wrong about that—the Packers were just too good."

• • •

The Raiders had picked up wide receiver Warren Wells during the 1967 season—another example of the way Davis kept track of players around the league. Like Clem Daniels in 1962, Wells was almost an unknown, though he had been named to a black All-American team by the *Pittsburgh Courier* while playing at Texas Southern. Wells had been drafted by the Detroit Lions in 1964 and was in the military the next two years. Cut by the

Lions, he was picked up by the Kansas City Chiefs. Hank Stram liked him, but he was eventually cut. Al Davis, to whom no player was an unknown, picked him up.

Wells was to become the centerpiece of the growing feud between Davis and his fellow general partner, Wayne Valley, but it was his on-field contributions that first caught everyone's attention. Not in 1967, however: because he hadn't been in training camp, he didn't know enough of the offense to be a factor. Wells played only at the end of lopsided games, along with George Blanda. The two of them connected for 13 pass completions, for a startling 302 yards and 6 touchdowns, but they occurred, after all, in "garbage time."

In 1968, though, with part of a season and training camp behind him, Wells became the deep threat the Raiders had needed since they traded Art Powell. Wells caught 53 passes for 1,137 yards (a 21.5-yard average) and 11 touchdowns, one of them a club-record 94 yards. The next season he was even better, averaging 26.8 yards on 47 receptions (1,260 yards) for 14 touchdowns. He complemented Fred Biletnikoff perfectly. Biletnikoff kept drives alive with key third-down catches, and, with attention focused on Wells near the goal line, he also caught 12 touchdown passes in 1969.

"Wells was the most amazing receiver I ever saw," said Raiders announcer Bill King. "No matter what the coverage, man to man or zone, he always seemed to be wide open. He didn't have the blinding speed of Cliff Branch, who was a world-class sprinter, but I never saw anybody who could get as open as he did." Blanda once described to me what he regarded as the key to Wells's success: "He can make cuts at full speed. The defensive back will be right with him, but he'll have to slow down to make his cut. Warren just keeps going, and he loses his man every time."

Wells gave balance to the passing offense, and the Raiders continued to dominate the AFL in 1968, playing five games in which they scored at least 40 points and another five in which they scored at least 30. A midseason stumble, though, in which they lost successive games to San Diego and Kansas City, proved costly. The Raiders and Kansas City tied at 12−2 for the AFL West title, which forced a play-off. The Raiders won the play-off easily, 41−6, but they could have better used that week to recover from injuries, as their next opponent, the New York Jets, did.

The site of the AFL championship game was rotated from year to year, and it was the Eastern Division's turn, so the game was to be played in New York. That was a critical factor, because the severe December weather in New York (the game was played on the 29th) was to the Raiders' disadvantage. (Knowing the winds would be howling at Shea Stadium, Davis planned to put up a wooden structure to protect his players on the bench and the sideline. AFL commissioner Milt Woodard first gave approval, but then retracted it under pressure from the Jets.)

The on-field matchup was a dramatic one, "Broadway Joe" Namath against Daryle Lamonica, also known as "the Mad Bomber." At dinner the night before the game, Davis told broadcaster Bill King that if his team won he could start a dynasty. "It was a great game, one of the most exciting I've ever seen," King remembered. "That was in an era when teams didn't pass as much as they do today, but both Namath and Lamonica put on a show that day."

The Raiders-Jets rivalry had started in 1967, when the Jets handed the Raiders their only loss of the season in New York and then lost to the Raiders in Oakland in the game in which Namath had his cheekbone shattered. The rivalry had accelerated in 1968 with the infamous "Heidi game," when NBC broke away from the game to show a movie just before the Raiders scored two touchdowns in 55 seconds to win. It was also fueled by the fact that Davis had more respect and fear for Namath than for any player in the league.

Namath was the first pro quarterback to throw for more than 4,000 yards in a season—4,007 in 1967—and the same year he had tied club records with 26 touchdown passes for the season and 5 in one game. Because he had done all this in the New York media spotlight, he was considered the player who had done the most to help the AFL survive. Still, there were many who downplayed Namath's achievements because they had come in the AFL, against pass defenses that were weaker than those in the NFL. His critics pointed to his high interception ratio as proof that he wasn't a polished quarterback, and they noted the fact that, until 1968, his team hadn't won a title.

Davis wasn't among the scoffers. "He's the best quarterback in football," he told me, in one of our earliest conversations in 1967. "The NFL guys can't touch him. He can throw any kind of pass you want, and he's got the quickest release I've ever seen. You can't get to him. He throws too many interceptions because he's *so* good that he thinks he can complete a pass even when his man is covered. He'll learn not to do that, but I'll tell you this—no lead is safe when he's throwing the ball."

On game day the wind blew as fiercely as expected, especially in the first half, when passes would sail or buckle, depending on whether they were thrown with or against the wind. That didn't deter either Namath or Lamonica, who threw an incredible 96 passes between them. Lamonica gained 401 yards on 20 completions in 47 attempts, Namath 227 on 19 in 49.

It was, one New York writer suggested, the first important AFL championship game—because it was played in New York instead of a cow town like San Diego or Oakland. Perhaps. For sure, it was much more exciting than most of the previous title games had been. And one pass, by Namath, was as good as any I have ever seen.

The Jets were on their own 42-yard line when wide receiver Don Maynard faked in, then up, and streaked down the right sideline. Defender George Atkinson stayed with him in very tight coverage, and Namath, throwing into the swirling wind, had no more than a six-inch hole to hit. He dropped the ball just past Atkinson's reaching hands and into Maynard's at the Oakland 6-yard line, 60 yards from where the pass had been launched. The pass set up a touchdown, again on a Namath-to-Maynard completion, that put the Jets ahead,

27–23. Just 3:09 remained in the game, but the Raiders had won games in less.

They should have won this one, too. Two big plays got them from their own 15-yard line to the New York 12. Lamonica first had hit Biletnikoff for 25 yards and then Wells for 36 yards; when Jets safety Jim Hudson was called for piling on after the catch, the Jets were penalized back to their own 12. On the next play Lamonica looked first for Biletnikoff and then for Wells. Both were covered, and the rush was coming, so Lamonica went to his third receiver, running back Charlie Smith, swinging wide to the sideline.

Had the pass been completed, Smith might have scored, because he had only linebacker Al Atkinson to beat to get into the end zone—but it was not the kind of pass Lamonica had ever thrown with much success, and this time it was a disaster. The ball went behind Smith, who could not handle it. Because it was thrown behind him, it was a lateral and still in play when it fell to the ground. Smith did not realize that and let the ball go, but the Jets' Ralph Baker fell on it on the 30. Jets' ball and Jets' game. The Raiders did get the ball once more, with 45 seconds left, but could get only to their 47 before the game ended.

So there would be no Raiders dynasty, and it would be the Jets who would go on to shatter the myth of NFL superiority by beating the Baltimore Colts in the upcoming Super Bowl. Instead, the Raiders were entering one of their most frustrating periods. In the regular season they had been dominant, losing only four games and tying one over three seasons, but for three years in a row they had lost in the league or conference championship game, always to the team that went on to win the Super Bowl.

"I have only one regret," Billy Cannon said when he was cut before the 1970 season. "I've always felt that this team had a chance to win every game in a season, and I wanted to be on the team when it did." Cannon's concern was misplaced. By the time he left, the Raiders were sliding from their peak and would have to be rebuilt before they could finally win the Super Bowl and lose the reputation of always choking in the big games.

• • •

Davis, in the press box, was beside himself, cursing Lamonica for throwing a bad pass, Smith for not realizing it was a lateral, and, most of all, John Rauch for everything.

Davis being Davis, he couldn't blame himself, although his unwillingness to coach the team he had built probably kept the Raiders from winning the Super Bowl, not just in 1968 but in subsequent years. I believe Davis could have coached that Raiders team to multiple championships.

And I believe Davis realized that, too. But he couldn't turn back, so he did the next best thing, fiercely second-guessing John Rauch during and after the game, not caring who was listening. That was the last straw for Rauch. Everyone knew he had been sending out résumés for some time; it was only a question of where he would go, and when. Shortly after the championship loss Rauch announced that he was leaving for Buffalo.

That made the second defection from the "team" Davis had put in place when he left the Raiders to become AFL commissioner. Scotty Stirling had resigned as general manager after the Super Bowl loss to Green Bay; with Davis back making all the decisions, Stirling had become little more than an office boy. Rauch's departure, though, was more newsworthy. It also enraged Davis, who said, "For Rauch's salary of $50,000, Buffalo is getting our offense."

Davis should have known better. Without Davis's system and Davis's players, Rauch was lost. He won only seven games in his two years as the Bills coach, and he was best known for his peculiar strategy of using O. J. Simpson as a decoy.

· 4 ·

The John Madden
Era Begins

Al Davis needed a coach. He wanted someone who would continue with his style and someone he could control. That inevitably meant that he would have to select a head coach from his present staff. Who? I thought back two years, to an eastern trip during which the Raiders had stayed nearly two weeks in Niagara Falls.

With nothing else to do, Bob Valli and I had lingered over lunch one day in the hotel coffee shop. John Madden, who had recently been hired as the Raiders linebacker coach, stopped by our table to talk.

That in itself was unusual. Although most of the players talked freely to the press, the tone for the coaching staff was set by John Rauch, who was suspicious to the point of paranoia, apparently afraid that whatever he said was being reported back to Davis. Ollie Spencer would sometimes talk books with me, but the other assistants remained aloof, answering questions when asked but otherwise avoiding the writers.

Madden felt no such constraints. He sat down and talked freely, asking several questions about what we were writing and what the press needed from the coaches. When he left I said to Valli, "He's going to be a head coach before too long."

Madden was only thirty-two at the time, and his coaching experience was minimal. He had been head coach at Allen Hancock Junior College in Santa Maria, California (about seventy-five miles north of Santa Barbara). In 1963 his team had won a league championship and been ranked ninth in the country. He spent the next three years as defensive coordinator for San Diego State and then moved to the Raiders.

Despite his youth and lack of experience, it was obvious that Madden was a good coach. He had great rapport with his linebackers (he'd take them to dinner when they played a particularly good game), and he had a vision far beyond that of most assistants. He was already thinking about the time when he would become a head coach and what it would take to succeed.

Now there was an opening, and a vacuum. The other Raiders assistants, handpicked by Davis, were valuable because of their technical expertise, but they were not head-coach material. Though the senior assistant was Ollie Spencer, Davis wanted Madden, despite his youth. When I predicted in the *Chronicle* that Madden would be the next head coach, Davis was enraged, erroneously thinking there had been a leak within the organization.

Davis delayed his announcement for two weeks to ease the shock for Spencer, who wanted the job. (Spencer eventually left coaching because he never got the head-coaching job he sought. He ran a successful insurance office in an exclusive housing development east of Oakland—ironically, just a few minutes' drive from Madden's home—until his death.) Davis may also have wanted to make Madden—and me—sweat a little before he made the announcement.

The date was April 4, 1969, six days short of Madden's thirty-third birthday. That same day Vince Lombardi came out of retirement to become the head coach of the Washington Redskins, telling the press that the biggest challenge was to build a champion. Davis sent Lombardi a telegram saying that the biggest challenge was to maintain success. It was typical Davis, implying that he was the more successful, even though Lombardi had won the first two Super Bowls.

Madden was labeled "Pinocchio" by one writer, who said that Davis would be calling all the shots. Madden didn't deny that. "I'm down the hall from the greatest football mind in the game," he told me. "I'd be a fool not to take advantage of that."

Knowing that he lacked the professional experience to take over all aspects of the job, Madden let Davis call most of the strategic shots for his first few seasons. The Raiders offense, to take the most obvious example, was run almost exactly as it had been run ever since Davis arrived. Davis continued to coach on the practice field and openly contributed to the game plans, not having to use subterfuge as he had with Rauch. He and Madden were almost a coaching tandem.

Even with his limited role, Madden had an impact. He had a personal touch with players that Rauch lacked, easing off somewhat on practice schedules and encouraging a more relaxed atmosphere. He was very much a players' coach. Many of them called him "Pinky," because of the way his face got red when he was angry or excited, but it was an affectionate term. It wasn't unusual to see Madden sitting with a player off the field and talking football.

That was no hardship for Madden, of course. He enjoyed talking to people, and he loved to talk football. The game consumed him. After practice he would often sit in his office with the writers and talk as long as we wanted to. (We *had* to be there in person; he seldom answered telephone calls and never returned them.)

Madden is not a sophisticated man (when I used the term *haute cuisine* in a story, he asked me what *hot* meant), but he is certainly one of the most intelligent men in sports. He has since used his intelligence to create a popular TV image, and even back then he knew how to exploit his image.

He was known, for instance, to have an explosive temper, and he sometimes used that temper in a calculating way. One time, when an *Oakland Tribune* photographer wanted to take a picture of the Raiders' all-black defensive backfield, Madden blew up and ordered the photographer off the field. He wasn't mad; he just didn't want the emphasis on an all-black unit at a time when some white fans were objecting to so many black players. Another time, after a morning practice in training camp, George Ross remembered Madden screaming at his players, "You guys stink! Get out of here! I don't even want to see your faces until tomorrow morning." When Ross asked Madden what that was all about, Madden replied, "Aw, they're tired and they need the break. But I couldn't let them think they were getting away with something."

"I always thought John was an outstanding coach and an outstanding man," Ross says today, and he's right. For many years Madden didn't get much credit for the Raiders' success, because he was overshadowed by Davis, but he was a fine coach.

Not because of any strategic brilliance. In fact, Madden's offensive style was based on winning the battle at the line of scrimmage—as anyone who watches him on TV might guess. He eventually moved away from the wide-open game Davis loved to a "smash 'em" game, running the ball off the left side and simply beating the other team to death. "I remember Al saying to me in 1971 that he hated this type of football," Ross said, "but he really liked John. 'If this is what he wants, we'll go with it,' Al said."

I felt that the Madden style hurt the Raiders in postseason games, when they played teams their physical equal. But running the ball off the left side, when he had power backs like Marv Hubbard and Mark van Eeghen behind Art Shell, Gene Upshaw, and Jim Otto, wasn't the worst idea a coach ever had.

Madden prepared his teams well, and the Raiders always played well for him. He was an excellent game-day coach. Not all coaches, even the best ones, are; neither Tom Landry of the Dallas Cowboys nor Chuck Noll of the Pittsburgh Steelers excelled on the sideline during games. Despite Madden's sideline histrionics—mostly aimed at intimidating officials—he was always in control. Neither he nor his teams ever panicked, and he was especially good at taking advantage of his time-outs at the end of a half or a game—one reason the Raiders were able to come from behind so often.

As Madden himself would probably admit, anyone could have coached the 1969 team successfully. The defense was still stingy, and the offense was more explosive than ever, with Daryle Lamonica throwing to Warren Wells and Fred Biletnikoff, who caught twenty-six touchdown passes between them. Although its 12 – 1 – 1 record wasn't quite as good as the 13 – 1 mark of the 1967 team, it was good enough to win the division title, and this one was the best of the early Raiders teams.

That wasn't just my opinion; it was also the opinion of the man who had built the team. I remember in particular a conversation Davis and I had late that season in a coffee shop in East Orange, New Jersey. His team had just beaten the Chiefs in Kansas City, in an enormously exciting game, and had flown from there to New Jersey, to stay for a week before playing the New York Jets at Shea Stadium. Buoyed by the win and sustained by his nocturnal disposition, Davis wanted to talk, and I was willing to listen. It was a long dissertation, as he went through the strengths and weaknesses of the top teams in football, not just the ones in his own league but those in the rival NFL (this was the year before the leagues were consolidated into a single two-conference league). I remember vividly Davis's main point.

"We're the best team in football, and we just beat the second-best team," Davis said. "The writers still think the NFL is better. Fuck. We've passed them up. The two best teams are in our league, and, with Namath, I'm not sure the Jets aren't better than anything in the NFL, too. We'll probably still have to beat the Chiefs once more to get to the Super Bowl. They're so much better physically than anybody in the NFL, but if we stay healthy, we should be able to do it. If we can beat the Chiefs, the Super Bowl will be easy."

The AFL that year had changed its play-off format from a simple division-champion-against-division-champion game to a two-week system. Each of the two division winners would play the runner-up from the other division in the first round, and the winners of those two games would meet for the championship. Why the change? So that NBC would have an extra round of AFL play-off games to televise (CBS already had three rounds of NFL games).

As expected, the Raiders won easily in the first round, with Lamonica throwing six touchdown passes in a 56–7 rout of the Buffalo Bills. But there was an ominous note—Warren Wells injured his shoulder during the game. In New York, the Chiefs beat the Jets, the Eastern Division champion. It was as Davis had predicted—the Raiders would have to beat the Chiefs a third time to take the AFL championship.

This was the most intense of the Raiders' early rivalries—two physically overwhelming giants butting heads. Al Davis had built his team in the same mold as Hank Stram's Chiefs, emphasizing size and speed to counter the Chiefs.

The Chiefs were a physically dominating team on defense, with a unit anchored by giant tackle Buck Buchanan and linebackers Willie Lanier and Bobby Bell; a case could be made that there has never been anyone better than those three at their positions. With Len Dawson throwing to Otis Taylor and with runners like Mike Garrett, Warren McVea, and Wendell Hayes, the Chiefs had a first-rate offense, too. But what made the rivalry most fascinating were the emotional differences between Stram and Davis, which set the tone for their teams.

Stram was a peacock, strutting up and down the sideline in his red blazer, a symbol for his team at home and a magnet for abuse from the fans in Oakland. On the road, his players were expected to be clean, shaven and to wear red blazers, white shirts, and ties. They were an imposing sight coming off an airplane.

Davis, of course, imposed no dress code on his team. How could he, considering the clothes *he* wore? It's difficult to look impressive when the dominant colors in your wardrobe are silver and black, but Davis seemed to go out of his way to look bad. On plane trips he might wear jeans and a sweatshirt, and he often had a day-old stubble. At games he might put on a sports jacket, but it would be an ill-fitting one, and he never wore a tie. The Raiders emulated their boss and tumbled off planes looking like a lost troop of the Hells Angels, an image that didn't bother Davis in the least.

On the field, the two teams were night and day. Davis's Raiders were a bombs-away group, always going for the jugular on both offense and defense. Stram's Chiefs, despite their offensive talent, played conservatively, content to let their defense control the game. For instance, in the second Raiders-Chiefs game of the 1968 season, played at Oakland, the Raiders had won, 38−21, and Stram had virtually conceded in the fourth quarter, running the ball rather than trying for a quick touchdown through the air to get his team back in the game. Afterward he had explained to reporters that he didn't want to risk an interception that might let the Raiders win by an even larger margin. That kind of thinking was entirely foreign to Davis, who never conceded anything.

The Raiders had won seven of their last eight games with the Chiefs, but the statistic was misleading. In 1969 there was almost no physical difference between the teams; the two Raiders wins had come by scores of 27−24 and 10−6. The score of the second game showed what was happening: the teams had come to know each other's tendencies so well that it was becoming almost impossible for either offense to move the ball.

The championship game, played in the Oakland Coliseum, started that way, too, with both defenses yielding ground very, very grudgingly—for the game, the two offenses combined gained just 440 yards. The Raiders scored first, just before the end of the first quarter, when Charlie Smith ran 3 yards to cap a 66-yard drive. The touchdown had been set up by a 24-yard pass from Lamonica to Warren Wells, but it was the only pass Wells caught in the game; his injured shoulder kept him out about half the time and limited his ability when he *could* play.

The Chiefs tied the game in the second quarter, a 42-yard pass from Dawson to Taylor setting up a 1-yard plunge by

Hayes, but it was a third-quarter play that gave the Chiefs their chance to win. Ironically, it came at a time when the Raiders seemed in position to take command, following Tom Keating's recovery of a fumble at the Kansas City 33-yard line.

Lamonica, under tremendous pressure, threw two incomplete passes. On the second one, as he followed through, his hand hit the helmet of Chiefs defensive end Aaron Brown. Lamonica came out of the game and George Blanda came in, without even a chance to warm up. Blanda threw an incomplete pass on third down, and then he missed a 40-yard field goal. On the next Raiders series, Blanda threw an interception at the Kansas City 5 when Wells fell down. No one knew it, but the game was turning.

Years later, the story of Lamonica bruising his hand on Brown's helmet is still remembered. What few people remember is the big break the Chiefs got three plays after the Blanda interception, a break made possible because the game was being played years before pro football adopted instant replay.

It was not usually the Chiefs' style to pass from deep in their territory, but on third down, at their 2, they had virtually no choice; if they couldn't get out of the hole, punter Jerrell Wilson wouldn't have room to drop 15 yards back from the line of scrimmage, as he preferred, and his punt might be blocked. Dawson faded into his end zone, and he hit Taylor upfield, at the Oakland 37. Movies of the game clearly showed that Taylor had only one foot in bounds, which should have made it an incomplete pass; instant replay would have overturned the officials' ruling of a completion. The Chiefs then drove all the way to score, with Robert Holmes going the final 5 yards.

Lamonica came back into the game, but he was not the same quarterback who had thrown for forty touchdowns during the regular season and one play-off game. His index and middle fingers were so swollen that he could hardly grip the ball. Lamonica being Lamonica, he kept throwing, but the statistics show what happened: before his injury, he completed

12 passes in 22 attempts; after the injury, he was 4 in 17. With a sore-handed quarterback at the controls, Oakland's bombs-away offense was defused. The Chiefs won, 17–7.

So the Chiefs went to New Orleans to meet the undersized Minnesota Vikings in the Super Bowl. The NFL mystique blinded the bettors, and the Vikings were 13-point favorites. I saw Davis the night before the game, and he hadn't changed his mind about the relative merits of the AFL and NFL champions. "If Lenny Dawson doesn't screw it up, the Chiefs win easily," he said. He was right; the Chiefs thoroughly dominated the Vikings in a 23–7 win. The Raiders would probably have done the same, but they didn't get the chance.

• • •

After the loss to the Chiefs, Madden was asked if he had thought of keeping Blanda in the rest of the game, since Lamonica's hand was so badly swollen. "No," Madden said. "Daryle wanted to go back in there, and I thought he should. He's the one who got us here."

Blanda had a different opinion. He told reporters that he thought he should have played and that the Raiders could have won if he had. This made headlines the next day and prompted a quick conference between Davis and Blanda, after which Blanda announced that he had been misquoted and would not talk to any more reporters. "Of course he hadn't been misquoted," George Ross said. "I had it all on tape. But George had to say something, and Al never objected to the press being made the scapegoat."

At the time the consensus was that Madden had made the right decision. Blanda was thought of as the placekicker, not a quarterback. He had quarterbacked the team to a win over Denver in 1968, when back spasms sidelined Lamonica, but otherwise he had played quarterback only in "garbage time." He had thrown only thirteen passes in the 1969 regular season. We all had underestimated Blanda's determination, as we learned the next season.

Because Houston Oilers fans wanted one of their own—

former Baylor quarterback Don Trull—playing quarterback, the Oilers had been looking to unload Blanda after the 1966 season, and Davis had picked him up cheaply for a defensive lineman, George Flint, who played very little for Houston. When he first came to the team Blanda was regarded as little more than a curiosity. At thirty-nine, it seemed obvious that his serious playing days were behind him. Blanda was usually brusque to reporters, and that earned him the nickname of "the Old Curmudgeon." The standard joke was that if Blanda missed a field goal he would bark, "You saw it. Write it the way you saw it"; then when we wrote that he had blown the field goal, he would yell at us for criticizing him. It took years before I understood Blanda's motives. He was a steady kicker and almost immune to pressure, so when he missed a field goal from a reasonable distance it was almost always because the snap or the hold was bad. But he didn't want to be the one who said so, and he hoped we would write it. We often didn't know, however, and made the assumption that he was at fault—and he didn't like being blamed when he wasn't at fault.

It wasn't just the press that got the sharp edge of Blanda's tongue. At a Raiders Boosters meeting in 1969 he took one look at the questions offered him and said, "It's certainly a pleasure to be here to answer these stupid questions. I get more intelligent questions from eleven- and twelve-year-olds." The Boosters thought he was kidding. He wasn't. As that episode indicates, Blanda could say almost anything. "He's like me," Davis said. "He'll pop off in the heat of the moment because he's such a competitor."

Those on the team who knew him well, especially Tom Keating, insisted that Blanda could be a warm, humorous person. The real Blanda, on the field and off, emerged in the 1970 season, in a remarkable streak of five games.

Starting against the Pittsburgh Steelers because Lamonica was injured, Blanda threw three touchdown passes and kicked a field goal as the Raiders rallied to win, 31–17. A week later he kicked a 48-yard field goal with 3 seconds left to give the Raiders a 17–17 tie with the Kansas City Chiefs. The following week he threw a touchdown pass to Warren Wells, with 1:30 remaining, to tie the game, and then he kicked a 52-yard field goal with 3 seconds remaining, to beat the Cleveland Browns, 23–20. The next week it was a 20-yard touchdown pass to Fred Biletnikoff with 2:28 left in a 24–19 win over the Denver Broncos. Finally, he kicked a 16-yard field goal with 7 seconds to go that gave the Raiders a 20–17 win over the San Diego Chargers.

All that made Blanda the Player of the Year in the AFL, and an inspiration to middle-aged men everywhere. In essence, what Blanda did was to give the Raiders a change of pace that year, much as a late-inning relief pitcher will do for a baseball team.

The Lamonica and Blanda styles were totally different. Lamonica would drop back seven steps, wait and wait and wait . . . until a receiver came open deep downfield. Blanda would take a quick three-step drop and fire the ball to a short receiver. Defenses accustomed to Lamonica were thrown completely off balance by Blanda. "There are a lot of throwers coming out of college who can throw the hell out of the ball," he explained. "They can hit you anywhere on the field—except they don't. You don't win pro games with a passer who can throw straight. You win by getting a receiver four yards open. Your sister can hit a target that's four yards open. You have to surprise the defense. A defense will stop you if they anticipate your play. You can only get a man open by surprising the defensive people."

Neither Lamonica nor Blanda, who again came on in relief, was enough to help the Raiders get past the Baltimore Colts in the AFC championship game. (The Colts had been put in the AFC in the 1970 realignment.) A blown coverage late in the game by defensive back Nemiah Wilson allowed Baltimore's Ray Perkins to score the deciding touchdown in the 27–17 Colts win. This loss, though, was much different than the heartbreakers to the Jets and the Chiefs the previous two years. It was painfully apparent now that the Raiders were not a great team. In just one year, too many key players had lost their edge. It wasn't just that the Raiders were 8−4−2 for the season, a mediocre year by their lofty standards, but the fact that they had outscored their opponents by a total of only 10 points.

This time Davis didn't blame his coach. "We've got to rebuild," he told me after the championship game. "We're not tough enough. We've got to get some tough guys. We've got to intimidate people again."

In the next draft the Raiders took defensive back Jack Tatum and linebacker Phil Villapiano in the first two rounds, to complement their strong safety, George Atkinson, a ferocious hitter despite his weight of only 175 pounds. In the next few years Villapiano would become known as one of the hardest-hitting linebackers in the NFL, Tatum would become known as "the Assassin," and the Raiders would be singled out by Pittsburgh Steelers coach Chuck Noll as a "criminal element" largely because of Atkinson.

That was what Al Davis had in mind, all right.

• • •

The almost perfect union between Al Davis and John Madden, who had come within one bruised hand of reaching the Super Bowl in 1969, started to unravel early in the 1970 season, before the Blanda heroics. The Raiders began disastrously, with two losses and a tie in the first three games—and the losses were to expansion teams, the Cincinnati Bengals and the Miami Dolphins. As it happened, both teams made the play-offs that year, but they were lightly regarded early in the season, and the Raiders losses seemed inexplicable.

The Dolphins game, in Miami, was particularly brutal. A torrential downpour made it impossible to pass the ball in the second quarter. The rain stopped at halftime, but the Raiders problems continued. A long touchdown run by Charlie Smith was called back because of holding. Davis later claimed that films disproved the holding call, but the reporters never got to see those films. The Raiders lost, 20−13.

To make a bad situation worse, the chartered plane on which

the team was to fly back to Oakland had mechanical problems. Before a replacement could be flown in, the team had to wait six hours in the Miami Airport. No one was happy about that, but Davis was probably more distraught than anyone. For a good part of the time he walked up and down the largely empty airport corridors, with me at his side, ranting and raving about the game. He second-guessed Madden and wondered aloud if he needed to make a change.

Any reporter experiences times when he has to make a decision as to whether a story or a source is the more important. In this case I chose the source. I reasoned that (1) Davis was not talking for the record, and I would be abusing a confidence if I wrote about what he had to say; (2) he was simply blowing off steam. I knew he wasn't really going to fire Madden. Davis was often very emotional after a game, particularly a loss, but he made his decisions in more rational moments. Madden would hear these same comments sometime, but he wouldn't be fired. So I didn't write the story. That caused me some anxious moments later because, unknown to me, Davis had made similar comments right after the game within the hearing of Miami reporters, who had written about them. Their stories, with the inflammatory quotes from Davis, implied that Madden would be fired, and my editor wanted to know why I didn't have the same story. Both Madden and I rode out the storm.

The next year, 1971, the Raiders had the same season record as in 1970, 8-4-2, but they missed the play-offs for the first time. They started off strongly, winning five straight games after a season-opening loss, and then faced Kansas City in their seventh game, at Oakland. The Chiefs were still the team the Raiders had to beat to win in their division, but Madden's caution was costly to him in this game. In a fourth-down-and-goal situation less than a yard from the end zone in the second quarter, Madden elected to kick a field goal, and the game ended in a 20-20 tie. After the game Madden said he'd make the same decision if he had it to do over. "The guy in the stands always says, 'Go for it,' " he said, "and then if you fail, he just goes out and gets another beer. We have to live with the decision."

It wasn't the guy in the stands Madden had to satisfy, though. His boss, Al Davis, approached the game with a much bolder philosophy, and he let Madden know about his displeasure afterward. The pressure from Davis increased when the Raiders lost three of their final four games, and I felt the pressure indirectly, in a confrontation with Madden after a Raiders loss to the Falcons in Atlanta.

There had been one key sequence of plays in the third quarter. The Raiders had been moving the ball downfield, largely by running it, but when they got inside the Atlanta 10-yard line, fullback Marv Hubbard came out and Daryle Lamonica suddenly started throwing, unsuccessfully. An interception ended the drive, and the Falcons won, 23 – 14.

The writers traveled on the team plane then, which meant that those of us working for morning papers had to write a story very quickly after the game and then update it, for later editions, by talking to the players on the plane. My story criticized Madden for taking Hubbard out at a vital juncture and Lamonica for his play calls inside the Atlanta 10 — the responsibility for calling plays rested, after all, with the quarterback.

I put my typewriter and copy on a table in the front of the plane, intending to work there after talking to the players in the back. Stupidly, I left my copy out on the table. I talked to Hubbard, who told me he had taken himself out of the game because of leg cramps, and to Lamonica, who told me the play calls near the goal line had been sent in from the bench. I returned to the front, intending to make the changes in my story, and saw Madden in full rage, his face as red as Hank Stram's blazer. He had read far enough into my story to see the criticism of him. I tried to explain that I was going to change the story, but the damage was done. I took my typewriter and retreated to a seat in the back. Madden called me two days later to apologize, which wasn't necessary. I knew his explosion had been simply a reflection of the heat he was getting from Davis.

By 1972 Madden knew he had to make extensive changes in the team. Only Tom Keating remained from the great defensive line that had been the key to the Raiders' Super Bowl year, and Keating had not been the same player since snapping that Achilles tendon in the AFL All-Star game after the 1967 season. Lamonica was increasingly hobbled by injuries, and his effectiveness had been curtailed by the zone defenses he was now facing. Warren Wells was gone and had not yet been replaced. Marv Hubbard, a sturdy up-the-middle runner and punishing blocker, was not the deep-pass receiving threat that Hewritt Dixon had been.

The changed personnel, coupled with Madden's more conservative approach to offense, was making the Raiders a different team. Madden knew he had to show the players that he was in control. Finally, in 1973, he confronted the problem directly by challenging Davis's authority over two players.

The first incident involved Jeff Queen, a running back and tight end for whom Davis had traded in 1972. Davis had always liked players who could play both those positions, because it gave flexibility to the offense. In Queen, a talented runner and pass catcher, he thought he had an explosive player who could come off the bench and make a big play. Queen was temperamental, though, and a spotty practice player. Going back to Art Powell, Davis had always been tolerant of that kind of behavior if the player produced. Madden was more traditional, feeling that "you practice as you play." Because Queen didn't practice hard, he played little.

Midway through the 1973 season, Queen called Madden one day and said he could not practice because of an injured ankle—an injury about which Madden was skeptical. When Queen appeared the next day Madden sarcastically asked him if he was healthy. Queen cursed at Madden and said, "You don't run this team, anyway. Al Davis does." Madden immediately suspended Queen, against Davis's wishes. When Queen returned he played only on special teams the rest of the year, and he was cut before the next season.

It was the Bubba Smith case, though, that was the real focal point of the dispute over control between Madden and Davis.

There were two types of players that Davis especially coveted: quarterbacks who could throw the ball 60 yards without a flutter and defensive ends who could destroy quarterbacks. The Raiders had one defensive end, Tony Cline, who was an excellent pass rusher but was undersized, at just over 240 pounds. At the other end, Horace Jones was a solid but unspectacular performer. Davis wanted more. In a conversation we had back in the summer of 1971, he had bemoaned the fact that the Raiders had given up on Richard Jackson after just one year, 1966, and that Jackson had gone on to become a great defensive end with the Denver Broncos. Davis was willing to take a chance to get one great player like Jackson, and so, after the 1972 season, he traded tight end Raymond Chester to the Baltimore Colts for Bubba Smith.

Smith was available only because he had torn up his knee in a collision with a downs marker in a 1972 exhibition game, an injury that had sidelined him for the entire season. An All-American at Michigan State, where he had inspired the chant of "Kill, Bubba, kill," Smith had been an overwhelming force at defensive end for the Colts, but they didn't think he would be the same player after such a serious injury.

It turned out to be a trade that didn't help either team. Chester, with his speed and good hands, had been the prototype of the great receiving tight end for the Raiders, split wide much like Kellen Winslow later with the San Diego Chargers. Chester had averaged about sixteen yards a catch and had caught twenty-two touchdown passes in his three years with the Raiders, but he fell off in Baltimore because he was used as a traditional tight end—a thoroughbred treated as if he were a Clydesdale.

The Colts had guessed right on Bubba Smith, who was healthy enough to play for the Raiders but had lost the explosiveness that had made him great. He was, in truth, no more than an average defensive end by then, far less than what Davis had expected. But Davis didn't want to admit his error by having Smith sit on the bench. Two-thirds of the way through the season, Smith was injured and missed a game. That gave Madden his opportunity. Although Smith could have played the next game, Horace Jones, his replacement, remained in the lineup.

Those decisions, particularly the second one, so enraged Davis that he told people in the Raiders office that Madden would be gone after the season. Again, a statement made in the heat of the moment was recanted when Davis thought rationally. Who could he get who would do a better job than Madden? Madden stayed, and his position was much stronger for his successful challenges of Davis.

The two had other confrontations. During training camp in 1975, Davis signed a player considered the best outside linebacker in pro football, Ted Hendricks, who had played out his option with the Green Bay Packers. During the season Davis signed tight end Ted Kwalick, who had been a star with the San Francisco 49ers before jumping to the World Football League. Madden hardly played either one for most of the year. "Everybody told me before I came here that Al Davis ran the team," Hendricks said, "but it doesn't seem that way to me. As far as I can see, John Madden is running it."

Hendricks finally got into the lineup in the last game of the season. When Tony Cline was hurt, Hendricks was put in as a combination end-linebacker. He played well in that role and then had a spectacular game against the Cincinnati Bengals in the play-offs, sacking quarterback Ken Anderson three times, once preventing Cincinnati from getting in range for a game-tying field goal. The Raiders won, 31–28. Having proved himself to Madden, Hendricks stayed in the lineup from then on and was elected to the Pro Football Hall of Fame at the end of his playing career.

Kwalick was not so lucky. The Raiders were overloaded with tight ends, with Bob Moore, Dave Casper, and Warren Bankston (who was used primarily on special teams). Kwalick had been an outstanding pass-receiving tight end for the 49ers, but he was not as good a blocker as Moore was. Casper, just beginning to assert himself, would be a great tight end for the Raiders in the years to come. Kwalick didn't catch a pass in 1975 and, though he stayed with the team two more seasons, played little.

In a sense Al Davis was now fighting a two-front war, with his coach and with his partner, Wayne Valley. Madden would eventually want out of the battle and retire from coaching, but long before then Davis would force Valley out and take total control of the franchise.

·5·

Al Davis 1,
Wayne Valley 0

In many ways, Al Davis's first ten years with the Raiders parallel the early life of the main character in Budd Schulberg's novel *What Makes Sammy Run?* Like Sammy Glick, Davis was never happy for long with one position. When he was coach, he wanted to be a partner; when he was the managing general partner, he wanted to be the sole owner.

Davis knew that time was his ally; he was a much younger man than either Wayne Valley or Ed McGah, the other general partner. George Ross remembered a time when the newspapers in Miami had been full of stories about a fight over ownership of the Dolphins between Joe Robbie, the general partner, and the limited partners (who included entertainer Danny Thomas). Davis had pointed out to Ross that Robbie would win because he had the power. "But Al wasn't so much concerned about Robbie," Ross said, "as about himself. 'You've got it all figured out, haven't you?' I said. 'You're going to have it all to yourself one day.' He just smiled."

It's doubtful that Davis, never a patient man, would ever have been willing simply to outwait his older partners, and his deteriorating relationship with Valley pushed up his timetable.

Valley and Davis had been like oil and water from the beginning, and they had grown further apart with the years. On road trips, Valley would harangue Davis if the itinerary issued by the club's front office was inaccurate. He often pointed out to beat writers that Rodger Bird's contract was only $10,000 less than Joe Namath's, though Bird was hardly as great a player; the implication was that "the Genius" wasn't always correct in his player evaluations. Dick Shutte, who at the time conducted the negotiations for radio station KNEW for the Raiders game broadcasts, remembered talking to Valley on one trip. "He told me that Davis would do anything to win, even push his grandmother down the stairs. 'He's a winner,' Wayne said, 'but he's the most obnoxious person I've ever met.' I was amazed that he would say that to me, because I hardly knew Wayne at the time."

While Valley disliked Davis, he was content to leave the operation as it was because he enjoyed the winning team Davis was producing. Davis was more circumspect about his dislike of Valley—only those closest to him, like Ross, ever heard him make openly disparaging remarks about his partner—but the deepening chasm between the two made it inevitable that Davis would soon make a move to take over the team completely. The catalyst for the final confrontation was the Warren Wells case.

Wells was an outstanding receiver for the Raiders, but he was a troubled man. He was a loner, without friends among his teammates. He had been raised in the tough Houston ghetto, and the attitudes he had learned early in life, particularly toward whites, had stayed with him.

Even when he didn't mistrust people, he could not communicate with them. I once interviewed him in his apartment for a magazine story, and he answered every question with one word or, at best, a sentence. He wasn't being uncooperative; he just couldn't articulate his feelings. At team parties he would sit off by himself drinking white port out of the bottle—an odd choice, but somehow fitting for this strange man who was so out of touch with society. His teammates gave him a wide berth, because he was known to be a "quick drunk" who became very angry on very little liquor.

Wells was an accident waiting to happen, and there was at least one accident that the public never knew about. Ross remembered Davis, on the team plane en route to a road game, saying that he had had a hard night. According to Davis's story, Wells had been arrested for taking out a pistol in a bar. Davis and the club attorney had been called down to the police station. After a long conference, it was announced that the pistol had no bullets in it, and Wells was released. "The widows-and-orphans fund must have been substantially richer after that night," Ross noted.

Then came the incident that nobody could hush up: Wells was convicted, on September 19, 1969, of attempted rape. Put on probation, he came back to the Raiders and seemed unaffected by his legal problems. His 1969 season was his best— 47 catches for 1,260 yards (a 26.8-yard average) and 14 touchdowns, and he followed that in 1970 with 43 catches for 995 yards, a 21.7 average, and 11 touchdowns.

The terms of his probation, set by sentencing judge Leonard S. Dieden, were strict. "I not only set down that he couldn't drink but that he couldn't be in an establishment that sold liquor," the judge (now retired) told me in an interview in Oakland. "But he was picked up twice on 502s—that's drunk driving—so I put him in jail."

That was on February 17, 1971. Wells got another chance; he was put back on probation on April 15 and entered a Synanon treatment center, where he seemed to be making progress. But after he left Synanon, he was involved in another incident, in Beaumont, Texas, in which he was knifed by a woman, the knife narrowly missing his heart. Wells was sent to prison on September 3, 1971.

"He was just a bad person," said Dieden, still bothered by the case twenty years later. "There are just some people who can't live by the rules of our society, and he was one of them. When I talked to him in my chambers, he just sat there. He was nonverbal—he just couldn't communicate. He just stared at me."

It was an ugly time, made uglier by what apparently were attempts by Davis to make the Wells case a racial matter. There was a demonstration by black activists at training camp one day, which Ross was certain Davis had inspired. Ross told Davis it was "disgusting"; Davis didn't comment.

Another time, Ben Davidson remembered, a black minister addressed the team. "I don't think John Madden quite knew how to handle that," Davidson said. "You just didn't have guys from outside talking to the team in those days. But John let him do it. So we had this big team meeting, and the minister started berating the white players, telling us that Warren's problems were caused by racial prejudice. Well, we knew better than that. Warren was quite capable of making his own problems.

"I was concerned that it would divide the team, blacks against whites. I was afraid the blacks would believe him, and I was even more concerned that there would be a backlash from the white players, because they knew they weren't responsible for this. But after the meeting blacks and whites alike went out of their way to be nice to each other and show there was no animosity. It wasn't spoken—it was just the way everybody acted. And at practice that day everybody was so polite. It seemed that every time one player hit another he'd be saying, 'Excuse me.' There was so much good will on both sides. I think on other teams this could have been very divisive, but we had the kind of leadership, with players like Willie Brown and Gene Upshaw, to avoid that. They let everybody know that it was winning that was the important thing, and we couldn't let this get in our way. So it didn't."

There may have been no animosity between the players, but there certainly was between Davis and Valley. Davis wanted Wells on the playing field, and he was convinced that Valley could get Wells out of prison and keep him out, because of Valley's friendship with Dieden; before being appointed to the bench, Dieden had acted as an attorney for Valley.

"Wayne never put any pressure on me at all," Dieden said. "He told me not to pay any attention to how this affected him, Ed McGah, or the Raiders, but just to treat it as I would any other case."

The last thing Davis wanted was for the Wells case to be treated like any other case. "Davis never made a flat statement that Valley was to blame," Tom Keating said. "He alluded to Valley's relationship with the judge and said, 'Some people in this organization are racist.' It was silly. Valley was a business-man; Wells could make him money, and he wanted him out on that field as much as anybody."

The schism between Valley and Davis over Wells became so apparent to the team that Keating called Valley in midsea-son of 1971 and asked him to explain the situation to the team. Valley agreed—but only if Davis was also there and reporters were allowed to attend. Davis refused.

The Wells case showed the dark side of Davis's nature, and perhaps an unrealistic element as well. Because envious rivals think he does it only to win games, Davis has received less credit than he deserves for his willingness to give players a second chance and to risk taking players who have been branded as renegades elsewhere. In Wells, however, he was all too will-ing to give second and third and fourth chances to a man who was manifestly dangerous to himself and society. It was almost as if he thought he could, by force of his personality, change Wells's character.

There was one more chapter in the Wells story. He had been sent to a work camp in Jamestown, in the "Mother Lode" area of California. "We heard that he had gotten along well there and had not made any trouble," Dieden remembered, "so there was some pressure to give him another chance. But I was concerned about Wells being out in the community." John Madden found that a religious retreat in San Ramon, near Oakland, would be willing to let Wells stay there during the football season, but that still left the question of training camp. "I didn't want to take the chance that he'd be out in the bars in Santa Rosa," Dieden went on, "and that something would happen. I asked Davis, Valley, McGah, and Madden to meet with me. They all came—except Davis. That set off an alarm because I felt Davis was the man who had to make the decision. I told Valley, McGah, and Madden that the Raiders would have to be responsible for Wells's behavior in training camp." According to Dieden, Sam Lacey, a probation officer who had worked with Wells, called Davis and reported that Davis said he would take responsibility.

"But then, the next morning," Dieden continued, "Davis called a press conference and said the Raiders couldn't take responsibility for Wells. So there I was, out on a limb, because I had let him out. I worried about that all day. When I got home, I got a call from Pete Rozelle, who said he was having Wells fly back to New York for a talk. He wasn't sure he would go along with my decision. But he called me the next day and said not to worry, that he'd work it out with Davis for the Raiders to take responsibility for Wells. I've never forgotten that episode. Wayne Valley was a very honest guy, tough but principled. John Madden really came through, too—John is a very upright type of guy. But Davis double-crossed me."

As it happened, all the maneuvering meant nothing. The prison and Synanon time had dulled Wells, emotionally and physically. In four years with the Raiders, 1967–1970, he had caught 156 passes for 3,632 yards, an average of 23.3 yards per catch, and had converted more than a fourth of those catches—42—into touchdowns. He was easily the most dangerous receiver in pro football in his last three years. But now, in training camp, he was lethargic, running his patterns as if he were running in water. If he had been just another receiver getting a tryout, he wouldn't have lasted beyond the first two days. As it was, Davis kept him until almost the end of the exhibition season, hoping to see just a few plays that would remind him of the player Wells had been. Wells never showed anything, and he was cut before the season started.

Back home in Texas, Wells returned to his pattern of bar-room brawls. Then he moved on to something more serious—armed robbery—and was sentenced to state prison.

• • •

Wells's legacy to the Raiders lived on in the relations between the partners. Although Valley never said it publicly, he hinted to both George Ross and me that he would try to get Davis out of the partnership when the ten-year agreement expired on January 1, 1976. He never got the chance, because Davis moved more quickly.

As early as 1970, the possibility of extending the contract, with Davis remaining as managing general partner, had been discussed at a meeting of both general and limited partners. The limited partners were enthusiastic, but they had no vote on the matter. Davis said he had "no objection." Valley said only that it was too early to discuss it, without saying whether he approved.

Because the terms of the general partnership allowed any two partners to make changes in the basic agreement, Davis didn't need Valley's assent if he had the vote of the third general partner, Ed McGah. And Davis had little doubt he could get McGah's vote.

McGah had been one of the original owners who wanted out in the second year of the franchise, when the team was losing and red ink was splashed through the books. But Valley had publicly shamed him into remaining, calling him "chicken shit" in front of friends at a country club. McGah had stayed in and had prospered financially, but Valley's humiliation of him remained in his mind. Davis, for his part, was solicitous of McGah when he came along on road trips. McGah knew little about football; all he wanted was a good time. He always brought with him a woman friend from Oakland, and the other Raiders partners, who knew McGah's wife, shunned him. But Davis would take him to dinner, flattering him and catering to him.

So when Davis came to McGah with a new contract in 1972,

McGah didn't even bother to read it before he signed it. He admitted to that in a taped telephone interview with George Ross, and he added that whatever Davis did was fine with him, because he regarded Davis as a football genius. (Later, in an acrimonious confrontation, he told Valley, "All I remember is that when you were running the team we were losing.") The tape was not admissible as evidence in a lawsuit later brought by Valley, but Ross used it as the basis for a story.

As with everything else in which the two were involved, Davis and Valley had different versions of when Valley learned about the new contract. Davis claimed he told Valley on July 6, 1972—at a partnership meeting called to discuss the possibility of expanding the seating at the Oakland Coliseum—that he and McGah were going to sign a ten-year agreement that McGah was "offering." A nice touch, that "offering," because the contract was Davis's baby from the beginning.

For his part, Valley at first claimed that he knew nothing about the new contract for some time, although he later testified that Davis had made an "obscure reference" to it at the July meeting. The reference, Valley testified, was a statement by Davis that "McGah has given me a ten-year contract." Valley claimed that there was then "dead air" for about thirty seconds and that Davis did not tell him the contract terms. He thought it was simply a trial balloon by Davis to pressure him into a new agreement. The next thing he heard, Valley testified, was from Buffalo owner Ralph Wilson, before a Raiders-Bills game in October. Wilson told Valley there was a new contract. "I don't believe it," Valley said. "I would know about it."

The following month, Valley said, his auditor discovered the new contract in the team's business records and read him some of the details. When he confronted Davis, Valley said, Davis replied, "Wayne, I could write a twenty-five-year contract myself, and you couldn't do anything about it." That was literally true, of course, as long as Davis had McGah's support.

The new contract was a beauty. Among other things, it included these provisions: (1) Davis was to get a $100,000 annual salary for ten years (the original contract had called for

$35,000), with a year added as each year was lopped off, for a maximum of twenty years, at which time Davis would be sixty-five. (2) The contract could not be terminated by other partners. If it were, Davis would be paid for the remainder of the contract and would be considered to have suffered "irreparable damage" to his reputation as a football expert, which could be the basis for a suit. (3) The contract could not be terminated by the death of a general partner. (4) Davis would have sole responsibility for hiring and for running the operation, on the field and off. He could hire a general manager at whatever salary he desired. He would set his own expense account, consistent with those of other clubs in the league, and he would be the sole judge of how much time and energy he put in on the job. (5) If Davis should be totally incapacitated for twelve months, the contract could not be broken; he would be paid for the remainder of it. (6) Davis would have the club's vote at NFL meetings. (7) Davis could engage in any other enterprise he chose, so long as it was not in direct competition with the Raiders.

Valley apparently did nothing about the contract when he first heard about it, although he did call the NFL commissioner, Pete Rozelle. As it happened, Rozelle planned to be in the Bay Area soon (to discuss a suit against the Raiders by limited partner Lou Borrereo, who was upset because the partnership agreement gave general partners the right to buy out limited partners if they chose), and a meeting was set up. There, Valley tossed around newspaper stories about the new contract, and he and Davis sparred verbally, as Rozelle and the league counsel, Jay Moyer, watched uncomfortably. Afterward Valley told Rozelle that he didn't want any league intervention, that he would settle the matter himself.

A month later the NFL owners gathered for their annual meeting, in Scottsdale, Arizona, and Valley used that forum to announce that he was filing a suit against Davis. The suit asked that the new contract be set aside, but in talking with others, including me, Valley left no doubt that he also wanted to get Davis out of the partnership.

The suit finally came to trial in May 1975. To reinforce Davis's reputation as a football genius, his attorney had Philadelphia Eagles owner Leonard Tose testify that he had tried to hire Davis in 1971 and 1972. Davis himself testified that he had entertained similar proposals from the Houston Oilers and the Los Angeles Rams, though no one from those organizations gave confirming testimony. The judge, Redmond C. Staats, ruled two months later that Davis's contract would be upheld but that his expanded powers would be disallowed. "A Solomonlike decision," an exasperated Valley said. "He cut the baby in half."

Talking to me in 1991 about his decision, the now-retired judge said that the key was his feeling that Valley had known about the rewriting of the contract to give Davis a raise but had done nothing about it. "Valley didn't want to acknowledge that Davis and McGah could do something behind his back," the judge said, "so he basically ignored it for months." In that belief, the judge ruled that Davis's new salary could not be rescinded, since Davis and McGah had proceeded on the basis of it for months, but he also ruled that the rest of the contract had to be submitted to Valley and the limited partners, and it had not been. "Davis wasn't dishonest, but he wasn't a true partner, in the sense that he didn't want anybody interfering with what he was doing," the judge added.

It's difficult to see how the Raiders could have continued with the split between Valley and Davis hanging over the club. Predictably, Valley was the one who finally conceded, agreeing to sell his share of the club to Davis at market value in January 1976. The sale meant that Davis now owned approximately 25 percent of the franchise shares. More important, there were no longer any dissenting voices in the organization. In the public's eye, Davis had long been the Oakland Raiders; now the image had become the reality.

Why did Valley bow out, when he had as much power after the lawsuit as he'd had before? His outside business interests almost dictated that he get out. As George Ross explained it, Valley had sold his construction business, Citation Building, to

Singer and was conducting seminars for Singer around the country; he thought it was unfair to drag Singer into a sports controversy it had nothing to do with. Ironically, Singer soon decided it didn't want subsidiaries like Valley's construction business, which were so different from its normal interests, and it sold the business back to Valley.

Valley had a great emotional attachment to football—he had helmets from every NFL team on his office walls—and he soon made an attempt to get back into the NFL. In 1975, when the San Francisco 49ers were for sale, he made an offer to buy the club, working with Lou Spadia, then the 49ers president and a minority stockholder. Franklin Mieuli, another minority stockholder, exercised an option to block the sale, believing that he could put together a deal with buyers in Sacramento. The Sacramento deal quickly fell through, but it gave Davis time to thwart his former benefactor once more. Davis found another buyer, Eddie DeBartolo. And when DeBartolo bought the team, Davis got a finder's fee of $100,000.

The confrontation with Valley drove a wedge between Davis and George Ross, his longtime newspaper buddy. Ross not only had written a story about McGah's not having read the contract before signing it; he also had quoted Davis extensively about the conflict, although Davis had thought his comments would not be printed. Davis stopped talking to Ross. "I was in a rock sandwich, between two people I greatly admired," Ross admitted. "I hoped to work it out, but I couldn't. Al was just relentless when it came to something like that. If you weren't his friend, you were his enemy."

The conflict so disturbed Ross that he got out of sports and became the assistant managing editor of the *Tribune*. Even that wasn't enough for Davis, who believed that Ross was sneaking back into the sports department and writing headlines critical of him. Eventually Ross took early retirement from the *Tribune*, a victim of the Davis-Valley war in a way he could never have foreseen.

Although it was not so traumatic an experience for me as it was for Ross, my own break with Davis over the same issue was just as final. When Valley filed his suit I wrote a column critical of Davis—after all, Valley had given him his chance for success. Davis stopped talking to me, too, and, except for isolated instances, has not talked to me since.

In a way he could not have understood, Davis actually helped me as a columnist, because I would no longer be blinded by my closeness to one powerful figure. It wasn't that I could no longer get information about either Davis or the Raiders. The players continued to be remarkably candid about their boss, as well as about their own play, and there were always front-office employees who would give me information about Davis as long as I protected my sources.

Davis's behavior in cutting off both me and Ross might seem extreme, but it was not unexpected. There were some writers, such as Wells Twombly, then a columnist for the *San Francisco Examiner,* whom Davis thought of as independent, and so any criticism from them didn't bother him. There was another group of writers he felt were loyal to him. That group included Ross, and it also included me.

It wasn't that we had never disagreed. In 1968, for instance, I had been very critical when he cut Clem Daniels in training camp—an emotional judgment on my part that was not supported by the realities. Davis had shrugged that off; he had known he would be criticized, but he also had known he was right. "How many thirty-one-year-old running backs are there in the NFL?" personnel man Ron Wolf had asked me. The answer, after Clem was cut: none.

There also had been times when Davis was not happy with what I reported. In 1971, doing research for *Newsweek* for a story on George Allen, who had made a winner out of the Washington Redskins, I quoted Davis as being critical of Allen's pattern of trading away draft choices. Davis, who always liked to be associated with winners, was embarrassed when the quote reached print. "I didn't want to be quoted on that," he told me. "I just got off the phone with George. I had to tell him I didn't mean it the way it came out."

When I had become a columnist I had to distance myself

from the Raiders, and I was mildly critical of Davis at times, though my heart was still with the team. That didn't bother him—but the Valley suit was a litmus test, and I failed it. Davis had had reason to think I would support him, because I was much closer to him than I was to Valley, but I felt strongly that Davis owed a debt to Valley for having given him an opportunity. I wrote that, and I was cut off.

Hank Stram was right. With Al Davis, you always know where you stand.

• • •

John Madden could defy Al Davis because Davis was concentrating on winning his battle with Wayne Valley for control of the franchise—but also because Madden was winning games, and that was primarily because of quarterback Ken Stabler.

No one ever exemplified the Raiders better than Ken Stabler, with his reckless, let-it-all-hang-out, never-concede attitude. In a 1978 game against the Denver Broncos he threw six interceptions—mainly because he never stopped throwing, each time thinking he could get the ball through for the winning touchdown. When I asked him about the interceptions after the game, he said, "That's the breaks. We'll get 'em next week."

"I always thought the Snake succeeded because he didn't fear failure," Raiders announcer Bill King said. "If he gave it his best shot and it wasn't good enough, he'd just say, 'Fuck it,' and go have a Scotch. To use a Bill Walsh word, he was resourceful. He always found a way to get the job done."

Resourceful, indeed. In a 1978 game in San Diego, the Raiders were trailing by 6 points with just 10 seconds left and had the ball at the Chargers 10-yard line. Back to pass, Stabler was hit by San Diego linebacker Woody Lowe. As he went down at about the 24, he purposely fumbled the ball forward toward Pete Banaszak, who tried to scoop it up and then kicked it toward the goal line. Dave Casper swatted the ball into the end zone and fell on it. Referee Jerry Markbreit, showing a naïveté unusual even for an NFL referee, ruled that all the fumbling had been unintentional and signaled a touchdown, giving the

Raiders the win. The next year, after Stabler admitted he had fumbled intentionally and Casper admitted he had intentionally shoved the ball forward, the NFL rule was changed to specify that a ball cannot be advanced by a fumble in the last two minutes of a game.

Time after time, Stabler brought the Raiders back from what seemed certain defeat, and yet Al Davis never liked Stabler as a player. "It seemed that way to you, too?" Stabler said, when I asked him about it some years later. "Ah, well, I've made my peace with the man. I've even found that I like him."

The year Stabler was in the draft, 1968, the quarterback Davis really wanted was Eldridge Dickey, from Tennessee State A&I. The Raiders took Dickey first and took Stabler, in the second round, only because some of those in the drafting room, notably Ron Wolf, wanted him.

Davis wasn't at all excited about Stabler. "Al talked three times about trading the Snake," the former offensive line coach, Ollie Spencer, remembered. "He kept saying, 'He can't throw sixty yards.' I said, 'But he can win for you.' Ron Wolf really fought for him, too, so Al kept him." Early in 1973, Davis was pressuring Madden to keep Daryle Lamonica in the starting lineup, even though Stabler seemed the better quarterback. When the Raiders declined after winning their first Super Bowl following the 1976 season, Davis publicly blamed Stabler. After the 1979 season he traded Stabler to the Houston Oilers for Dan Pastorini, a quarterback for whom the phrase "unfulfilled potential" was invented. Crazy, and yet, if you knew Davis and his thinking, it all made a strange kind of sense.

"It wasn't personal," Stabler says now, from the advantage of perspective. "I was never his kind of quarterback—physically, anyway. Mentally, I probably was, because we both really want to win, but he didn't like my style of play. He liked a guy who could throw long. Really, Daryle Lamonica was his kind of quarterback, a bombs-away type of guy, or like Jay Schroeder is now. That wasn't my style. I was a very accurate, high-percentage type of passer. I liked ball control. I'd throw the short and intermediate-range passes and occasionally go deep.

I liked to use all my receivers. Davis would stand behind me at practice and say, 'Take a look downfield,' or 'Look downfield first.' I had a tendency to throw under the coverage without even looking deep. But my style worked for me, so I stayed with it."

For all his skill in evaluating players, Davis has some glaring blind spots. One is his liking for big linemen. "We used to joke that if you wanted to get a raise just take your shirt off before you went in to talk to Al," Tom Keating remarked. The Raiders have had some great linemen, but they've also had some spectacular failures, big men like Charles Philyaw, Greg Kent, Kelvin Korver, Richard Sligh, and Tom Gipson.

Another big blind spot is for the enormously talented athlete who never develops into a good football player. The best example is Eldridge Dickey, the quarterback drafted ahead of Stabler. Dickey could flick a ball sixty yards with an all-wrist motion, and he was fast enough to be tried as a wide receiver and looked as if he could play either running back or defensive back. "He had more ability than any player I ever saw," said Marv Hubbard, who was chosen number eleven in that same draft. Yet Dickey never made it at any position. He was tried first at quarterback, but he was totally undisciplined and had to be shifted to wide receiver. He might have made it there, but he "heard footsteps," as the football saying goes. He was released in 1971, the day after he dropped what should have been a touchdown pass in a game against the Kansas City Chiefs because he knew he was about to be hit by Willie Lanier.

Before Dickey played himself off the team, he was just one more obstacle in the path of Stabler, who also had to work his way past George Blanda and then Daryle Lamonica. Stabler was a topflight athlete. Before injuring his knees he was a shifty, elusive runner; he got his nickname of "Snake" from his running style. He was also a good pitcher, and the possibility that he might turn pro in baseball—he was told there were far more successful left-handed pitchers in baseball than left-handed quarterbacks in football—probably kept other teams from taking him on the first round of the draft, before the Raiders could grab him.

Talented as he was, Stabler was totally unsuited to Davis's offense. "I remember when I came out of college," Stabler said, "I was going through a passing drill with John Rauch and Bill Miller, a wide receiver on the team. That was my first try at throwing Raiders patterns. They were running patterns seventeen or eighteen yards deep, and if you figure you're throwing from behind the line and the middle of the field to the sideline, you're maybe talking about a forty-yard pass. Well, I'd come out of a system at Alabama where I was throwing nothing but short passes, and I didn't have the arm strength to throw those passes. Everything came up short. But in those years I was behind Lamonica, and George Blanda, too, for a while. I worked on lifting weights, mostly out of boredom, I suppose, and that really built up my arm strength. I still couldn't throw downfield like Lamonica, but I could throw the other stuff."

For several years it didn't matter what Stabler could throw. He hardly played at all until the 1972 season, and it wasn't until the fourth game of the 1973 season, when he led the Raiders to a 17 – 10 win over the St. Louis Cardinals, that he finally took over for Lamonica, who never started another game for the Raiders.

The change was a dramatic one, in style and personality. Lamonica was a loner, friendly with everyone on the team but close to none. "A quarterback can't be close to another player," he told me more than once, "because you never know when you might have to chew out a player." That thought never seemed to have occurred to Stabler (or to Blanda, for that matter). He was especially close to Fred Biletnikoff and Pete Banaszak, roommates and soulmates. He played hard and he partied hard. As unsuited as he was to Davis's style on the field, he was perfectly suited to the unrestricted atmosphere Davis allowed *off* the field. Other teams would have put restrictions on his personal life that Stabler would have found intolerable.

Stories were always circulating among the Raiders about Stabler's wild partying, and, as he said in his own book, *Snake,* most of them were true. For most of his time as a Raider he was married—although to different women—but, as he admitted, he didn't feel like a husband. Certainly he didn't act like one. He and his Raiders roommates gloried in their ability to score with women, posting such mementos as women's panties on the walls of their room at training camp in Santa Rosa. Silly, yes, but Stabler was always a very likable man—or boy— caught up in the fantasy world of professional sports. He was a genuine person; what you saw was truly what you got.

He carried that attitude over to the playing field, and he could make memorable remarks in the heat of battle. Just one example: The 1977 play-off game against the Baltimore Colts went into a second overtime period. As the Raiders were driving for what became the winning touchdown, the Colts called a time-out. Madden was gesturing furiously on the sideline, but Stabler was looking up at the stands. Madden yelled, "You've got to concentrate, Snake." Stabler responded, "You know, John, I was just thinking, these people are seeing a helluva game today."

Even in the midst of the tremendous excitement generated by a Super Bowl, Stabler could remain calm. In the game of January 9, 1977, the Raiders' first drive against the Minnesota Vikings was slowed, forcing a field goal. "I came off the field," Stabler told me, "and John was bitching and moaning and throwing his arms around like he always did, and I told him, 'Relax. There's plenty more points where that came from.' "

Perhaps Stabler could keep calm because he always knew what he was doing on the field. The Raiders quarterbacks called almost all the plays, and even when Madden sent in a call, the quarterback, whether Lamonica or Stabler, had the freedom to change it. The reasoning was that the quarterback, on the field, had a better feel for what was happening in the game. But that system is only as good as the quarterback. Lamonica would make some calls that had the players (and observers) shaking their heads. "Sometimes, when he calls a play in the huddle, I wonder where that came from," Pete Banaszak once told me, "but he always makes it work." Lamonica made the plays work—at least in the first part of his career—because both he and his teammates were good enough to overcome bad calls.

Stabler, from the start, had a better feel for the game, an intuitive knowledge of what would work. Because he had confidence in his game, Stabler could bring the pass receivers together in practice and get them to cut their patterns short, from seventeen or eighteen yards down to twelve or thirteen. That was still enough for a first down, and Stabler was able to find the openings between the zones. And a psychological ploy of Madden's saved Stabler from plays suggested by receivers who thought they were open. During film sessions Madden would stop a play just as a pass was being released and ask the receivers, "All right. Which of you were open?" When he ran the film again it usually showed that receivers who thought they were open actually had come open only after the pass was thrown and the defenders were released to go for the ball.

It was the period when offensive coordinators, such as Bill Walsh with the Cincinnati Bengals, were becoming a major factor, but, for the Raiders, Ken Stabler was the offensive coordinator. He decided during the week what plays he wanted to use, and those were the plays he called during games—basically the same plays game after game. Stabler changed the complex Davis offense into a simple one and, because of his ability and his teammates', the Raiders won.

When quarterback Jim Plunkett came to the Raiders in the 1978 season, he had a hard time believing what he saw. "Stabler actually survived on a very few pass routes. We'd be sitting in meetings with Tom Flores, the backfield coach then, and he would say, 'We'll do this' and 'We'll do that,' and Snake would be nodding his head. But in the game he'd use two deep routes. If the coverage was zone, receivers would adjust and run hooks, and we always had the post patterns, so he could always go to that. There wasn't much beyond that, and Snake would use those same patterns no matter who we were playing.

It didn't matter to Madden, so long as we won. John in those years was a lot like Art Shell today. Get the guys ready, and let everybody do what they were supposed to do."

Stabler's independence was an annoyance to Davis, though, because much of the game plan Flores was proposing had come from Davis. As he had done with Madden and Ollie Spencer when they were assistants under Rauch, Davis was trying to put his ideas in place through Flores, but Stabler was discarding most of them. Davis fumed, but he couldn't do much as long as Stabler and the Raiders were winning.

The Raiders had changed from a bombs-away team to a ball-control team, with a bruising running attack to set up Stabler's pinpoint passing. Davis didn't like it, but it fit the personnel, because Stabler had two possession-type receivers to throw to, Biletnikoff and Mike Siani, and the hard-running Hubbard running behind a massive offensive line.

Three of those linemen—Upshaw, Shell, and center Jim Otto—are in the Hall of Fame, but the most fascinating was a fourth member of the group, Bob Brown, a right tackle obtained from the Los Angeles Rams in 1971. Once again Davis had showed his willingness to resist the conventional wisdom, which said that Brown was too difficult to contend with, and go for ability.

Brown was the strongest offensive lineman I have ever seen—I saw him knock down a goalpost one day in practice. He dominated defensive players, driving them well off the line of scrimmage. "I had this theory that the common denominator of man is pain," Brown told me, "and I was determined to administer as much pain as possible. Instead of being the shock absorber, I wanted to be the one who gave the shock. I was reasonably quick, so I could attack, and if my balance was a little bit off I could recover. Plus, I wanted to beat up on this guy so he wouldn't rush as hard in the fourth quarter as the first."

Stabler told of Brown complaining during one game because the Raiders were running most of the time behind Shell and Upshaw on the left side. "Run the ball to the right side

for a change," Brown growled from the line of scrimmage.
Knowing the other team would be looking for just that, Stabler
thought he'd teach Brown a lesson and had Hubbard run over
the right side. Brown knocked his man back four yards. "As
an athlete, you want to be part of the game, the principal part,
not just cutting off the back side," Brown told me. "But, re-
flecting back, how do you say it's a mistake to run play after
play after play to the left when it was always successful?"

Nobody messed with Bob Brown, an intimidating man with
a 6-foot-5, 295-pound frame, of which about 250 pounds
seemed to be in his chest and shoulders. He was a presence,
with a stare that could have melted an iceberg. "He was the
most intimidating player ever to play this game," Upshaw said.
"I remember one player—I won't mention his name—who
Brown ripped with his forearm, with his thumb, and the guy
said to me, 'Please don't let him hit me again.' Bob didn't take
any shit. He marched to a different drumbeat. 'If I'm hurt,
don't call my doctor, call my lawyer,' he used to say."

The NFL's Lineman of the Year with both the Philadelphia Eagles and the Los Angeles Rams, Brown had been labeled troublesome because he dared to question the often petty
rules of many NFL teams. He was relieved to learn that he
wouldn't have to worry about petty rules with the Raiders.

"It was the best athletic experience I had, being here," said
Brown, who still lives in Oakland, "and working with the people
I worked with. You couldn't ask for a nicer person than John
Madden. For the first time since my experience with Joe Ku-
harich, who was my first coach in Philadelphia, I was treated
as an adult." Brown also enjoyed his teammates. "It was a group
of guys who were fanatically committed to the same purpose,
and that purpose was winning. A group of guys who were different—I don't know if you'd say free spirits or just weird—
who cared about each other. They were uniquely different from
the guys I played with on the Eagles and Rams. When I was
with the Eagles in the early sixties, it was a difficult time for
the country, and there were two different camps. There wasn't
a lot of camaraderie. There were blacks over here and white

guys over there. With the Raiders, everybody was together. If I was a guy who liked to kick back and drink beer, I would have loved to have sat down with Ken Stabler, for instance."

Ironically, Brown used his freedom to criticize the one person who was responsible for that freedom, Al Davis. That made him popular with the anti-Davis writers—but it also caused his earlier-than-necessary departure, in 1975. "I left under unique circumstances," Brown said. "I wasn't invited to training camp. John Vella was coming up to replace me. Athletes are like gunfighters—they don't want to stand aside and let a young fellow come up. If I had been more agreeable or demonstrated a personality that suggested I could have been a backup, I think I could have continued to play. But I think, because of some of the things I had said and done, Al was uncomfortable. He probably thought that if I'd stayed around I'd have been more of a disruptive force than a positive one. But I think I could have helped John."

Brown's comments about Davis alienated him from the Raiders owner for several years, until Davis's close friend Sam Bercovich brought them back together. Now Brown has a considerably more mellow view of Davis. "I never had any problems with Al," he told me. "Al never did anything to me. He treated me like an adult and he paid me well, and that's the God's honest truth about my relationship with Al Davis."

Brown might have seemed out of place on another team, but not on the Raiders. This was, after all, a team with a defensive back, Skip Thomas, who had picked up the nickname of "Doctor Death" and liked it so much that he had it painted on the side of his car. It had a defensive end named Otis Sistrunk who shaved his head, prompting broadcaster Alex Karras to say, during a Monday night telecast, that he was from "the University of Mars."

It also had one of my favorites, fullback Marv Hubbard, who was a bruising runner from a school known more for its academics than its football, Colgate. In time Hubbard would be succeeded by another fullback from Colgate, Mark van Eeghen. Envious critics around the NFL had always said that

Al Davis would take players from anywhere, but I don't think Colgate was what they had in mind.

Nobody ever savored playing football the way Marv Hubbard did. "I loved him," announcer Bill King said. "Running backs usually are glamorous, even though they can take a terrific pounding, but there was no glamour about Marv. He was strictly blue-collar. And he was a great postgame interview because he'd still be so high. You never knew what he was going to say. I remember after one Kansas City game he told me, 'The best thing about that game was just sticking my helmet between the numbers on number 63' "—Willie Lanier.

It took Hubbard two years to make the team; his first year he was cut and went to play in the Continental League. "The first year I came to the Raiders," Hubbard remembered, "I didn't feel like I belonged. I thought, 'These guys made a mistake drafting me.' I looked around and saw guys like Ben Davidson, Daryle Lamonica, Jim Otto, and I thought, 'What the fuck am I doing here?' But in the Continental League I played against some guys who had played in the NFL, and I suddenly realized that I was good enough to play in the NFL. When I came to training camp the second year, I was determined to make the team. It was like, get out of my way, I'll step on your fucking foot if I have to.

"I was always a player who went all out in practice. I remember linebacker Bill Laskey used to bitch at me because it happened that I blocked him a lot, and he didn't like the fact that I hit him so hard all the time. That kind of attitude helped me, but I think it was another incident that made the difference.

"We were going through a drill in practice, and I was running when Greg Kent grabbed me. Kent was a defensive tackle who'd been a high draft pick, but he was a stiff. He was big, but he couldn't play, and everybody knew it. He grabbed me by the back of my jersey and started spinning me around until I finally lost my balance and fell down. I was really pissed, and I got up and charged him. He fell down on top of me, so I reached back and punched him right in the family jewels. I knew exactly what I was doing. Everybody was watching us, and Kent just kind of collapsed in sections. From that point, I was accepted as an Oakland Raider."

Hubbard didn't have an extended career—his prime really lasted only four seasons. No one could have sustained his style of play for long. He wasn't fast enough to run away from tacklers, or elusive enough to dodge them. He didn't want to, anyway. He simply wanted to run into and over tacklers. He was the backbone of the Raiders attack, because he gained the toughest yards. When the Raiders needed 3 yards for a first down or a touchdown, Hubbard was the man. In 1972 he broke Clem Daniels's season record by 1 yard, with a total of 1,100, but the most remarkable aspect of his career was his average gain of 4.8 yards. (In 1972 it was an even 5 yards.) He couldn't fatten his average with long runs, as some runners did; in 1971, for instance, his longest run was only 20 yards. He did it with his consistency, getting 4, 5, or 6 yards on almost every run, even when the defense knew he was coming.

The Kansas City rivalry brought out the best—or worst—in Hubbard. In 1974, when Hubbard was interviewed in the dressing room after a game in which the Raiders beat the New England Patriots, most of the questions were directed toward the next week's game in Kansas City. Hubbard answered the questions by praising the Chiefs. "I gave all the right clichés," he remembered, "about how tough Kansas City was, what a tough game we'd have. Then, when the reporters were finished, I turned to Pete Banaszak and said, 'We're going to whip their ass!' " The reporters were still close enough to hear that comment, and it got into their stories and was picked up in the Kansas City papers. The Chiefs fans turned out the next week with "Mother Hubbard" banners on which were written various obscene sentiments, and Hubbard was booed every time he carried the ball, in a 7 – 6 Raiders win.

It wasn't just the fans who were ready for Hubbard. "The whole Kansas City team was looking for me," he remembered ruefully. "I had a tremendous day—I think I might have gained all of twelve yards in twenty-seven carries, or something like that. On one play, their tackles pinched in and just stood me up. I wasn't going anywhere. As soon as Willie Lanier saw where the ball was, he came running full force at me and hit me straight on. His helmet hit the top of my chest and up into my chin. I think only the fact that his helmet had a leather strap in the middle kept me from getting my chin split wide open. We all fell down. I felt like I was free-falling. It was just like in the comic strips—I was seeing stars. I think one eye was going one way and the other was going the other. When I came to, we were all there in a pile. Lanier's face mask was butting up against my face mask. I said, 'Is that as hard as you can hit?' Willie just started laughing."

Hubbard's running was a perfect complement to Stabler's passing because Hubbard forced linebackers, and sometimes defensive backs, to come up toward him. So a play fake to Hubbard would open up the passing lanes for Stabler. The Raiders were once more a force.

• • •

Most teams would have been happy with the 8−4−2 records the Raiders posted in 1970 and 1971, but that was a slump for this team. The next year, when the Raiders went 10−3−1 in spite of an unsettled quarterback situation, was more like it. In 1973, Stabler's first full year, the Raiders were only a game worse, at 9−4−1, and in both years they won their division title. Again and again they were frustrated in postseason play, however, losing to the Pittsburgh Steelers in the play-offs in 1972 and to the Miami Dolphins, 27−10, in the AFC championship game after the 1973 season. The Dolphins had gone on to win the Super Bowl, the fourth team to beat the Raiders in a championship game before going on to win the ultimate championship.

It seemed that 1974 might finally be different. Once he knew the quarterback job was his, Stabler had taken command in 1973, completing nearly 63 percent of his passes. In 1974 his percentage fell off to 57.4, but he threw for twenty-six touchdowns and had only twelve interceptions—helped greatly by a new deep receiver, Cliff Branch.

Branch had been drafted on the fourth round in 1972, amid much skepticism from many in pro football, who thought he was a sprinter first and a football player second. He certainly was a sprinter, having been timed twice, in high school, at 9.3 seconds in the 100-yard dash. He was small; listed at 5 feet 11 and 170 pounds, he was probably both shorter and lighter. And this was when the bump-and-run defense was still legal, allowing defensive backs and linebackers to knock small receivers to the ground before a pass was in the air.

There was reason to question the acquisition of Branch, because he had played for a college team (Colorado) that did not pass much. In his two college years he had caught passes for a total of 665 yards, while returning punts for 733 yards and kickoffs for 755. His first training camp did nothing to change the minds of the skeptics. In practice and in games, Branch seemed to drop more passes than he caught. Ominously, he was also getting the cold shoulder from both Davis and Madden, which usually meant a player had no future with the Raiders. Branch certainly felt so. Waiting in the airport after the club's final exhibition game, in Dallas, Branch told me he was sure he would be cut. "Nobody's talking to me," he said.

That was situation normal with the Raiders top command. When a player couldn't help, it was almost as if he had leprosy. Such behavior might have been expected of Davis, but even Madden, who had a deserved reputation for being close to his players, could sometimes act that way. For instance, once he had decided that Stabler was his quarterback, Lamonica became a nonperson. "He can't even say hello to me," Lamonica said.

Branch wasn't cut, after all. The club desperately needed a fast receiver, and Davis, who always put a high value on speed, decided to keep him. Branch caught just three passes in 1972 and another nineteen in 1973, but from watching and working with Fred Biletnikoff, the master, he learned how to concentrate on passes. From being an uncertain receiver, he went on to become an excellent pass catcher and could finally make use of his great speed.

By 1974 he was ready. He became the club's first deep threat since Warren Wells went to jail. He didn't have the exceptional cutting ability of Wells—but he didn't need it because of his sheer speed. "You'd hear the crowd start to scream even before the ball was in the air," King remembered, "because they'd see Cliff opening up that gap between him and the last defender." In 1974, Branch opened up that gap often enough to catch 60 passes for 1,092 yards (an 18.2-yard average) and 13 touchdowns.

Branch had almost too much speed for Stabler, who had worked with Biletnikoff so long that the pair had developed almost a sixth sense of communication. Sometimes, on a deep pattern, Biletnikoff and Stabler would realize virtually at the same moment that Biletnikoff couldn't beat his defender. So he would slow down, letting the defensive back get in front of him, and then catch a pass that Stabler had deliberately underthrown. In Branch's case, any underthrowing was not deliberate. As Stabler later admitted, there were times when he simply could not throw as far as Branch could run, and Branch would have to come back after the ball was in the air, often making a spectacular catch. "He was one receiver I never overthrew," Stabler said.

After losing their season opener in 1974, the Raiders won the next nine straight, clinching another division title. With an overall 12–2 record, the Raiders were at home for all their play-off games, including the first-round game against the Miami Dolphins—later called "the greatest pro football game I've ever seen" by veteran TV announcer Curt Gowdy. I'll second that.

"That was such a great game because we were playing a team that had great coaching and great players," Stabler

remembered. "Like Bob Griese, Paul Warfield, Nick Buoniconti, Larry Csonka, Jake Scott, Dick Anderson. And it was in
the play-offs. I'll never forget the excitement of that game."

The Dolphins had been "the team of the decade" until that
point, with three straight Super Bowl appearances and two
straight championships. In 1972 they had won every game they
played, fourteen in the regular season and three in the postseason. They had come down a little since then, but they had
still finished 11 – 3 in the 1974 regular season. And they had
an added incentive this time: it was probably their last chance
at a championship for a while, because Csonka, Warfield, and
Jim Kiick would all be going to the World Football League
after the season.

The fans had hardly taken their seats before Nat Moore
ran the opening kickoff back 89 yards for a Dolphins touch-
down. The Raiders, too, had their share of spectacular plays:
Biletnikoff caught a touchdown pass with his left hand while
Tim Foley of the Dolphins was holding his right arm, and
Branch went 72 yards on a play in which he caught the ball,
fell down, got up, and then outran defensive back Henry
Stuckey to the end zone.

The score leapfrogged all day. The Raiders tied the game
at 7 – 7, fell behind on a Miami field goal, went ahead on Biletnikoff's touchdown, fell behind to 19 – 14, went ahead again
on Branch's touchdown, but then fell behind again at 26 – 21.
With the ball on the Oakland 32, there was 2:08 left.

Plenty of time. With 18- and 20-yard catches as the big
plays of the drive, the Raiders drove to a first down at the
Miami 8-yard line. There were 35 seconds left. On the next
play, the Raiders flooded the right side with three receivers—
Biletnikoff, Branch, and Bob Moore—but the Dolphins covered all three. Stabler drifted to his left. He felt someone grab
his ankles as he spotted Clarence Davis on the left side of the
end zone. He let the ball go.

"My first thought was, 'Oh, shit,'" Stabler remembered,
"because the ball didn't have much on it. It just hung out there.
I knew it was in the general area, and I could see Clarence

Davis there, but he was surrounded, and there was really a wrestling match for the ball." Davis won the wrestling match and the Raiders won the game, 28–26, on a play that would be known as "the sea of hands." Stabler gave all the credit to Davis. "Clarence basically just took the ball away from everybody. He was the one who made the play; I didn't have anything to do with that."

Raiders fans celebrated in the Coliseum parking lot for hours, and many of the players joined them. Because the stadium was small—a growing complaint of Davis's, which would eventually play a key role in the franchise's future—season-ticket holders remained virtually identical year after year. It was an extended family, in which the players were certainly included.

In the parking lot after games, Tom Keating recalled, "game after game, we'd see the same people, and so we got to know them. Sometimes we'd stop off and have a drink. Sometimes it was more than one. Hubbard was always late to the team party because he'd go from one group in the parking lot to another. 'I can't be rude to the people,' he'd tell us."

Because the Raiders fans tended to be heavily blue-collar, they were sometimes perceived as a rough crowd. That was far from the truth. In fact, it was the San Francisco 49ers crowds across the bay who were the tough ones: hard-drinking fans who poured abuse and sometimes beer on their erstwhile heroes. (The entrance to the tunnel at Kezar Stadium had to be covered in the 1960s because fans would hurl bottles and cans at players, coaches, and officials.) The Oakland fans were loud and supportive, but they were mannerly—when they had to sit next to the same people year after year, they tended to be polite.

The fans' celebrations this time were short-lived, though, because the next week the Raiders lost to the Pittsburgh Steelers, 24–13. It goes without saying that the Steelers went on to win the Super Bowl.

It was much the same in 1975. The Raiders were 11–3 for the season and beat the Cincinnati Bengals, 31–28, in the first round of the play-offs. But again they lost to the Steelers in the conference championship game, in Pittsburgh, 16–10.

It was a brutal day, with a wind-chill factor of minus 12 degrees. Even Biletnikoff's "stickum" froze. The sidelines were solid ice, so that all the pass patterns had to be run in the middle of the field. Not surprisingly, there were eight fumbles and five interceptions.

The one bright spot for the Raiders was the play of tight end Dave Casper, who caught five passes. Casper was another of those strange personalities that the Raiders seemed to attract, an intelligent man, who could keep three conversations going more or less simultaneously but who until now had had trouble concentrating on the game. He often said that he'd rather play tackle than tight end—an incomprehensible sentiment to his listeners. "He was a real flake," announcer Bill King said. "I remember one time he signed late in the exhibition season. He came on the show with me after the game and said that training camp was overrated. 'The only thing I need to train is my eyes,' he said, and then he went into this long dissertation about training his eyes to see the ball to catch it."

Gene Upshaw remembered that Casper had an innovative mind. "He'd come into the huddle and say, 'If everybody gets out of the way, I can block the nose tackle.' We'd look at him like he was crazy, but now that's a standard play, the tight end taking out the nose tackle. A bright guy, but a little off center. But then, you had to be off center to play for the Raiders in those days."

Casper would go on to be the Raiders' best tight end yet, but no one was thinking about that after the second straight loss to the Steelers in the championship game. The Raiders had outlasted the Miami dynasty only to see a Pittsburgh dynasty take root. When would their turn come?

·6·

The Raiders Are
Finally Super

Each year Al Davis made certain that the Raiders media guide compared the team's record since he had taken over to the records of other clubs in the NFL. The Raiders record, of course, was better than anyone else's. In time Davis extended the comparison to other sports, and the Raiders again came out on top.

There was only one problem with the comparisons: they were limited to regular-season play. The Raiders were dynamite in the regular season—four losses was a bad year for them. In postseason play, though, they always fell short. They had lost their only Super Bowl game, after the 1967 season, and they hadn't been able to get back since.

They had been defeated by some great teams. The Green Bay Packers, who beat them in their only Super Bowl appearance, and the Miami Dolphins and the Pittsburgh Steelers, who beat them in AFC championship games, are among the best teams in NFL history. Six times the Raiders lost in conference or league championship games to teams that won the subsequent Super Bowl. But none of that mattered to the sportswriters and broadcasters, who labeled the Raiders as "chokers." Because Davis was unpopular with so many in the media and around the league, his attempts to portray the Raiders as the most successful organization in sports only made matters worse, giving his detractors a chance to laugh at the Raiders—how could a team be the best if it couldn't win the championship games?

Davis was thinking of all that when he praised Ken Stabler to beat writers, before the 1976 season, as the most accurate passer in the game. Davis seldom had a good word to say about his quarterback in those days, to the media or to Stabler himself. No matter how well Stabler played, Davis always told him he could have done better. But this time he added his ultimate praise: "He's a winner."

Despite that, 1976 didn't seem to be the Raiders' year to break through. The early news about the team, in fact, was more concerned with who would *not* be there than who would be. George Blanda, for openers, was finally gone. Blanda, whose forty-ninth birthday came on September 17, was four years older than anyone else who had ever played professional football, but even he couldn't defy time forever. He had not had any significant playing time at quarterback since the 1971 season, throwing a total of seven passes in his last three seasons. His kicking leg, though still accurate, had lost strength. The Raiders had used punter Ray Guy on kickoffs in the 1975 season, and Blanda had kicked only one field goal of more than 40 yards, a 41-yarder in the AFC championship game.

Davis had drafted a left-footed soccer kicker, Fred Steinfort, on the fifth round, but to protect himself he told Blanda to come to training camp. Blanda just sat, while Steinfort got all the kicking opportunities. Finally, when it seemed that Steinfort could do the job, Blanda was sent home.

It was not Davis's finest moment. At the least he should have called a press conference to announce the Blanda cut. Considering how much Blanda had meant to pro football, it would have been a nice touch to arrange a special ceremony for him—but that was not Davis's style, probably because it would have put the emphasis on a player instead of on the genius who had built the team. So one day Blanda was in camp; the next day he was gone, with no announcement.

Steinfort later pulled a groin muscle and could not kick. Erroll Mann, brought in to replace him, was erratic all year. It was as if Blanda had put his curse on the team. But it is only fair to note that when Blanda was inducted into the Pro Football Hall of Fame years later, he chose Davis to be his presenter. "He gave me nine extra years on my career," Blanda said.

If Blanda's departure was predictable, other losses were not. Fullback Marv Hubbard, the key to the Raiders running attack, had twice dislocated his left shoulder during the 1975 season, and that shoulder brought a premature end to his Raiders career. Hubbard's replacement, Mark van Eeghen, was the same kind of bruising, straight-ahead runner that Hubbard had been; he gained 1,012 yards in 1976 without a run longer than 21 yards. But temperamentally the two were poles apart. Van Eeghen was distinctly quiet, on and off the field.

The defense was altered dramatically because of key losses. Defensive end Tony Cline, always a dangerous pass rusher despite his relatively light weight for a lineman (about 240 pounds), was waived because of bad knees. Knee injuries also sidelined end Horace Jones and tackle Art Thoms for the season, leaving Otis Sistrunk as the only player returning from the 1975 defensive line. That forced the Raiders to go to the 3–4 defense—which turned out to be the best thing that could have happened, because they had excellent linebackers: Ted Hendricks and Phil Villapiano on the outside and Monte Johnson and Willie Hall on the inside.

The injuries also proved to be a motivating tool. "One of our biggest motivators was adversity," Madden said after the season. "When something bad happens, you have two alternatives: either let down and fold up, or just go out and play all the harder. When we had all those injuries early, everyone talked and wrote about them. This really became an indirect affront to the guys who were still out there playing. They looked around and said, 'Hell, I'm not hurt. I'm still playing.' "

Now the 3–4 defense is the base defense for virtually all NFL teams, and in fact the Raiders had experimented with it as early as 1965, but—for the Raiders and every other team at the time—the 3–4 defense was no more than a change of pace. If their defensive linemen had stayed healthy, the Raiders would have stayed with the 4–3 defense. Going to the 3–4 meant a complete change in their defensive philosophy.

In the 4–3, the four defensive linemen are responsible for rushing the passer and stopping the run; the three linebackers occasionally blitz but usually are used to cover the backs on pass patterns and to stop runs that get past the line of scrimmage. In the 3–4, which has three linemen and four linebackers, the defensive linemen are often double-teamed, so their main responsibility is to tie up the offensive linemen and plug the middle. The outside linebackers often rush the passer, and it is the linebackers who make most of the tackles and get most of the attention. That is why defensive linemen hate the 3–4.

Starting the season, Madden chose to go with Sistrunk, Dave Rowe (picked up in a trade with San Diego), and rookie Charles Philyaw as his defensive linemen.

Philyaw was one of the more spectacular of Al Davis's mistakes. As noted earlier, Davis has a weakness for the truly massive player, and Philyaw seemed to be a computer model of one. He was 6 feet 9 and was listed at 270 pounds, though he was probably heavier, without any noticeable body fat. He was fast for a big man, and agile; in high school he had averaged sixteen rebounds a game in basketball and had won the state (Texas) shot-put championship. Davis drafted Philyaw just before the Dallas Cowboys could.

There was only one problem: Philyaw's mental development didn't approach his physical, and that kept him from being an effective player. The players often broke up into position groups for meetings, and more than once Philyaw showed up in the offensive linemen's meetings. Defensive line coach Tom Dahms said, "Let him stay there. He doesn't learn anything in our meetings anyway."

Philyaw stories quickly circulated among the Raiders. One

time, when he suffered a cut in training-camp practice, Madden told him to go see the doctor. Philyaw went to the room of teammate Skip Thomas—the one whose nickname was "Doctor Death." Before a road game, Philyaw asked Fred Biletnikoff if he could borrow a pair of shoes, because he had forgotten his. Biletnikoff asked Philyaw what size he wore. It was 16; Biletnikoff's was 11. The players wore their last names on the back of their uniform shirts, and Philyaw asked Madden why one player had his first name, too—pointing to a uniform reading "Van Eeghen."

Philyaw did fit the Raiders image in one way, though; before a game with the Oilers in Houston, he was arrested for passing bad checks while in college, at Texas Southern. The Raiders made good on the bad checks, and Philyaw played one of his rare successful games for them, getting two sacks and blocking four passes. Perhaps that was what it took to motivate him.

Al Davis is not a man who freely admits mistakes, so Philyaw lasted four years with the Raiders, but he was never much more than a large body. In fact, he was part of what was probably Davis's worst draft, in 1976. Philyaw was Davis's first pick on the second round; his *second* second-round pick was Tulsa quarterback Jeb Blount. Virtually every other Raiders official in the drafting room was against the pick, but Davis's vote was the only one that counted. Blount was so dismal that he never even made the active roster. He was put on injured reserve before the final exhibition game, supposedly because of an injured shoulder, but when a reporter asked him which shoulder was injured, Blount answered, "I don't know."

In all, the Raiders had eighteen picks in that draft. Not one of them ever made a significant contribution. The only pick that helped was the one the club didn't have: the Raiders had forfeited their number-one pick as compensation for Ted Hendricks, who had been signed in 1975 as a free agent. That was an excellent exchange, because they could never have drafted a number one as good as Hendricks—especially not that year, judging by what Davis did with his remaining picks.

Fortunately for the Raiders, Philyaw was injured in the fourth game of the season and was benched. To replace him, Madden put in John Matuszak, the latest of Davis's reclamation projects. Matuszak had been the very first player drafted by the Houston Oilers in 1973. He was a mountain of a man, only an inch shorter than Philyaw and close to 300 pounds, with the strength expected of someone that size. He was also a troubled man who had nearly self-destructed before he was picked up by the Raiders.

Matuszak had been an immediate starter in Houston and was named to several all-rookie teams, but he tried to jump to the Houston Texans of the World Football League after a contractual battle with the Oilers. A court ruling sent him back to the Oilers, who traded him to Kansas City in midseason of 1974. He played well for the Chiefs that season and in 1975, but his off-field actions deeply disturbed Chiefs coach Paul Wiggin, especially an episode in which Matuszak, arrested for speeding, was found to be mixing alcohol and drugs. There was even a report—never verified—that Matuszak's heart stopped beating once and Wiggin had to pound on his chest to get it going again.

The Chiefs released Matuszak. At that point, no one else in football would have signed Matuszak, whose reputation for wild living was widespread throughout the NFL. But Davis gave him a last chance, and Matuszak extended that into seven years with the Raiders, playing in two Super Bowls. It was far longer than anyone expected, probably including Matuszak himself.

Matuszak's life-style didn't change when he came to Oakland, but Davis, as always, did not interfere as long as "big John" played well, which he did for the extent of his Raiders career. He was arrested once for shooting up road signs, he was sued by a male stripper who claimed that Matuszak had harassed him during a performance, and he had a capacity for liquor and Quaaludes that was as big as his body. He would start celebrating on Sunday night after a game and go right through the next day, a day off for the players, to Tuesday morning. In other words, the ultimate Raider.

There was a difference, though. The Raiders had always had more than their share of hell-raisers, but Matuszak took his celebrating far beyond what Stabler or Hendricks or Hubbard or anyone else did. With him it wasn't fun, it was a competition—and he was competing only with himself. No one else was in that league. In 1979, Tom Flores, in his first year as head coach of the Raiders, would ask Stabler, of all people, to room with Matuszak to quiet him down. That tells it all.

When he was sober Matuszak was a gentle giant, soft-spoken and considerate. When he was drunk he was totally out of control. Which was the real Matuszak? Nobody knew, least of all the man himself. One time in training camp he told me plaintively that he felt people didn't understand the real John Matuszak—but he never gave them a chance. He was playing the role that he felt everyone expected of him. It was no accident that he became a fairly successful actor after his football career.

It always seemed to me that there was an undertone of sadness to his life. It didn't take extraordinary intelligence to see that he would not live a long life. As it happened, he died in 1989 from an overdose of a tranquilizing drug he was taking for the back pain that was his legacy from his football career—but there was undoubtedly a cumulative effect from the abuse his body had taken for so many years.

Had he worked at his craft, Matuszak could well have been the best ever to play his position, but his almost endless partying eroded his physical skills. By the time he reached the Raiders he was probably little more than 50 percent of the player he had been capable of being. Even at 50 percent, though, he was a big improvement over Charles Philyaw. Matuszak was perfectly suited for the Raiders' 3–4 defense (or what they called their "orange" defense) because he couldn't be moved. Sometimes, if a pass play was slow in developing, he would simply overwhelm his blockers and get to the passer. Mostly he was just there, an immovable object that kept the opposition from advancing on his side of the line. The Raiders would not have made it to the Super Bowl without him.

• • •

The NFL schedule makers always like to start a season with a matchup that provided a dramatic game in the previous season. It was no surprise, then, when the Raiders and the Pittsburgh Steelers, who had met in the 1975 AFC championship game, were paired in the opener of the 1976 season. But there were some important differences to this game, starting with the fact that it was played in Oakland.

Many teams over the years had accused Al Davis of having the field overwatered at the Oakland Coliseum, because it was almost always slow and soggy. That was one element of the anti-Davis paranoia that he encouraged. Many coaches also thought that he had their locker rooms bugged; when Harland Svare was coaching the San Diego Chargers, he once shouted at the ceiling of the Chargers' locker room in the Coliseum, "God damn you, Al Davis!" No doubt Davis would have watered the Coliseum field if he had thought it would give the Raiders a competitive advantage, but he didn't have to. The field was actually below sea level, and it took years for engineers to solve the problem of water leaking into the ground. They had not yet solved it by opening day in 1976, and the field was soggy for the important game against the Steelers.

A wet field was just one of the Steelers' complaints that day. To try to stop Raiders players from stealing practice footballs and giving them to youngsters, equipment manager Dick Romanowski used to write "Fuck" on them. One of those balls got into the game by mistake, and when the Steelers center bent over it and saw the obscene message, he was convinced it was another of the Raiders' psychological schemes.

Raiders guard George Buehler had to play against "Mean Joe" Greene, then the top defensive lineman in the league. Buehler, a good player who got little recognition because he was at the opposite end of the line from Gene Upshaw, always did particularly well against Greene, but this day he felt he needed some extra help. To keep Greene from grabbing his jersey and tossing him aside, Buehler smeared the top half of his uniform with Vaseline. Inevitably some of the grease got on the ball—another Raiders plot, the Steelers thought.

This was one of the great rivalries in the NFL at the time, and the game was far more than a chess match. The Raiders' George Atkinson put Pittsburgh receiver Lynn Swann in the hospital with a concussion after a particularly violent hit. The Steelers' Mel Blount retaliated by grabbing Cliff Branch low after a reception, turning him, and dropping him on his head. Raiders safety Jack Tatum grabbed Steelers tight end Randy Grossman, after what Tatum thought was a late block, and threw him to the ground, punching him after Grossman landed.

Following many NFL games, even very close ones, the crowd will see players from the opposing teams shake hands and hug each other. No one ever saw the Raiders and the Steelers hugging. For the Raiders, the rivalry in the 1960s with the Kansas City Chiefs had been intense, but the rivalry with the Steelers in the 1970s transcended that. These two teams hated each other.

The Raiders won the game, in what had come to be their typical style. The Steelers were ahead by two touchdowns, with only three minutes to go, when Stabler threw a touchdown pass to Dave Casper and then ran in a second touchdown from 2 yards out, to tie the game. With 1:05 left, Dave Rome tipped a Terry Bradshaw pass that was intercepted by Willie Hall at the 13. Fred Steinfort kicked a 21-yard field goal to win the game, 31–28.

The Raiders were 3–0 when they traveled to Foxboro, Massachusetts, to meet the New England Patriots, who demolished them, 48–17. Only Dave Casper, who caught a team-record 12 passes for 136 yards, played well for the Raiders. Amazingly, it was the only game the Raiders lost that season, as they tied the franchise record by going 13–1. More important, the team that hadn't been able to catch a break in the postseason was going to get two huge ones this time around.

Because the Raiders had the best record in the AFC, they would host all their play-off games. That was the good news. The bad news was that in the first round they had to play the

Patriots, the team that had embarrassed them in the regular season.

The tone of the game was set early when George Atkinson nailed Patriots tight end Russ Francis between the bars of his face mask and broke Francis's nose. That was not an unusual incident for Atkinson, a vicious tackler—he preferred the term "aggressive"—who was often embroiled in controversy.

"I had been an aggressive player since high school," said Atkinson, who is now marketing a water-purification system in Oakland. "That was just the way I played. And it was well known around the league at that time that if you weren't aggressive you didn't survive, either as a team or as an individual. If you weren't aggressive you didn't win. And in the heat of battle things would happen." Atkinson played at just 175 pounds, 50 or 60 pounds lighter than the tight ends he covered, and, as he put it, "If I hadn't been aggressive, I wouldn't have even made the team in the first place."

It was, in fact, Atkinson's aggressiveness that caused him to be playing strong safety to begin with. Davis had drafted him as a cornerback and punt returner; as a rookie, in 1968, Atkinson set an AFL record for punt returns in one game, with 205 yards against the Buffalo Bills, a mark exceeded only once in NFL history. Davis had him moved to strong safety in 1971 because he felt that Atkinson and free safety Jack Tatum would discourage receivers on patterns in the middle of the field.

With just over a minute to go and trailing by 21 – 17, the Raiders had a third down and 18 on the Patriots 28-yard line. A field goal would do them no good; Stabler had to throw. Rushed hard, Stabler threw an incomplete pass, but Ray "Sugar Bear" Hamilton crashed into him after the pass and was called for roughing the passer, which gave the Raiders an automatic first down at the New England 13.

The penalty was a gift. Films later showed that Hamilton's momentum had carried him into Stabler and he could not have stopped short. Stabler had suffered only the normal punishment for a quarterback who releases a pass late, but he had been rewarded by an overzealous official.

The great teams take advantage of their breaks. Five plays later, from the 1-yard line, Stabler rolled to the left looking for Casper. When the big tight end could not get open, Stabler dived into the end zone behind Gene Upshaw's block. The Raiders had won, 24–21, and they would have another shot at the Steelers in the AFC championship.

The Steelers had started slowly that year, losing four of their first five games, but once they righted themselves they looked even better than the team that had won the Super Bowl the previous year, winning their last nine games and yielding only 28 points in that stretch. For the season they outscored their opponents by a whopping 342–138; by comparison, the Raiders point differential was 350–237. As the Raiders were squeezing by New England, the Steelers were crushing the Baltimore Colts, 40–14. In the victory, though, the Steelers lost their two running backs, Franco Harris and Rocky Bleier, because of injuries. Neither could play against Oakland, forcing the Steelers to use a one-back (Reggie Harrison) alignment that was no threat at all to the Raiders.

What should have been a hard-fought game was really no game at all. Without Harris and Bleier, the Steelers had to depend on the passing of quarterback Terry Bradshaw. Later, in the Steelers' great streak of four Super Bowl wins in six years, Bradshaw became their main weapon, with receivers Lynn Swann and John Stallworth, but at this point he couldn't carry the team; he had only 14 completions in 35 attempts—hardly championship-caliber statistics. In the fourth quarter Bradshaw in effect conceded, calling running plays when he should have been passing on every down.

For their part, the Raiders simply ran at the Steelers. There was little deception. The Raiders were determined to show the Steelers that they could beat them at their own physical game. It was a street fight, pure and simple, and this time the Steelers won, 24–7. The game was so one-sided that after Stabler came out late in the third quarter, with bruised ribs, his replacement, Mike Rae, didn't have to throw a pass the rest of the way.

The Raiders were finally in the Super Bowl again, nine frustrating years after their first appearance.

The cynical billed the game—played at the Rose Bowl in Pasadena—as the "Losers Bowl," because the Raiders had just missed getting there so often and their opponents, the Minnesota Vikings, had lost all three Super Bowls in which they had played. The label was unfair, since both teams had successful records. The Vikings had won eight divisional titles in nine years and had not had a losing season since 1967. The Raiders had won nine divisional titles in ten years and had not had a losing season since 1964. Most of the NFL teams, it was safe to say, envied the Raiders and the Vikings; certainly, *they* did not regard either of them as losers.

Perhaps the Vikings' lack of success in the Super Bowl had begun to take its toll on Bud Grant, the Minnesota coach. Usually a low-key coach—he traditionally started training camp later than anyone else, and he often gave the players days off during the season because he wanted to go hunting or fishing himself—Grant seemed tense the whole week before the Super Bowl, complaining about the team's hotel, the bus ride to the game, and everything else.

Madden may have been just as tense, but he didn't show it. He was always a master at masking the turmoil in his gut—until he finally had to quit coaching, because of an ulcer, two seasons later. "John made it easy for us," Stabler noted. "We didn't even have curfew for the first two or three days we were there, and our practices were easy, as they generally were. We weren't going to leave our game on the practice field."

In fact, at the last practice, the day before the game, some of the players had gotten a tennis ball and were playing baseball with it. "Davis was going crazy," remembered Upshaw, one of the baseball players. "He looked at us and wondered if we were prepared to play, but we were prepared all right.

"Madden really emphasized that we'd finally gotten back to

Coach Eddie Erdelatz sits alongside quarter-back Tom Flores, with backup Babe Parilli on the right, in the first regular season Raiders game, played at San Francisco's Kezar Stadium on September 11, 1960.

Davis looks over his team at his first practice session in 1963. By the next season, only Jim Otto (00), Wayne Hawkins (65), and Clem Daniels (carrying the ball) would remain.

Shortly after being named coach of the Raiders in 1963, Davis meets with his star running back, Clem Daniels, left, and quarterback Tom Flores.

Jim Otto, the Raiders Hall of Fame center, gets ready to snap the ball in training camp in 1961, the first year he wore 00.

Russ Reed

A disconsolate Davis sits alone in the stands at North Platte, Nebraska, after his Raiders lost to the Denver Broncos in an August 1967 exhibition game. Two weeks later, in the regular season opener, the Raiders beat the Broncos, 51–0.

Raider defensive end Ben Davidson knocks the helmet off New York Jets quarterback Joe Namath in a 1967 game. Later in the game, Ike Lassiter broke Namath's jaw, but Davidson got the credit/blame because of this celebrated photo.

Quarterback Daryle Lamonica and coach John Rauch confer during a timeout in a 1967 game. Davis's offensive system went far beyond anything Rauch, a former quarterback, had previously known.

Davis poses with fellow Raider general partners Ed McGah, left, and Wayne Valley in 1968. By this time, Davis and Valley were deep into the feud that broke up their partnership.

George Blanda kicks a field goal just over the outstretched hands of Kansas City linemen, including John Matuszak, soon to become a Raider defensive lineman. In 1970, Blanda won Player of the Year honors.

Ben Davidson and Tom Keating prepare for a motorcycle trip to Mexico in February 1971, looking even fiercer than they looked when they lined up side by side in the Raiders defensive line.

A handcuffed Warren Wells is led out of the courtroom after being convicted of rape in 1969. The case involving the Raiders wide receiver became the catalyst for the final break between Davis and fellow general partner Wayne Valley.

John Madden beams as Davis holds the Vince Lombardi Trophy, signifying the Raiders' first Super Bowl win on January 9, 1977.

Russ Reed

Fred Biletnikoff zeroes in on the ball as the Raiders beat the San Diego Chargers in their 1976 championship season. Notice Biletnikoff's intense concentration.

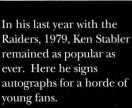

In his last year with the Raiders, 1979, Ken Stabler remained as popular as ever. Here he signs autographs for a horde of young fans.

Ron Riesterer

Jim Plunkett runs for his life as Philadelphia Eagles defensive linemen pursue him during the 1981 Super Bowl, won by the Raiders, 27–10. Plunkett was the game's MVP.

Russ Reed

Davis warmly welcomes Raider running back Marcus Allen as he comes off the field in a 1982 game. The relationship between Davis and Allen later soured.

In a game near the end of the Raiders' last season in Oakland (1981), fans show their support, but the decision had already been made to move the team to Los Angeles.

Davis joins hands with Los Angeles city and county officials in 1980 after announcing that he would move the Raiders to Los Angeles. With him, from the left, are John Ferraro, city councilman; Bill Robertson of the Coliseum Commission; supervisor Kenneth Hahn; and mayor Tom Bradley.

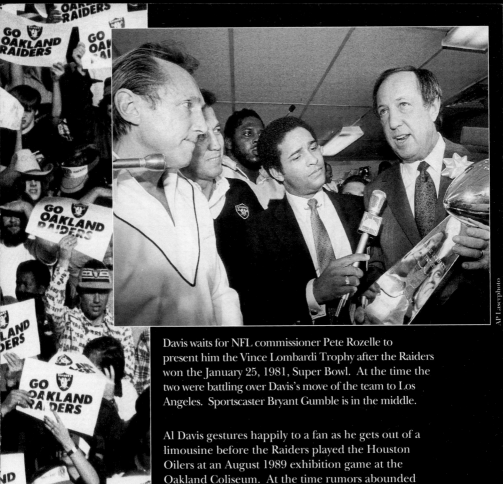

AP Laserphoto

Davis waits for NFL commissioner Pete Rozelle to present him the Vince Lombardi Trophy after the Raiders won the January 25, 1981, Super Bowl. At the time the two were battling over Davis's move of the team to Los Angeles. Sportscaster Bryant Gumble is in the middle.

Al Davis gestures happily to a fan as he gets out of a limousine before the Raiders played the Houston Oilers at an August 1989 exhibition game at the Oakland Coliseum. At the time rumors abounded that Davis would be returning the team to Oakland.

Ron Riesterer

Oakland Tribune photo by Mike Macor

A tired-looking Al Davis announces at a 1990 press conference that the team will stay in Los Angeles.

the Super Bowl, and we were here to play a football game. That was our theme—we were there to win. The first year we went, we were there just to enjoy it, not to win. I walked into the Packers dressing room after that game and talked to some of the great Packers—Henry Jordan, Ray Nitschke, Bart Starr—and I said, 'You've got a great football game.' They told me, 'You guys are going to be back a lot more times.' I never thought it would take that long, especially when we got into all those championship games but weren't able to get over that final hurdle. But now we were finally here, and we were going to make the most of it. Madden had talked to other coaches who had had teams in the Super Bowl, and he really had us prepared.

"Because Minnesota had been there four times and hadn't won, you had to figure the law of averages was on their side. They had to win sometime, but we didn't want it to be this time. We had gone through all those times of being the bridesmaid, and we didn't want to be disappointed again. What we knew about Minnesota was basically that on defense all they had was the front four, 'the Purple People Eaters.' If you could get through that front four, the rest of their guys weren't too anxious to make tackles. That's how we got Clarence Davis through for those big gains. We felt we had a big edge because of our size. Alan Page was giving away a lot of weight to me. I knew he was capable of dominating a game, but I was determined he wouldn't do it against me. It was the same way with Art Shell. His man, Jim Marshall, was the smallest of all, and Art was up to almost 300 pounds. If we could neutralize their quickness, we had it made."

The Raiders faced some early frustrations, when Errol Mann missed a 29-yard field-goal attempt on their first possession and Ray Guy suffered the first punt block of his career minutes later, giving the Vikings first-and-goal on the Oakland 3-yard line. But two plays later the Vikings gave the ball back, on a fumble by Brent McClanahan, and the Raiders were on their way. They won their first Super Bowl, 32 – 14, in a virtual mirror image of their 33 – 14 loss to Green Bay in the second

Super Bowl. There was another ironic comparison: Willie Brown returned an interception 75 yards for a touchdown, a Super Bowl record; the record he broke was a 68-yard return by Herb Adderly against the Raiders in January 1968.

The two big stories of the game for those who had watched the Raiders through the years of frustration were the play of offensive tackle Art Shell and wide receiver Fred Biletnikoff.

Shell played as well as any offensive lineman could ever hope to, in the biggest game of his life: he pitched a shutout against Vikings defensive end Jim Marshall, who didn't get a single quarterback sack or even an unassisted tackle. It was almost as if Marshall hadn't come to the game. Behind Shell and Gene Upshaw, Clarence Davis also had the best day of his career, rushing for 137 yards and being named by the Associated Press as the game's Most Valuable Player.

Meanwhile, the remarkable Fred Biletnikoff—who had been the heart and soul of the Raiders passing offense for ten years and who was so nervous before the game that he smoked two packs of cigarettes—capped his Hall of Fame career by catching 4 passes for 79 yards, setting up 3 touchdowns, and being chosen the game's MVP by a panel of writers from *Sport* magazine.

Though he may have been the slowest wide receiver in the league at that point, Biletnikoff still had the moves that had baffled defensive backs for so long and the hands that seemed to suck in passes like a vacuum cleaner taking up dirt. He made the most memorable play of the game, and the one that took away what little suspense remained by the third quarter. It was a play he called himself. He had spent hours going over Vikings game films on his own, studying the moves of the defensive backs, particularly Nate Wright. He knew Wright's moves almost as well as he knew his own. With the ball at midfield, he came into the huddle and told Stabler he could get open. "Freddie never said anything in the huddle," Stabler recalled. "So when he came in and said he could beat his man, I put it down as gospel. Sure enough, he was wide open when I threw him the ball."

Biletnikoff caught the ball at the Minnesota 35-yard line and began a footrace to the goal line with Wright and Bobby Bryant and, it seemed, Father Time. The thirty-four-year-old Biletnikoff seemed to be running in sand as he fought his way downfield, flailing his arms wildly, trying desperately to pull out more speed. "I was looking for a gas station out there," he admitted later. He was finally downed at the 2.

Because Shell, Upshaw, and the others had done their usual job in protecting Stabler, he was still standing after he threw the ball and had time to reflect as he watched the play unfold. "As I saw Freddie running downfield, I thought, 'Damn, we're kicking some serious ass today,' " Stabler said.

That play was the game. On the next play Pete Banaszak scored, and the point-after made it 26 – 7. The rest was only a formality. When the game ended the players started to carry Madden off the field—and dropped him. "That was the hardest part of the game," Upshaw remembered.

"I remember Freddie crying when the PA announcer said he'd won the MVP award," Stabler said, "and then crying at his locker when his son came in. Those are great memories." Biletnikoff was smoking and crying at the same time. "We got a ring for the first Super Bowl, but I never wore the damn thing," he said. "It was a second-place ring. This is the one I wanted, the winner's ring."

And Al Davis? For Al Davis, the man who had put the team together and had finally seen it live up to the grandiose statistics he kept putting in the media guide, there was the great irony: his most successful team was the one over which he had the least control. Despite their success, he was only biding his time until he could get rid of John Madden and Ken Stabler.

·7·

Goodbye,
John Madden and
Ken Stabler

In the middle of the 1978 season came an event that overshadowed football, even for the obsessive Al Davis.

About 1:00 A.M. on October 19th, the day the Raiders were scheduled to fly to New York to play the Jets, Dr. Robert Albo got a frantic call from Davis, from his home. Davis's wife, Carol, had collapsed in the hallway between the bathroom and bedroom.

Albo, a close Davis friend for many years and still one today, drove immediately to the Davis home. When he got there, Carol Davis was unconscious and her heart was not beating. "She was dead, for all intents and purposes," said Albo. He started cardiopulmonary resuscitation and had Davis phone for an ambulance.

Carol Davis was taken to Merritt Hospital in Oakland and put on a respirator. Albo remembered that she was "shocked" three times to get her heart beating, twice on the way to the hospital and once a few hours later in the intensive care unit of the hospital. She was in a coma for seventeen days, the first fifteen on the respirator. "Then, she started to breathe for herself and started some weird movements on the pillow, which destroyed virtually all the hair on the back of her head," said Albo. Soon after that, she started making movements in which her head went back and her arms turned out. "It's a very common thing we see in spinal or cerebral injuries that are very severe," said Albo, "which is why the specialists we called in thought that recovery would be very unlikely. However, we took a brain scan and she did not show a dead brain."

Albo recalled that, while his wife was in a coma, Davis rarely left the hospital, taking the room next to her. "On the morning of the seventeenth day, I came on my morning rounds, and Al said, 'You know, she seems more alert this morning.' I walked into the room and said, 'Carolee,' and she opened her eyes. I said, 'How are you doing?' and she said, 'Pretty well.' I was flabbergasted. I ran back into the other room and Al came in, and she was awake. Which was almost like a miracle."

A long rehabilitation program began, which eventually restored Carol Davis to full health. Albo estimates that in his thirty-year medical career he has heard of no more than two or three people who were similarly stricken who recovered as completely as she has. "The remarkable thing is her recovery," he said. "It happens in children who are unconscious that long and come back, but in adults, it's very, very unusual. We've had people who have had strokes and come out of it, but they aren't the same as they were before."

Davis often talks of his frustration at not being able to overcome death. In this case, by sheer force of will, he seemed to.

•   •   •

His wife out of danger, Davis returned to the mission he had been pursuing for some time: getting his football team back from John Madden and Ken Stabler. It wouldn't take much longer. Madden would retire from coaching at the end of the season, and Stabler would be traded a year later.

That wouldn't have seemed possible the year before. As long as Madden and Stabler won, they were secure, and in

1977 they were still winning. To win two consecutive Super Bowls didn't seem as challenging then as it became in the 1980s—Green Bay, Miami, and Pittsburgh had already succeeded, and the Raiders appeared quite capable of it, too, when they finished 1977 a strong 11–3, a game behind the Denver Broncos in the AFC West.

Raiders fans remember that season primarily for the playoff games, the first of which, in Baltimore, was the third longest in NFL history. The night before the game Davis gave the players miniatures of the Vince Lombardi Trophy that the team had won at the Super Bowl the year before. The message didn't have to be spelled out.

The game, which went into a sixth quarter, was the one that will always be known for the "Ghost to the post" pattern run by Dave "Ghost" Casper. The Colts led, 31–28, when the Raiders took the ball with just over three minutes left in the fourth quarter. After a first down, Stabler looked to Casper for the big play the Raiders needed. Casper had been running short hooks all day, so the Baltimore defense was set up exactly as Stabler wanted it. He sent "the Ghost" deep to the post. The pass—which Stabler later self-deprecatingly referred to as a "wounded duck"—floated through the air as thousands in the stadium and millions watching on television held their breath. Finally it dropped just over Casper's shoulder into his hands. The Raiders had a 42-yard gain, and moments later Errol Mann kicked a 22-yard field goal to tie the score and send the game into overtime.

With 4:16 remaining in the second overtime period, the Raiders drove to the Baltimore 12, and, with the Colts bunched to prevent an expected run, Stabler passed to Casper for the winning touchdown. The final score was 37–31. Even now, Madden calls that game "the most exciting game of my career. It had everything."

The AFC championship game the next week, at Denver, also had its exciting moments, but for an entirely different reason: the game was decided on a bad call by the officials. Midway through the third quarter, the Broncos had the ball on the Oakland 2-yard line, after recovering a Clarence Davis fumble on the 17. When Denver running back Rob Lytle, diving for the end zone, fumbled the ball, Raiders defensive lineman Mike McCoy picked it up and started running. But the play was whistled dead, and the officials said there had been no fumble. The Broncos subsequently scored.

Everyone but the official who made the call thought there had been a fumble; the Broncos defensive unit had even started out on the field, before realizing that their team still had the ball. Television replays clearly showed a fumble, and the miscall was so embarrassing to the NFL that it set in motion the process that led to instant replay, to avoid such obvious misjudgments. The league office sent a written apology to the Raiders.

None of that was any consolation to the Raiders, who lost the game, 20–17. Instead, it was the Broncos who were in the Super Bowl. The Raiders would not return to it until both Stabler and Madden were gone.

• • •

A cloud was cast over the 1978 season even before it officially began, in an August 12 exhibition game in Oakland between the Raiders and the New England Patriots.

Patriots wide receiver Darryl Stingley ran a crossing pattern into the middle of the field. It was the type of pattern the Raiders seldom ran because of the danger of injury to the receiver. On this play, Raiders safety Jack Tatum hit Stingley head on, and the Patriots receiver crumpled to the ground.

Tatum himself thought at first it was just another tackle. It was a hard hit but a clean one. Tatum was known for his hard tackles, much as Ronnie Lott would become known as the San Francisco 49ers "enforcer" in later years. Tatum knew, from his talks with Al Davis, that he was expected to be an intimidating force, to make receivers "hear footsteps" when they came into the Raiders secondary. In fact, after Tatum's hit on

Stingley, Raiders executive Al LoCasale, doing the commentary on the telecast at the game, told his audience that it was an example of Raiders football.

Stingley did not get up. As he lay there a hush came over the stadium; it was obvious this was not just another play. A stretcher was brought out to take Stingley off the field and get him into an ambulance. At the hospital, doctors determined that Stingley's spinal cord had been damaged. He would never walk again. For months Stingley remained in an East Bay hospital, where doctors sought vainly to restore movement to his limbs. Virtually every day John Madden came to see him, quietly and without publicity; it wasn't until Stingley talked about it much later that the outside world knew of the visits.

In any football game, there are several collisions as hard as that of Tatum and Stingley. On this play, Stingley's spinal cord was hit at just the wrong place. He was paralyzed, and neither Madden nor Tatum nor any of the Raiders players could forget that. This pall may have been a factor as the Raiders started their season slowly and finished it with a disastrous (by Raiders standards) 9 – 7 record. But, as always, it was the quarterback and the coach who took the brunt of the criticism.

The Raiders were 2 – 2 after their first four games of 1978. Stabler had completed only 46 percent of his passes and had thrown twelve interceptions. Everyone wondered why, and he wouldn't give any explanation. He stopped talking to the press.

Just another spoiled athlete who would talk to the press only when everything was going well? Not at all. Stabler had always been accommodating, win or lose; he had talked at length after throwing seven interceptions in the 30 – 7 loss to Denver just the season before. But Stabler knew that if he talked now about his own problems, he would also have to point to weaknesses in the team, and he didn't want to do that. He hoped the writers would look at what was happening and draw the right conclusions without his pointing a finger at anyone. Few did. The story became: what was wrong with Stabler?

What was wrong with Stabler was basically that his most reliable receiver, Fred Biletnikoff, had been benched and that injuries and inexperience in the offensive line had broken down his protection on pass plays, forcing him to hurry his throws. Biletnikoff had been benched because of a Davis ultimatum that Madden could not fight: Davis wanted to play Morris Bradshaw, his latest project.

Bradshaw had been a running back at Ohio State, but Davis was convinced that his size and speed would make him an excellent receiver. Davis was wrong, and it cost the Raiders dearly over the next two seasons, but Davis managed to deflect the blame for his decision onto Stabler and Madden.

Biletnikoff, though nearing the end of his career, was still able to get open for those critical first-down catches, and he and Stabler had the kind of unspoken communication that can develop only after years of playing—and, in this case, partying—together. Bradshaw was younger, faster, and bigger than Biletnikoff, but he didn't catch the ball very well. It was not just the tough passes but the routine ones that he couldn't handle. He caught forty passes, because so many were thrown his way, but he probably dropped twenty, and nothing is more psychologically damaging to a team. Bradshaw played eight seasons for the Raiders (1978 was his fifth), but he never developed as Davis had hoped.

It was an ugly time. As the chasm with Madden deepened, Davis spent less time on the practice field—and when he was there, Biletnikoff would curse at him. In the locker room Biletnikoff frequently launched tirades against Davis, with which his listeners could only agree. It was Biletnikoff's last year with the Raiders. He played in Canada the next year, and then he retired.

On the front line, tackle John Vella and guard George Buehler were injured. Henry Lawrence, another Davis favorite, replaced Vella. In future years Lawrence would justify Davis's faith and become an outstanding tackle, but at the time his teammates gave him the ironic nickname of "Killer" because he so obviously wasn't. Again and again, defensive ends would go right through Lawrence on their way to the quarterback. It didn't help that running back Clarence Davis, a ferocious blocker, was also injured. His replacement, Art Whittington, couldn't block at all.

The lack of protection for the quarterback took away the Raiders' long passing game; Cliff Branch, who had caught forty touchdown passes in four years, caught only one in 1978. Yet when the season ended Davis blamed the team's passing problems on Stabler. "You've got to point to someone, so blame Stabler," Davis told writers. "He makes the most money. He gets paid to take the pressure. I'm certainly not going to make excuses for him, but he doesn't do any work in the off-season. I'm dissatisfied with the condition of the team and with the coaching staff for allowing the players to get out of shape. It has been our offense that has controlled the game. The defense played the same this season as it always had. But this year Cliff Branch caught only one touchdown pass. If you can't get the long ball to your wide receivers, you can't win. It all starts with the left-hander."

That was vintage Davis, putting the blame for the mediocre 1978 season squarely on Stabler and the coaching staff. It sealed Madden's decision to retire.

Madden had had a great run, winning 103 games in his ten years as the Raiders head coach. Only Don Shula, with 105 wins in his first ten seasons at Baltimore and Miami, had done better. But the pressure had become intolerable for Madden— the pressure from Davis, and also from himself.

The pressure from Davis was obvious to outsiders, for Davis had never been able to curb his tendency to second-guess on game day. In the thirteenth game of the season, for instance, the Raiders had led, 16–14, over the Seattle Seahawks when Madden called for a long pass on third-and-one from the Seahawks 38, hoping to get the touchdown that would put the game out of Seattle's reach. The pass failed, and a run on fourth down fell short. Seattle won the game with a field goal, starting a three-game Raiders losing streak that doomed their chances for a division title.

"Going for the touchdown pass on third-and-one," Davis told a writer later, "was like going for a home run when you need a sacrifice fly. I've got nothing against running on fourth down, but I would never have thrown that pass on a third-and-one. And it wasn't Kenny's call." Of course, it had always been Davis's philosophy to go for the end zone inside the other team's 40-yard line, and he loved the long pass. The irony wasn't lost on Madden. "If Ken connects, the game's over," said Madden. "But he didn't, so now I'm the jackass."

In the last few weeks of Madden's time, he and Davis scarcely talked. Madden glossed over that period in his first book, and he is circumspect in his comments about Davis now, aware that he has nothing to gain by open criticism. Despite their differences at the end, Madden has a genuine admiration for Davis's mind and ability. Madden's son, Mike, worked for the Raiders until the fall of 1990, when he came to work for his father. Madden also appreciates the fact that it was Davis who hired him as head coach, the first step in what has become a very successful career. When Madden was inducted into the Bay Area Sports Hall of Fame in February 1991, he had Davis present him, and he told the audience, "Al Davis had the guts to make me the head coach when I was only thirty-three."

By 1978, though, Madden had developed an ulcer, and that, along with his fear of flying, forced him to make the decision to leave coaching at the age of forty-two.

Anyone who traveled with the Raiders then knew of Madden's flying phobia. Bob Bestor, an administrative assistant with the team in the late 1960s and early 1970s, remembered Madden screaming because a flight to an exhibition game in San Diego had a stop in Los Angeles; like all those who hate flying, Madden had his worse moments at takeoff and landing. I vividly remember one instance when I was traveling with the team. Madden had waited for his nerves to settle before he accepted a meal tray from a stewardess. He took a seat near me. Just as he started his meal, the pilot announced, "If you look out the right side of the plane, you can see lightning flashes." Madden turned a shade of green that clashed with his usual red. He didn't eat another bite.

Madden's phobia was quite understandable. Many of his

former college teammates died in 1959 in the crash of an airplane carrying the football team from Cal Poly of San Luis
Obispo. Madden had played for Cal Poly only the year before.
He can certainly be excused for thinking of what might have
been.

"I wasn't surprised that John quit, after that last year," said
Tom Flores, who replaced Madden. "He was really in bad shape
with his ulcer, and his fear of flying had really intensified. I
remember flying into Denver, which was always tough, and
John just about passed out on us. He was just terrified."

After Madden's retirement Davis kept him on the payroll,
not because Davis needed Madden's services but because he
didn't want Madden to change his mind about retirement and
accept a coaching post with another team. There was, in fact,
a clause in Madden's contract to prevent that—another example of Davis's fear that his secrets would be given to another
team.

Madden had little to do. When Davis decided to move the
team to Los Angeles, Madden scouted practice sites and possible office locations, but that was hardly a full-time job. He
seldom came into the Raiders offices. It was a difficult time for
Madden, because he hadn't thought about what he would do—
he had only wanted to get out of coaching. He taught a few
classes on football at the University of California extension
school in Berkeley (he did well—I sat in on one session) and
thought briefly about returning to teaching.

When Madden got a chance to do the "color" commentary
on telecasts of some preseason games, he wasn't confident about
his abilities. At halftime of one game at the Oakland Coliseum,
I came out of the press box and saw him puffing nervously on
a cigarette. "Did you see anything out there I could talk about
in the second half?" he asked.

Since then, of course, he has found many things to talk
about and has deservedly become the most popular of the color
commentators on NFL games. It is the perfect job for Madden, who remains obsessed with football. That obsession kept
him going through the long hours as Raiders coach, and it

serves him well now. He spends more time talking to coaches and players than any other commentator does, and that is reflected in his analysis. It's not work to him. Near the end of a tight game between the Washington Redskins and the New York Giants in 1990, his broadcasting partner, Pat Summerall, commented that no fans were leaving. "Why would they leave?" Madden demanded. "Where could they go that would be better than this?"

•   •   •

There was little suspense about who Madden's successor would be. Davis's building-wide search procedures were well known by now. Although one or two television reporters speculated about Davis going for a name coach like George Allen (the thought of Davis and Allen working together was certainly a delicious one), the only serious candidate was Tom Flores, the team's chief offensive aide and a former Raiders quarterback.

Flores was a solid coach and personality and was well versed in the Raiders' organizational and playing systems. He had been an assistant coach since 1972 and had been thinking for some time about becoming a head coach. "I thought I was prepared," he said, a dozen years later, "but I was only thinking in terms of the football part of it. No assistant understands the emotional part of head coaching, and the stress. You spend your time on a lot of things you shouldn't bother with."

Flores wasn't as independent-minded as Madden had become, so Davis was once again in control of his coach. It would take him only another year to reach the other part of his goal, getting rid of Stabler—and Stabler helped the process along with some comments he came to regret.

Davis started the war of words after the 1978 season, telling one writer that Stabler was like a 24–8 pitcher who had a 17–10 season. (Davis, who had played baseball in high school, loved to make baseball allusions.) Stabler fired back in an interview with the *Birmingham News*. "I have lost all respect for the organization," he said. "I don't want to stay where I'm not appreciated. I have contractual obligations to the Oakland

Raiders and I will fulfill them. I'd be letting down my team-mates if I took a powder. I will play as hard as I can because I have loyalties to my teammates and myself. I have two years left on my contract and an option year. I'll honor that and go from there."

Stabler's comments, made in the heat of the moment, were honest ones. Davis's were more calculated. His criticism of Stabler diverted attention from the fact that Davis's drafts had not been brilliant in recent years—the major reason the team had slipped—and that he had erred in forcing Morris Bradshaw into the starting lineup.

Davis was probably also trying to goad Stabler. Those around Davis knew he was seriously concerned about Stabler's lack of conditioning, and with reason. Stabler's theory on condition-ing was at least thirty years out of date; he believed that he had only so many throws in his arm and that throwing—or any other kind of training—in the off-season would lessen his ability to perform in the regular season. In fact, athletes have learned that off-season conditioning programs can lengthen their careers. With his football intelligence and resourceful-ness, Stabler could have been an effective quarterback into his forties, like George Blanda, if he had worked on his condition-ing. As it was, he was finished as a topflight quarterback by his mid-thirties. Although he was a tremendously exciting quar-terback, ranking with Joe Montana and Roger Staubach in his ability to pull out games that seemed lost, his time at the top was too short to merit serious consideration for the Hall of Fame.

When Stabler read reports, originating from the Raiders, that Jim Plunkett and Randy Hedberg, his backups, were throwing well in off-season workouts, he just yawned and had another drink. That wasn't going to change his thinking or his life-style. Stabler stated in a magazine interview that Davis had talked to Stabler's attorney, Henry Pitts, and said he wanted to bury the hatchet. "I'd like to bury the hatchet—right between Al Davis's shoulder blades," Stabler said.

Strong stuff, but this was the Raiders. On another team, a

player would have been gone right after such a remark. Davis *did* shop Stabler around some, asking for two first-round draft choices and two quality players in return; obviously he wasn't serious.

Hoping to be traded to a team in the south, Stabler reported late for training camp in 1979, but he still had one of the best years of his career, completing 61 percent of his passes and throwing for twenty-six touchdown. Flores thought it was his best year. (In 1976 Stabler had somewhat better numbers, completing 66.7 percent and throwing for twenty-seven touchdown, but he had much better support. Even with Stabler throwing so well, the Raiders were just 9–7 in 1979.

Perhaps Davis's verbal jabs had inspired Stabler. Some writers speculated that he had worked harder on conditioning, but that was imagination working overtime; Stabler's weight and conditioning were the same as they'd always been. He simply was able to reach back for one final great year.

It was also his last year with the Raiders. Davis asked Stabler after the season if he still wanted to be traded. Stabler said he did, and so Davis traded him to the Houston Oilers for Dan Pastorini. Would Davis have done that if Stabler hadn't made public statements about wanting to leave? Probably. Stabler's comments just made it easier for Davis to do what he had wanted to all along.

Never forget that Davis's motto is "Just win, baby." He will overlook almost anything if a player produces. Stabler's strongest comments had been made between the 1978 and 1979 seasons, but Davis had made no serious attempt to trade him then. He thought Stabler had one good season left, and he wanted to get that out of the veteran quarterback. After Stabler's strong season in 1979, Davis didn't think he had much left and decided to trade him while he still had some value.

Davis had always liked Pastorini, who had the strong arm Stabler lacked. In 1971, three quarterbacks were the first three choices in the draft: Plunkett (the Heisman Trophy winner) from Stanford, Archie Manning from Mississippi, and Pastorini from Santa Clara. Because he had played at a small college,

Pastorini hadn't been tested as the other two had, but a conversation I had with Davis that year (in Baltimore, before the AFC title game) convinced me that he thought Pastorini had the most potential.

Maybe, but Pastorini lacked the discipline to develop his potential. He'd had some great moments with the Houston Oilers, but no consistency. Davis thought that playing for a better team would bring out the best in Pastorini, but it never did. He was undisciplined on and off the field, once driving his car into a tree. It's cruel to say so, but the best thing Pastorini did for the Raiders was to break his leg in the fifth game of the 1980 season, making room for Jim Plunkett, who took the Raiders to the Super Bowl that season and in 1983.

Meanwhile, Stabler was exiled to Houston, where he had two good seasons before the inevitable decline set in. As much as he enjoyed playing for Bum Phillips, the Houston coach, it wasn't the same. His heart was still in Oakland.

"I don't know if Al would have traded me if I hadn't said I wanted to be traded," Stabler told me in a 1990 conversation. "He got the kind of quarterback he wanted—he traded a junkball pitcher for a flamethrower. Maybe he would have done that whatever I said. I do know this, I wish I'd never said it. If I had one thing to do over, I'd take back those words. I wish now that I could have finished my career in Oakland. We had some great times in those years, and I've got a lot of great memories."

It was probably no consolation to Stabler, but the Raiders didn't last much longer in Oakland, either. Al Davis had plans.

·8·

The Raiders Move
to Los Angeles

Ironically, the contract that made it possible for Al Davis to move his Raiders from Oakland to Los Angeles was one signed by the man Davis had forced out of the Raiders ownership, Wayne Valley.

The contract with the Oakland Coliseum, signed in 1966, was ostensibly for twenty years, but Valley, then the managing general partner, had insisted that he have the opportunity to move the team if fan support did not develop in Oakland. Valley, who had been raised in Oakland and made his home in the area, was skeptical that Oakland would ever support pro football. So, after the first five years, the contract gave the Raiders an option every three years.

Despite Valley's doubts, Oakland had supported the Raiders very well, and if he had remained as managing general partner the Raiders would still be there. Al Davis did not have Valley's ties to the area. For all his public claims of loyalty to "little ol' Oakland," Davis thought his stature suffered because his team was not in a major city. "If we played anywhere else, there would be a street named after him," said Davis's echo,

Al LoCasale. By 1979 Davis was determined to move to Los Angeles—though he has not had a street named after him there, either.

The Oakland contract called for the option to be exercised by April of the second year of each three-year extension. This meant that the Raiders should pick up the next option by April of 1979. When they didn't, the Coliseum's general manager, Bill Cunningham, was nettled but hardly surprised.

"In theory," said Cunningham, who had been the general manager since 1964, "any option is an extension of the existing contract. Davis never used it that way. He always used it as a lever to get a better deal. He never exercised the option on time; he always tried to change the deal. Because the Raiders were so good, and we thought we had such a good relationship, we always sweetened the deal. One year it might be an improvement to the facilities. Another time we made a deal with the Port of Oakland to get the Raiders a practice field for a dollar a year. It was a continuing process. So when we got into a lot of trouble in 1979 and 1980, we thought, 'Well, here we get into another deal like the last one.' "

Cunningham had kept notes on the various contract negotiations, and they showed that Davis had never exercised the option on time. In 1970 and 1973, he sent undated letters in December to renew, eight months after the supposed deadline. In 1976, he didn't renew at all. Then in August of 1977, he sent a letter to the Coliseum Board claiming that the Raiders had a binding lease, and the board decided to accept that as the equivalent of the Raiders' exercise of their option.

There was one big difference in 1979: Davis had an alternative to Oakland. In the previous negotiations he had only been trying to get the last possible concession from Oakland— his normal negotiating style. This time the Los Angeles Coliseum was seeking a client to replace the Los Angeles Rams. Their owner, Carroll Rosenbloom, was moving the Rams to Anaheim, starting with the 1980 season—primarily because Anaheim had offered him the chance to buy a hundred acres surrounding the stadium at a price well below market value.

Rosenbloom's move was also important to Davis as a precedent. The National Football League's constitution required that team owners approve the move of a franchise. (At the time Rosenbloom announced his intention to move, 100 percent approval was required; that was later amended to require 75 percent approval.) But Rosenbloom did not seek approval until after he had signed the agreement to move, by which time approval would be a mere formality. NFL commissioner Pete Rozelle ruled that the move was a "suburban" one, like the moves of the Dallas Cowboys to Irving and the New York Giants to the Meadowlands in New Jersey. Because Anaheim was within a seventy-five-mile radius of the Los Angeles Coliseum, the Rams were considered to be still in the same metropolitan area, and therefore, Rozelle said, the move did not require a vote. Rosenbloom, a powerful man within the NFL, had clashed with Rozelle in the past, and Rozelle did not want another fight.

In fact, Anaheim is not a suburb of Los Angeles but a separate city. Rozelle certainly knew that—he had been general manager of the Rams before being named commissioner. And Rams fans proved unwilling to drive to Anaheim for games; the team's list of season-ticket holders was almost completely new within two years.

The Rams move left the NFL vulnerable when Davis finally decided to move his team without seeking the permission of his fellow owners.

Davis negotiated with both Los Angeles and Oakland throughout 1979 and into 1980—although the Oakland negotiations were largely a charade—before he announced, in March of 1980, that he was going to move the team to Los Angeles. There was much more to come before the team actually moved, however. The city of Oakland filed an eminent-domain suit to keep the Raiders. The Los Angeles Coliseum had earlier filed an antitrust suit against the NFL, claiming that the league was illegally conspiring to keep an NFL team out of the Coliseum, and the Raiders had joined that suit. And the NFL owners, in a vote Davis had not sought, voted 22−0 against allowing the Raiders to move—nine days after Davis had formally agreed to move his team.

While the legal and political maneuvering was going on, the Raiders played their 1980 and 1981 seasons in Oakland. Ed Heafey, the attorney for the Oakland Coliseum, dubbed the team "The Raiders of the Lost Park." The next year, after Oakland had lost its eminent-domain suit and the Los Angeles Coliseum Commission and the Raiders had won their antitrust suit against the league, Davis was finally free to move the team, in time for the 1982 season—though the team kept its practice facility in Oakland that year, and many of the players, coaches, and executives kept their homes in the Oakland area.

Davis's action led to further changes in the NFL, since owners knew they could no longer prevent franchises from moving. Robert Irsay moved his Colts franchise from Baltimore to Indianapolis without permission, literally leaving in the middle of the night. Bill Bidwill asked for permission to move his Cardinals from St. Louis to Phoenix, but got it primarily because the owners knew he could move without it.

Rozelle had tried to persuade Davis not to move without permission, most notably at a meeting in Dallas on March 3, 1980, but Davis wasn't listening. Soon Rozelle himself was being attacked, by Davis's friends and supporters in Los Angeles. Rozelle was biased, the charges went—he had helped owner Max Winter campaign for a new domed stadium in Minnesota for the Vikings, under the threat that the Vikings would move if they didn't get it, but he hadn't helped Davis in any way.

"Al never asked me for any help at all," Rozelle noted wryly. "Max Winter did. Al would never ask me for anything. He'd take what he could get." Rozelle was in the position of the polite man who does not know what to do when a rude man comes up to him at a party. He was bound by what he thought of as society's rules; Davis was not.

Rozelle denies now that the lawsuits resulting from Davis's move to Los Angeles forced him into retirement. "Those suits, and others like the USFL suit, were very trying, but I was getting to an age and had been on the job so long, almost thirty years, and it was always somewhat stressful."

There is no question, however, that Rozelle felt the strain of the lawsuits. His friends worried about his health, especially his constant smoking. When I interviewed him after his retirement, in Rancho Santa Fe, California, he looked 100 percent better than the last time I had seen him as commissioner, though he was still carrying the extra pounds he had put on after he stopped smoking. Now doing consultant work for the NFL, he was relaxed as he talked about his tennis game and the building of his new home just half a mile from his office.

Meanwhile, Davis still looks stressed out—but that's his normal look.

• • •

As far back as the late 1960s, during our talks at the Raiders training camp, Davis had spoken fondly of two cities—New York and Los Angeles. It was clear that he thought those were the only two cities in the country that counted, and Los Angeles was his favorite. He had enjoyed living there when he was an assistant at Southern Cal and in his first year with the Chargers, before the team moved to San Diego. When Rosenbloom moved the Rams to Anaheim, Davis finally had his opportunity to return.

There was another factor in his decision. For all his reputation as a "genius," Davis has never been an innovator. His strength has been an ability to take somebody else's idea and make it work. His offense when he came to the Raiders was Sid Gillman's, and even in the 1990s the Raiders were running the same basic offense. Growing up in Brooklyn, Davis had seen Walter O'Malley move the Brooklyn Dodgers to Los Angeles, and he used O'Malley's maneuverings as a blueprint for his own. In both cases, the owner claimed the city he was leaving had forced him out because it wouldn't give him what he needed. In both cases, the owner said he had to leave the smaller city for the larger one because the economics of the sport made it impossible for him to succeed in the smaller city. In both cases, the owner left behind a fervent, almost a rabid, fan base.

"I think Davis wanted to come to a major city," said Bill Robertson, who negotiated the original deal for the Los Angeles Coliseum and the agreement in 1990 for the Raiders to stay. "He wanted to be a big fish in a big bowl, instead of a big fish in a little bowl."

Davis argued publicly that he needed more revenue than Oakland could provide if he was to continue fielding topflight teams. He especially stressed the need for luxury boxes—suites that rent for $45,000 or more per season. All the NFL owners have sought luxury boxes, primarily because the money they bring in does not have to be shared with visiting teams, as the money from ticket sales does (60 percent for the home team, 40 percent for the visitors). Some thought that Davis was looking ahead to the time when cable-television revenues would be an important factor. Robertson thought, as I did, that Davis's desire for recognition was more important than either of these.

"Finances obviously had a lot to do with it, but that wasn't the most important thing," Robertson said. "I thought the cable-TV market would be important to him. Network TV money is divided evenly among teams, but I thought owners would be reluctant to split up cable money. I just felt that this was a natural, to come into the second-largest media center in the country, and the cable TV would be a bonanza. But he told me, no, it was not a factor, that when it came to that, the league would do the same thing it had done with regular TV. He felt that he could come down to this big community and really get recognition. I think that was important. All of us have egos and like to be recognized."

Oakland faced an uphill battle throughout the contract negotiations. Davis wanted to go to Los Angeles, if that city could come up with any sort of offer he could live with. Davis dealt directly with Robertson about Los Angeles arrangements; he almost always had his assistant, Al LoCasale, deal with the Oakland officials. He wouldn't discuss anything beyond five years with Oakland; he talked about seven years and then ten years with Los Angeles.

Robertson would have preferred an even longer contract. "I wanted as long a contract as I could get," he told me, "but I was satisfied with what we got. I felt that if we got the luxury boxes, there was no question that Al would stay. I had confidence the Raiders would be a winning team and that the fan support would be very good."

Although his supporters claimed that Davis left Oakland because he couldn't get his luxury boxes, in fact the final Oakland offer included sixty-four of them. Although he said he couldn't compete in the NFL money market if he stayed in Oakland, in fact the Raiders were seventh in the league in home revenues there (with the highest average ticket price of $11.97 at that time) and first in road revenues. Most telling, Davis was always direct with Robertson, who has praised him for his honesty, but he was evasive in his dealings in Oakland and used the media to blast the Oakland negotiators and make misleading statements.

On the rare occasions when Davis himself met with the Oakland negotiators, he would put nothing in writing. "He'd write on a blackboard, and then as soon as we'd read it he'd erase it," remembered George Vukasin, who is now the president of the Oakland Coliseum Board but was then an Oakland city councilman and a member of the city's negotiating committee.

The whole period was especially frustrating for Cunningham, who could not get Davis to sit down and agree to anything. The Oakland Coliseum management in general, and Cunningham in particular, took a beating from the Bay Area media, which tended to accept Davis's version of events, so it's important to understand that Cunningham was well respected within his profession. He had served as president of the International Association of Auditorium Managers in 1973 and 1974 and had been given the group's highest honor, "for contributions to the profession," in 1977.

"There were really two periods," said Cunningham, who resigned in September 1980 to become a consultant. "One was from March or April of 1979 up to the first preseason game. That was the period when the Raiders should have exercised the option but had not. We were trying to get meetings, and I could meet with Al LoCasale, but I could never get with Davis. It was always 'Mr. Davis is busy, Mr. Davis is doing this, Mr. Davis is going to war with Kansas City, so he can't talk to you.' "

Cunningham and Bob Nahas, the president of the Coliseum Board, knew that Davis would want more than a simple extension of the contract, but he needed to know how much more. The Coliseum had a reserve fund of $1,350,000; if Davis wanted improvements that cost more than that, Cunningham would have to go to the city and the county for money.

"In the summer," Cunningham remembered, "there started to be some articles written that Davis was talking to Los Angeles and considering moving. People began to get a little nervous here. Before the first preseason game there was a blast in the newspaper, Al Davis taking the Coliseum apart. We never had had that before. There was a public offensive on things he hadn't talked to us about. At this time, Bob Nahas and I realized there was more to this than we'd thought. We'd received a list of improvements from Al LoCasale that they wanted. We estimated that they would cost between $12 million and $15 million. We told LoCasale that we'd have to go to the city and county, and that it would mean a long-term contract."

LoCasale had delivered the list at a meeting in his office with Cunningham and Jack Maltester, who was about to become president of the Coliseum Board, on May 31, 1979. The Raiders list included luxury boxes and changes in early-season scheduling, so the Oakland A's would not automatically have priority on September and October dates. But the Raiders would not commit to a long-term contract, the only basis on which the Coliseum could afford the improvements.

Cunningham remembered the meeting vividly. "LoCasale had a yellow pad, seven or eight pages, with all these things

156

written down. So I wrote them down and then sent a confirming letter to Al Davis asking if there were any deletions or corrections. No response. But later, when we released the list on September 8—after telling him we would have to because the city and county wanted to know what was going on—he just went bonkers, saying the list was a real fabrication."

The negotiations—or lack of them—were complicated by the fact that Nahas was planning to resign as president of the Coliseum Board, a position he had held for twenty years, at the end of 1979, and Maltester was scheduled to take over. Unfortunately, Maltester was a friend and political ally of Wayne Valley, and that made Davis automatically suspicious of his intentions. It was impossible for the two men to work together. Years later, Davis told Nahas, "I'd still be in Oakland if you'd stayed on the board. When you left I didn't have anybody to talk to." There was some truth to that—Nahas had always been able to work with Davis—but when Davis moved the club, Nahas told him in a private letter that he'd made a mistake because "you turned your back on the Oakland fans."

Cunningham and Nahas had reason to be nervous. Davis was even then talking seriously to Bill Robertson, president of the Los Angeles Coliseum Commission, who had been looking for an NFL team to move into the Los Angeles Coliseum. Mel Durslag, then a columnist for the *Los Angeles Herald-Examiner*, had also been campaigning for an NFL team, but, as he told me later, "I didn't have the slightest idea Al Davis would come down here. I thought he was just using the guys down here to get a better deal in Oakland. In fact, I lost a bet with Bill Robertson. Bill told me the Raiders would come down here."

Robertson, the executive secretary of the Los Angeles County Federation of Labor, has been an elected official in the labor movement since 1957. He is a patient man, no doubt because of his history as a labor negotiator, and a straightforward man, without pretension, respected for his honesty. He and Davis had an immediate rapport. "I like Al because he's an honorable man," Robertson told me. "He's never lied to me, which I think is an admirable characteristic."

Nonetheless, their negotiations did not go smoothly, primarily because Robertson could not promise Davis much at first. "The Coliseum didn't have any money," he said. "I went to the city council and the county board of supervisors and Jerry Brown, the governor. Our concept was to get $5 million from the city, $8 million from the county, and $5 million from the state. Our initial concept was that we would build a hundred luxury boxes." But then, Robertson continued, California passed Proposition 13, which froze property taxes throughout the state at 1975 levels and sharply reduced city, county, and state revenues. "We'd had approval, but that proposition knocked everything out. I had to tell Davis we didn't have any money. He didn't say anything decisive on the phone. We got back together a couple of days later, and he said he would build the boxes."

In later depositions by architect Robert Bennett, it was disclosed that Davis had met with Robertson, Los Angeles Coliseum general manager Jim Hardy, and Bennett as early as January 1979 to discuss the possible move of the Raiders—this at a time when Davis was supposedly negotiating with Oakland for an extension of his contract there. According to Bennett's testimony, Davis and John Madden were meeting with architects on the design of the luxury suites in March; by April 18 plans for the boxes, a practice field, and improvements in parking and dressing rooms were detailed enough that the Raiders' approval was all that was needed for work to begin. During this period Davis also told both Hardy and Bennett— again according to Bennett's depositions—that his deal with Oakland was finished, that he would not pick up the option on the contract with the Oakland Coliseum.

There was one potential problem: Rams owner Carroll Rosenbloom opposed the idea of another NFL team moving into the Los Angeles Coliseum, so close to his team's new home in Anaheim. Davis and Rosenbloom had known each other for a quarter of a century; Davis had worked for the Baltimore Colts in the 1950s, when Rosenbloom owned them (before his legendary trade of the Colts for the Rams). Rosenbloom was probably the only man in the league who had any influence with Davis, who often deferred to the older man. Many people think that Davis, who was willing to defy the rest of the league, would not have dared to move against Rosenbloom's wishes. Even Robertson said he wasn't sure Davis would have tried.

It never came to that. On April 2, 1979, Rosenbloom, the one man who might have stopped Davis, drowned, while swimming in the Atlantic Ocean off the coast of Florida.

Davis was only playing for time with Oakland while he worked out a deal in Los Angeles—but then the negotiations took a surprise turn. Near the end of 1979, problems developed in Los Angeles. Both USC and UCLA, the other Coliseum tenants, objected to the removal of seats to make room for luxury boxes. "UCLA was just looking for an excuse to leave," Robertson said. "USC's concern was more legitimate, because they had high-priced seats in the area that would have come out to make room for the boxes." Some of the county supervisors, including Pete Schabarum, a member of the Coliseum Commission, opposed any deal with the Raiders, too.

And a dramatic new offer was about to be made in Oakland.

• • •

In mid-January of 1980, Oakland Coliseum Board members George Vukasin and Bill Moorish had a talk with Cornell Maier, the chief executive officer of Kaiser Aluminum, the biggest corporation headquartered in Oakland. They wanted Maier, who had always been closely involved in civic affairs and was an avid promoter of Oakland, to look at their latest proposal to the Raiders and give them his opinion.

"I didn't think it was attractive enough, that it needed to be improved," Maier, now a consultant to Kaiser Aluminum, told me. "If they improved it, I committed that Kaiser Aluminum would contribute $2 million. There would be no strings—the money could be used in whatever way the negotiators wanted to use it. And I would try to get money from other businesses. A little later Clorox committed another $1 million."

"That was very helpful," Bill Cunningham recalled, "because there were things we couldn't do because of the restrictions on the way the Coliseum could spend money. Davis wanted money for his practice field, for instance, and to pay for the club's indemnification for the 49ers"—a legacy from the AFL-NFL merger settlement. "There was no way the Coliseum could do that. The feeling at the time was that Cornell had saved the day. Some of the politicians thought it would be a slam dunk, that Davis would love this."

Maier recalled a series of meetings, first with him, Vukasin, Moorish, and Oakland's mayor, Lionel Wilson, to refine the package, and then with Maier, Vukasin, Wilson, and Davis. The last meeting with Davis was, ironically enough, in Los Angeles; Davis was there for the Super Bowl game between the Pittsburgh Steelers and the Los Angeles Rams in Pasadena. "The Raiders—meaning Davis—liked some things and didn't like others," Maier noted. "There were revisions and revisions and revisions, but we were all fairly optimistic."

Following his first meeting, Davis called Robertson and, according to Robertson, told him that Oakland had made him such an attractive offer he might have to take it. "I told him that if he did, I would naturally be disappointed," Robertson said, "but there would be no hard feelings. I felt he had been negotiating with us in good faith, and if Oakland came up with a better offer there was nothing I could do about it."

Oakland made two specific proposals to Davis, the first one at the meeting in Los Angeles on January 19, the day before the Super Bowl, and the second at a meeting five days later in Oakland.

The first proposal called for a five-year contract, $1 million in stadium improvements during the 1980–1982 period and another $1.75 million in improvements in 1983–1990, and $500,000 in immediate improvements to the practice field and $1.5 million for past improvements made by the Raiders, the latter to be financed with the Kaiser money. Most important, it also called for a $4 million nonrecourse loan to the Raiders to build the luxury suites, which meant that the suites themselves were the only security for the loan; if the Raiders moved or defaulted on payments, the suites would belong to the Coliseum. "Of course," Cunningham noted, "they wouldn't be of much use to us if we didn't have a football or a baseball team." The proposed loan was for thirty years; if the Raiders left after five years, the Coliseum would have had to pay on the loan for another twenty-five years.

After Davis responded, the second proposal restructured the improvements to make $1 million available immediately, proposed an 8 percent rental fee on ticket revenues for regular-season games and 10 percent for play-offs, and gave the Raiders 45 percent of the net from concessions and 85 percent of the money from advertisements on the message board for Raiders games, all of which had previously gone to the Coliseum.

Under this proposal, the Coliseum would have raised its share of the money by allowing Charles Finley, then the owner of the baseball A's, to buy out his lease. Finley had been trying to sell the club to Marvin Davis, who wanted to move it to Denver, but had been blocked by the lease, a very strong one—in sharp contrast to the lease with the Raiders. The A's were a weak team then, and their season attendance had dropped to 306,763.

Al Davis countered that he wanted a $1 million rent rebate, to be paid in five yearly installments of $200,000, and no guarantee on the loan for the suites.

"We thought we were getting down fairly well," Maier said. "We were about a million dollars apart, which I didn't think was very much." Then one day Maier had a call from Joe Bort, the chairman of the Alameda County supervisors and the representative of the county on the Coliseum task force, though he had not taken part in the Maier negotiations. "He came to my office," Maier said, "and told me that as county representative he couldn't support it. He said he didn't think his constituents would go for the proposal, and he couldn't go for it."

Bort's objections had been noted at an earlier meeting of the task force. Bort's main argument was with the thirty-year loan under only a five-year contract. To protect the city and the county, he had wanted an $800,000 penalty clause if the Raiders left before the loan was repaid, but such a clause had not been included in the second proposal.

"If you owned a building and your tenant wanted you to remodel it, you'd certainly want a lease that would give you time to recoup your investment," the now retired Bort told me. "In this case I was willing to split the difference—I would have gone for a fifteen-year lease. But Davis would never commit to more than five years. Cornell didn't seem to think that was important, but I was sure that at the end of five years Davis would leave. Bill Cunningham had supplied me with information about leases around the country, and in every case, where teams had gotten good deals on their leases, they had committed to at least twenty years and sometimes thirty years.

"There were other questionable aspects of that proposal. The city and county would have to borrow money at somewhere between 11 and 13 percent, and we were going to loan money to Davis at 4 percent. Later he asked for another half million, with the same repayment schedule on the loan. I calculated that his interest would then be down to not much more than 3 percent."

The county board of supervisors never got a chance to vote on the proposal, because Maier realized that Bort's opposition doomed it. Maier called Mayor Wilson and asked him to meet with Bort in Maier's office. "I left him alone," Maier said. "I then talked to Lionel a few minutes after that. I said, we don't have a proposal, and I think we have an obligation to Al Davis to tell him that.

"I always believed that if you've got a dirty job to do you should do it in person, so we made an appointment with Al. We walked into his office, opposite the Coliseum. He was all smiles, very chipper. I knew what he was thinking—these guys are here to close the gap and make it go. I had been elected the spokesman, and I said, 'Al, I'm sorry to tell you the county has withdrawn its support for the proposal.' Well, Al got very upset. He thanked us for coming, and we left."

Shortly after that Davis phoned Robertson. "He told me, 'We've got to talk again. Oakland has taken its offer off the table,'" Robertson told me.

Only now are the full details of the negotiations on the Maier proposal becoming public. Because the negotiations were private, the failure of the deal spawned many rumors. One that still persists is that Pete Rozelle told the Oakland negotiators to stand firm because Davis couldn't move. For instance, in a 1990 book, *Black Knight*, author Ira Simmons writes, "When Pete Rozelle learned of the generous offer that Wilson and Maier were discussing with Davis, he called Bill Moorish of the Coliseum Board and said something like, 'Don't give him so much, we won't let him move anyway.'"

"That's the exact opposite of the truth," Moorish told me. "I had been named head of the board's football committee, so I thought the league should know what we were doing. I called Rozelle to report what was going on. Rozelle said, 'That's a good idea,' and thanked me for calling." Moorish added that when he testified in the antitrust trial, lawyers for both Davis and the Los Angeles Coliseum tried to get him to say that Rozelle had told him to have Oakland cut back on its offer. "That was nonsense," Moorish said. "I had called Rozelle; he didn't call me. He didn't know me from Adam at the time, so there was no reason he would call me."

Moorish's story corroborates what Rozelle told me. "I certainly wouldn't have told anybody not to go up in an offer, because I always wanted teams to get as much as they could, including Al," Rozelle said.

After the Maier deal was aborted, Cunningham remembered, the Coliseum task force met once again. "There was a whole atmosphere of despair," he said. "Out of that meeting came a decision to put together the best deal Oakland could make, put it into a legal document, and send it over to Davis."

On February 4, 1980, a clerk from the office of Ed Heafey, the Coliseum counsel, attempted to deliver that document to the Raiders offices. At the door, Al LoCasale refused to accept it and threw it out into the parking lot. "I testified later that it was one of the five best deals in the league at that time," Cunningham said. "We had gone beyond what we really thought we should."

The proposal LoCasale threw out called for a ten-year contract, but the Raiders could end it after five years if they put their decision in writing. It still had the $4 million loan for sixty-four luxury suites, but it also had the $800,000 penalty Bort had wanted. The Raiders would get all the revenue from the boxes and from the game tickets that box renters would have to buy, at higher than normal prices. The rent was reduced to 7 percent for the first $7 million gross, 10 percent after that. The Raiders would get 45 percent of the net from concessions.

The combination of a short-term contract, the low rental, and the concession money made the proposal a favorable one, but not as good as the previous offer because of the $800,000 penalty and the loss of the $3 million that Kaiser Aluminum and Clorox had promised. A letter to the Raiders noted that they were free to negotiate for that money directly with the two companies, but by now Maier had dropped out of the negotiations in disgust, and it's doubtful that the money would have been recommitted.

Less than a month later, on March 1, Davis signed a memorandum of agreement with the Los Angeles Coliseum.

The agreement—in reality, an agreement to agree—would have been an $18.5 million deal if it had all come to fruition, which it did not. It was to be financed with money from the county ($5 million), the Olympics committee formed for the 1984 games in Los Angeles ($5 million), and the city ($8.5 million). It was to include money for luxury suites and improvements to the Coliseum, plus $4 million for unspecified relocation costs. In some ways the Los Angeles agreement was inferior to the Oakland proposal. Although Robertson had agreed verbally to build ninety-nine luxury suites, the Coliseum Commission was not committed to that in writing; Davis had only promises. "I was advised by counsel not to put anything in writing," Robertson said, "because of the antitrust lawsuit. But I had made a commitment to Al, and others later joined me."

It seems strange that Davis would be so trusting, especially considering the history of the Coliseum Commission, a political body whose composition changes with the election results. It has never had a consistent philosophy and has lost pro football, basketball, and hockey tenants, largely because of inept management. To expect this politically charged board to honor commitments made by Robertson shows a naïveté that would not be expected of a hard bargainer like Davis. It only underscores how strongly Davis wanted to move to Los Angeles. The Oakland deal proposed by Maier was so sweet that it had made him pause, but once that was withdrawn, the move to Los Angeles was inevitable.

"I've always felt that he was only using Oakland for leverage in getting a better deal in L.A.," Bort said. But Maier defends Davis. "I have never blamed Al Davis for moving because of what happened in those negotiations," he told me. "I thought he was justified. I said that to a number of people. After the antitrust lawsuit started, I had a number of conversations with Pete Rozelle and the lawyers involved in the suit, and I told them the same thing. There's no way anybody could say that Al Davis asked for too much. I thought we were very close to a deal."

The Maier negotiations had one significant side effect for Oakland. "After they had fallen apart," Maier remembered, "I got a phone call one day from Charlie Finley. He told me, 'You're the only one who's making sense in this deal. I'm impressed, and I want you to find a buyer for me for the A's.' I asked around and found out that Walter Haas was interested, so I helped put together a deal for the Haas family to buy the A's." The irony is that if the Maier negotiations had gone through, the Raiders would have stayed in Oakland but the A's probably would have left. It would be difficult to argue today that Oakland would be better served by having the Raiders and not the A's.

• • •

When Davis's Los Angeles agreement became known, Pete Rozelle and the NFL owners didn't take long to counterattack. Rozelle called a special meeting of the owners in Dallas, at which he asked Davis to make a presentation. When Davis replied that he intended to move and did not feel he needed any approval, citing Carroll Rosenbloom's move of the Rams to Anaheim, Rozelle appointed a fact-finding committee to report at the owners' next regularly scheduled meeting, to be held in Palm Springs the following week.

The owners Rozelle appointed were Art Modell of the Cleveland Browns, Herman Sarkowsky of the Seattle Seahawks, George Halas of the Chicago Bears, Wellington Mara of the New York Giants and Bill Bidwill of the St. Louis Cardinals. Davis immediately attacked the committee as being stacked against him, which was true enough. Rozelle would have found it impossible to put together a committee that was not anti-Davis, as was shown at the owners' meeting, when the vote—which Davis, of course, had not requested—was 22−0 against him.

The battle lines were drawn. It would be a bitter fight for the next few years. The crossfire extended even to the media. Arguing vehemently against Davis's move, I found myself debating Mel Durslag in print and on radio talk shows, though he had been my role model when I started my newspaper career. Now I can see that Durslag probably had the more balanced view. Unlike some of those close to Davis, Durslag has been able to see his flaws and weaknesses, but he also admires Davis for his accomplishments and his willingness to take risks.

"It wasn't easy backing Al," said Durslag, who has never been one to shy away from a fight. "I got a lot of people pissed off at me. Just being a supporter of Al Davis can get you hung. A lot of newspaper guys got mad at me because they didn't like Al Davis." (I myself remember Dave Anderson of the *New York Times* calling Durslag "mouthpiece" at a pregame party in 1980.) "The NFL basically cut me off. The irony was that I had known Pete Rozelle since 1946, when he was making $50 a week doing public relations for Compton Junior College. We had even been social friends with Pete and his first wife. So it wasn't a personal thing with me at all.

"There was no way I could back down and not support a team coming to L.A. I was the one who had started the move to get a team to L.A. after Carroll Rosenbloom pulled his slick move to go to Anaheim, and I'd even lined up the lawyer, Max Blecher, for the Coliseum. There was just too much history of teams moving for the Raiders to be stopped."

It was Durslag's contention that, although Davis angered the other owners by the way he moved without their approval, he was neither better nor worse than they were. "These guys aren't Eagle Scouts," he said. "You're dealing with cutthroat guys. If Davis disappointed Oakland, the only thing I can do is hearken back to sports owners for the past fifty years. Look at O'Malley leaving Brooklyn—who could ever have thought that? Bill Bidwill was on the committee that said it was terrible that the Raiders left Oakland and their loyal fans, but what happened when he got his chance? He moved to Phoenix. They're not very nice people, but I guess that's why they got to where they are.

"Al is not motivated by money. He just wants to make a difference. That's the way these guys are. Why would Carroll Rosenbloom make the deal he made in Anaheim? He was born with money and certainly had all the money he would ever need, so what was he going to do with real estate in Anaheim at seventy-two? But he wanted to be a factor. I argued with Tex Schramm about the move. He said, 'If Al had just gone about it the right way . . .' I said, 'You mean, Al should have been a good boy?' He's not that kind of guy. Instead of smoothing things over, he wants to spit in somebody's eye. And Al never explains. He just does what he thinks he should do, and that's it."

Oakland fired the first legal salvo even before Davis signed his agreement in Los Angeles: an eminent-domain suit to take over the Raiders, filed on February 22, 1980. The case was dismissed by Monterey Superior Court Judge Nat Agliano. The main event, though, was the antitrust suit against the NFL. The Los Angeles Coliseum had brought the suit in August 1978, after the Rams left for Anaheim, claiming that the NFL was depriving the city of major-league pro football. It became a viable suit only after the Raiders joined it, however, because then Los Angeles could legitimately claim that the NFL was trying to prevent a team from coming in.

Unlike baseball, which was granted antitrust immunity in 1922 in a U.S. Supreme Court decision, the NFL has no protection against antitrust suits. Rozelle had successfully campaigned for a limited exemption in 1966, to allow the league's merger with the AFL, but that exemption did not apply in this case.

Specifically, the Los Angeles Coliseum's suit challenged Rule 4.3 of the NFL constitution, which at the time required a unanimous vote of the twenty-eight owners before a franchise could move. Having been advised by NFL counsel that the rule's 100 percent approval requirement violated antitrust law, the owners amended the rule, at a special meeting in Chicago in October 1978, to require three-quarters approval. Davis did not vote on the rule change, and the statement he made at the meeting was later a matter of dispute at the trial. Davis claimed that he said, "I reserve my rights to move." Others remembered his saying only, "I reserve my rights." Whatever he said, he abstained from voting, and the vote to amend the rule was 27–0.

At that same meeting the owners formally approved the Rams' move to Anaheim, even though Rosenbloom had already signed his agreement with Anaheim. Again the vote was 27–0, with Davis abstaining.

Despite the change in Rule 4.3, the Los Angeles Coliseum did not drop its suit, but it did nothing much about it, either, until Davis announced his decision to move. At that point the suit became an active one. The Raiders not only joined the suit as an active partner but filed one of their own against the NFL for $160 million. They also added a side issue by formally charging Pete Rozelle, the new Los Angeles Rams owner, Georgia Frontiere, and San Diego Chargers owner Gene Klein with a "conspiracy" to keep the Raiders from moving to Los Angeles. Klein and Davis had long been enemies; Klein had once threatened to sue Davis, when the Raiders were slow to send the Chargers their share of the gate receipts from an exhibition game in Oakland.

The NFL's primary defense was that of "single entity"— the claim that the twenty-eight teams were actually one unit, rather than competing businesses in the same field. The NFL did, of course, conduct some activities on behalf of all the teams, like running the draft of college players and sharing TV revenues equally, but the case involved far more than legal issues. Pete Rozelle wanted to keep it a league battle; Davis made it a personal one.

Davis has a great ability to portray himself as a victim, and even Bill Robertson told me that he thought Rozelle was pursuing a "vendetta" against Davis. "I always thought it was the other way," Rozelle told me. "Al didn't like me after the merger, because of what happened with the commissionership." My belief is that Rozelle had regarded Davis as simply another annoyance, and probably not his worst one. Dealing with NFL owners is not easy, because all are independent and wealthy people accustomed to doing things the way they want. Rozelle's greatest accomplishment as commissioner was that he was able to keep them working together, for the benefit of the league, until Al Davis decided to move his team to Los Angeles.

"It became a suit between Al and myself," Rozelle said, "but the NFL owners felt as strongly as I did. I felt very strong about keeping the league together. As long as we worked together, we could really progress. I was really upset because Al and the Raiders had come into the merger, and they signed certain documents accepting certain conditions, and he just disregarded them. He came in and took the benefits, including television, but this one rule he didn't like, so he went to court. That was what concerned me. Any time you have a league flaring off, you have problems. There was a very strong precedent with the league. The feeling was that if people just felt they had the right to move anywhere they wanted, it would be like the early days of pro football, when you wound up, for instance, with two teams in Chicago, the Bears and the Cardinals. There had to be some sort of order. The league's considerations had to be taken in along with the club's consideration."

• • •

It was more than a year before the antitrust trial began. In the interim Oakland was able to get court injunctions that kept the Raiders in place for the 1980 and 1981 seasons. The NFL sought a change of venue to move the trial out of Los Angeles, arguing that potential jurors, even if they knew nothing about football, would be biased toward Los Angeles because of the economic benefits to the city. Federal court judge Harry Pregerson denied that request, and the trial began on May 11, 1981.

The first of what would be two trials lasted three months. There were many star witnesses—Kansas City Chiefs owner Lamar Hunt, Miami Dolphins coach Don Shula, and Dallas Cowboys general manager Tex Schramm among them—but the trial itself was slow moving, as are most trials apart from those on "L.A. Law." The witnesses on both sides generally just reiterated their basic positions. There was one dramatic event: after testifying, on May 27, Gene Klein suffered a heart attack and was rushed to the hospital. (He survived that attack but died of a later one, on March 12, 1990.)

Davis was a star witness for the Raiders and the Los Angeles Coliseum. His counsel, Joseph Alioto, the former mayor of San Francisco and now one of the leading antitrust attorneys in the country, persuaded him to forsake his normal silver-and-black attire, and he appeared dressed in conservative business suits and ties. On the stand, he usually spoke in the mock-southern accent he adopts when he wants to be at his charming best. I spent some time at both trials, and it was hard for me to reconcile the humble, soft-spoken man on the stand with the forceful man I had known, whose "Fuck!" punctuated his speech with great frequency.

Carefully taken through his testimony by Alioto, Davis made several telling points in favor of the move. He remained unflappable in cross-examination, and several jurors later commented that they had been impressed by him. Alioto said that Davis was the best witness he's ever had.

The key factor in the trial, though, was neither Davis nor Rozelle. It was a ruling by Judge Pregerson on July 28, just before the jury was to start deliberations, that the NFL was not a single entity, but was twenty-eight competitors, thereby undercutting the NFL's primary defense. At the same time the judge dismissed the Raiders' conspiracy charges against Rozelle, Frontiere, and Klein.

Then, before a verdict could be reached—the jury was deadlocked at 8−2 in favor of the Raiders and the Los Angeles Coliseum—a mistrial was declared. An attempt had been made to select jurors with no previous knowledge of the NFL (and therefore no bias either way), but it was discovered that one juror, Thomas Gelker, was a cousin of an owner in the defunct World Football League. Gelker said that he had not talked to his cousin in ten years—long before the cousin bought the WFL team. But some jurors maintained that Gelker, one of the two favoring the NFL, was biased against Davis and toward the league. Judge Pregerson decided there was no chance that the deadlock could be broken, and he declared a mistrial.

While everybody waited for the second trial, rumors surfaced of an impending compromise between the NFL and Davis. Sometimes, the rumors hinted that there would be a financial settlement. Other times, reports held that Davis would be given an expansion franchise in Los Angeles and the Raiders would stay in Oakland, which ignored the fact that Davis and the Raiders were an inseparable combination.

Then, almost on the eve of the trial, just two days before jury selection was to begin, there was even a report that the Los Angeles Coliseum would abandon Davis, drop the lawsuit, and take an expansion franchise. Mike Frankovich, president of the Los Angeles Coliseum, told Mel Durslag for his syndicated column that he would favor a deal that would give Los Angeles an expansion franchise and leave Davis in Oakland. "I have a responsibility to the [Coliseum] Commission and to the people of Los Angeles," Frankovich said, "and I want to make a deal. But Al Davis would have to be taken care of."

Bill Robertson quickly squelched that. "We have a strong lawsuit," said Robertson. "We won eight of the ten votes in the first trial, and we don't have to be humble to anyone. Al Davis is an ally who gave our cause credibility. Without him, we drew nothing but blanks from the NFL. The very least the league should do is offer the expansion franchise to a group headed by Davis. We have no assurance he would take it. But our chances in court are too good for us to cave in at any price the NFL might dictate."

Robertson's comments put the case back in perspective. With the NFL's single-entity defense thrown out, there was almost no chance the Los Angeles Coliseum and the Raiders could lose the case. Robertson wasn't going to abandon Davis, and the Raiders owner was determined to show the league that he could do what he wanted.

Rozelle tried to get Congress to pass legislation exempting the NFL from the antitrust statutes. That attempt failed, and the second trial began on March 29, 1982. This one lasted just six weeks, and on May 7, 1982, a six-woman jury ruled in favor of the Raiders and the Los Angeles Coliseum, deciding that the Raiders had been damaged by $11.5 million and the Coliseum by $4.9 million. (The automatic trebling of damages in antitrust cases brought the total to $49.2 million.) The NFL appealed the verdict all the way to the U.S. Supreme Court, but the Court refused, without comment, to hear the appeal.

Rozelle was to see his worse fears realized as a result of Davis's move and the NFL's defeat in court. "Robert Irsay left Baltimore on the heels of the precedent Davis created in California," he said. "Bill Bidwill got approval to move from St. Louis to Phoenix, but the owners really had no choice. I think it would have been better if the league had prevailed. Phoenix was our number-one site for an expansion team, but it went to the Cardinals. This has created great ill will in Oakland, Baltimore, and St. Louis. In those cities, at least, people don't feel the league has operated with a lot of integrity."

While all this action was taking place in the courts, the Raiders continued to play in Oakland. The legal byplay eventually crippled Davis's ability to keep the team competitive—"They're taking away my football time," he complained to announcer Bill King—but it didn't affect the team's play on the field.

"Al was always good about isolating the players from that problem," Gene Upshaw said. "That was his problem, not ours. We wanted to play. It didn't matter if it was Oakland, if it was Santa Rosa, if it was Los Angeles, if it was a barge floating up and down the coast of California. I was closer to it because of my relationship to Davis, but I didn't think it really bothered anybody."

In fact, in the midst of all the uproar, a surprising, almost shocking, event occurred: the Raiders won their second Super Bowl.

·9·

The Underdogs
Win Another
Super Bowl

Perhaps the biggest single factor in Al Davis's football success
has been his willingness to trust his own judgment—as when
he signed Jim Plunkett as quarterback in 1978. The conventional NFL wisdom was that Plunkett was through, another
potential star ruined because of injury and circumstance, but
Davis thought otherwise. Although even Davis couldn't have
realized it at the time, his decision to sign Plunkett would bring
him a second Super Bowl ring.

Plunkett, a Heisman Trophy winner at Stanford and the
first player taken in the 1971 draft, had had a disappointing
pro career. Playing for a terrible team in New England, he
took a pounding. Traded to the San Francisco 49ers in 1976,
he had only a fair season. He was still suffering from a shoulder injury he had sustained while with the Patriots and played
in just twelve games, completing 51.9 percent of his passes while
throwing 13 touchdown passes and 16 interceptions. He ranked
eighth among the quarterbacks in the fourteen-team conference.

Before the start of the 1978 season he was released by the

new general manager of the 49ers, Joe Thomas. It was a shocking move, one of many mistakes made by Thomas, who was determined to remake the 49ers in his own image. He certainly did, taking a team that had just missed the play-offs in 1976 to a 2–14 record in 1978, before he was fired by owner Ed DeBartolo, Jr. Plunkett was as shocked as anyone. "I was so down and discouraged," said Plunkett, now a beer distributor and still living in the San Francisco Bay Area. "My agent, Wayne Hooper, talked to a couple of teams, but I didn't want to pack my bags and go somewhere else. I'd already played in one cold-weather city, and I didn't want any part of that again."

Then Al Davis came calling. Davis looked beyond Plunkett's problems with the Patriots and the 49ers and thought that, if given time to recuperate emotionally and physically, as well as the chance to play behind a good offensive line, Plunkett might surprise everyone. Davis also knew that he wasn't risking anything by signing a quarterback who was a free agent and therefore didn't cost the Raiders another player. "When the Raiders showed interest," Plunkett said, "that's what I wanted. I could stay in my home."

Most observers thought it was a meaningless move, but that ignored Plunkett's character: he is a fighter. Even at Stanford he'd had to fight to stay a quarterback; John Ralston, his coach, had thought of switching him to tight end as a freshman, because of his size and toughness. Plunkett was never a picture passer, and he threw a fairly high number of interceptions. But he had a knack for making the big play, and he was a leader, as he had proved in taking Stanford to an upset win over Ohio State in the Rose Bowl.

For his first two years with the Raiders, Plunkett sat on the bench watching Ken Stabler, learning the offense, and becoming part of a team that was totally different from any he'd been on. "It was a much looser organization," he told me. "It would have been hard for me to go from a Raiders-type situation to a more disciplined situation, but to go from a more structured organization to the Raiders, well, at my age, it made it much easier.

"There was another thing I noticed right away. At San Francisco and New England, they were in awe of other teams. They didn't want to be embarrassed. But with the Raiders, they had a reputation, and they lived up to it, for the most part. They went out and had a good time during the week, but every Sunday they expected to beat the hell out of the other team, so they went out and played. Their attitude was tremendous. They expected everybody to be in awe of them. Their reputation got around the league. And I think the Raiders still have that mystique about them."

Even though Stabler had changed the offensive concept from long passes to shorter, controlled ones, the style was still Al Davis's: it depended on the quarterback's being given more time to throw than in most systems and being able to wait for his receivers to get open, instead of throwing to a designated spot where a receiver was supposed to be. Plunkett had a difficult time making the adjustment.

"It was hard for me just to hold the ball," he said. "They had a lot of strength in the offensive line, and I remember 'Snake' would drop back and pat the ball in his right hand, just waiting for somebody to get open. In New England and San Francisco, I had to just go back, plant, and throw, on timing patterns. I'd learned all my life to anticipate, to know where the receiver is going and throw the ball on the break. But when I came to the Raiders, they told me not to throw until I saw the receiver's front numbers, after he'd turned toward me. That was hard for me to get used to. I'd throw the ball, and the receiver would turn around and be surprised to see the ball.

"The offense was confusing, too, the way they numbered and called things. They said it was for the players in the early years who didn't know what was going on. It was more difficult for the quarterback, because instead of calling their number and letting them do it, you had to call all the routes, which meant much more to learn. I would have had trouble if I'd had to step in right away. I still wanted to play when I went to the Raiders, but the fortunate thing was that there was no hurry. They had Stabler, an established quarterback, and a very good team. The year gave me a chance to concentrate, work hard, and get myself back together again, physically and mentally.

"Of course, that was the first year. By the second year I was ready to play, but I still had to sit." In fact, it began to seem like more of the same in Plunkett's third year, 1980. Stabler was gone, but Dan Pastorini was playing; having made the much-publicized trade, Davis wasn't going to have Pastorini on the bench.

Plunkett played well in the exhibition season, but when it looked as if he wouldn't be playing in the regular season, he went to coach Tom Flores and asked to be traded. Flores talked to Davis, but Davis wouldn't consider a trade. Plunkett had little trade value, and Davis knew that he could still play. Very quickly, he got his chance.

Oakland Raiders fans were as loyal as any fans I've ever seen. From 1967 on, I saw every game played at the Oakland Coliseum, and I had heard only one Raider booed—Daryle Lamonica. In 1980 the fans added a second to their boo list—Dan Pastorini. In this case the fans seemed to know more than Davis did. Pastorini didn't appear to have a clue what to do. He clearly didn't know the offense, and he seemed to just wind up and throw the ball. With him at quarterback, the Raiders split their first four games and were on their way to a third loss, at home against the Kansas City Chiefs, when Pastorini went down with an injury.

The fans cheered as Plunkett came on the field. (It turned out that Pastorini had a broken leg, but the fans couldn't have known that. All they knew was that another quarterback was coming in.) Plunkett was not an immediate success in the Kansas City game. "I had to throw fifty passes in three quarters," he remembered, "and I threw five interceptions. I was pretty down, because I didn't feel I'd have many more opportunities. When you're my age and you get an opportunity, you have to take advantage of it, and I didn't feel I did."

There would be more chances. With Plunkett making big plays, the Raiders went on to win six straight, and Pastorini became the forgotten man. His leg healed faster than expected, and he told Davis he was ready to play again, but Davis chose not to have him activated. Pastorini did accompany the team on road trips to Seattle and Philadelphia and was reported to be drinking on the team plane, which is against club rules. On the Philadelphia flight he confronted Davis, insisting that he be activated, but he failed to make his case.

That weekend was a bad one for Plunkett, too, as the Eagles beat the Raiders, 10–7, in a game that threatened to tear the team apart. "Philadelphia just kicked my butt," said Plunkett, who was sacked eight times. "The offensive line was on me, said I didn't set up in the right place, and that was why they gave up the sacks. So, all of a sudden, there's a little division between me and Art Shell and Gene Upshaw, proud men who had played well for years and years. We had our little internal hassle about that. Art and Uppy demanded and got a lot of respect from everybody, and they put the fear of God in people. I'd get in the huddle and call a play, and they'd look up at me like, 'Are you sure you want to call that play?' It took me aback a little. I'd always been from the school that the quarterback called the play and everybody else shut up. They didn't go by those rules—they didn't go by any rules but their own. It was quite an experience for me with those guys."

The Raiders got past that internal problem to win three of their last four games, and their 11–5 record tied them with the San Diego Chargers in the AFC West. The Chargers were the division champion because of a better divisional record, but the Raiders also went to the play-offs, for the first time in three years, as a wild-card team.

No wild-card team had won the Super Bowl since the merger of the NFL and AFL in 1970, although the Los Angeles Rams had made it that far the year before but lost to the Pittsburgh Steelers. The Raiders would have to win three games, the last two on the road, even to get to the Super Bowl.

They were confident they could do it. "We were 9–2 since I'd taken over," Plunkett told me, "and our defense, which had started the season giving up almost more points than anybody in the league, by the second half of the season was giving up the fewest. Our offense was moving the ball. Kenny King, the fullback, was new from Houston, and he was having a great year. Defenses just weren't adjusted to that kind of speed from a Raiders' fullback. Bobby Chandler was a great addition at wide receiver. Cliff Branch was still making the big pass plays he was known for before I came. There was no doubt in our minds that we could do it."

The Raiders had another plus—smart coaches. Over the years they had always been well prepared for games because of the work of their assistant coaches. Al Davis believed in continuity, and his assistants generally stayed for many years, but the big contributor to the Raiders' first play-off game, against the Houston Oilers, was defensive coordinator Charley Sumner, an exception to the rule of continuity.

Sumner was and is an independent man. He had already left the Raiders once and returned, and he would leave them again in 1984 to become the head coach of the Oakland Invaders in the USFL. He had had some battles with Davis over defensive strategy, and when he left the Raiders after the 1968 season, to go to the Patriots, there was a considerable breach between him and Davis—which only widened when Sumner told his former colleagues what the salaries of the Patriots assistants were. It had seemed likely that Sumner would never again coach with the Raiders, but Davis recognized his ability, and, as always, winning was more important to Davis than personality differences. He rehired Sumner in 1979, and Sumner's defensive strategies would play an important part in the Raiders' success in the early 1980s.

His strategy against Houston was simple: blitz the former Raiders quarterback, Ken Stabler, from his blind side with defensive backs. The Oilers sometimes ran a formation without a wide receiver on one side of the field. Whenever they did, the Raiders would blitz with either cornerback Lester Hayes or safety Mike Davis, who each got two sacks. In all, Stabler was sacked seven times. Hayes also intercepted two Stabler passes, the second one for a touchdown, and the Raiders cruised to a 27 – 7 victory.

"I also blocked a punt and scored a touchdown," Hayes reminded me later. "Charley Sumner had the coaching personality of a pit bull. He'd blitz everyone. That fortified my confidence, because we didn't give the passer time to throw." It was the continuation of an amazing year for Hayes, who had intercepted thirteen passes during the regular season and would get another four during the play-offs. "That didn't include the five I intercepted that were called back because of penalties," he said. "I didn't drop a pass all year. It was an auspicious season."

It seemed only fitting for Hayes, who had a remarkable playing career and personal life. He started his college career as a linebacker, shifting to safety in his junior year and also playing a little at cornerback. The Raiders made him exclusively a cornerback, and he had made a success of it against heavy odds.

Since the Raiders still played more man-to-man coverage than most teams did, their requirements for defensive backs were more stringent. Other teams, playing zones, took backs who weren't able to cover tightly, but the Raiders couldn't afford that. They usually drafted college cornerbacks and tried them first at corner; if they weren't good enough there, they would be shifted to safety. With Hayes, the Raiders switched directions, moving him from college safety to pro cornerback, and it seemed a disastrous idea when he was a rookie in 1977, and even into the 1978 and 1979 seasons. Trying to cut off every pass, Hayes was often faked out of position.

"I think I could have made it earlier if I'd gotten any help from Willie Brown," he told me, "but Willie's ego got in the way. I think he talked to me once the entire 1977 season. I had to watch films of cornerbacks like Pat Thomas and Mel Blount, who played the tight bump-and-run I had to play. And George Atkinson and Jack Tatum taught me all the dirt. I watched films of receivers, and I kept track of coaches. They all have patterns and tendencies. So I was self-taught."

By 1980 he had learned his tough position and had become the best cornerback in the league. Using the same "stickum" that had been Fred Biletnikoff's best friend, he led the league in interceptions. "My career was based on stickum," Hayes said. "It did change my entire life. It was a gift from God. I was invincible with the help of stickum."

He was also solving a personal problem—stuttering. Hayes was a gregarious man and a funny one, with many pet expressions. He liked to refer to play-off bonuses, for instance, as "twenty thousand pictures of dead presidents." Newspapermen could listen patiently through Hayes's halting speech, but the stuttering eliminated any chance for radio or television interviews. That was intolerable to the publicity-conscious Hayes, so he went to a speech therapist and conquered his handicap.

His on-field performance had been one of the big reasons for the Raiders' improvement, as he dramatically displayed in the win over Houston. For the frustrated Pastorini, it was just another lost weekend. The night before the Houston game he got into a shouting and shoving match with Houston sportswriter Dale Robertson, who covered the Oilers. It was not Pastorini's first disagreement with Robertson; a year earlier, when Pastorini was still with the Oilers, two days before the AFC championship game between Houston and the Pittsburgh Steelers, Pastorini had grabbed Robertson and shoved him through a door.

This time, Pastorini first confronted Robertson in the parking lot of the hotel where the Oilers were staying. After a brief exchange of words, Robertson headed into the hotel, and Pastorini followed. Robertson was standing at the bar when Pastorini came up, shoved him in the chest, and pulled his coat down around his arms. Others in the bar grabbed Pastorini before anything more could happen. About thirty minutes later, according to police reports, Pastorini drove his car into a tree in nearby Alameda, suffering cuts and bruises but no broken bones. No charges were filed against him.

None of this was extraordinary behavior for a Raiders player so long as he produced on the field, but Pastorini had not. He didn't play another down for the Raiders and was traded after the season.

The Raiders played their next game, against the Browns in Cleveland, in weather conditions perhaps the second worst in NFL play-off history—behind only the famed "Ice Bowl" championship game in Green Bay, after the 1967 season, between the Packers and the Dallas Cowboys. The temperature in Cleveland was 1 degree above zero, or minus 30 degrees with the wind-chill. Raiders trainer George Anderson called the U.S. Army's base at the Presidio in San Francisco seeking tips on cold-weather gear. "They didn't have any ideas beyond what we already had," he said. "We used two different kinds of skin cream to put on the players' faces or any exposed areas. We had little heating capsules that you break in your hands, and heating pads on the benches. And of course we had all kinds of thermal underwear." Underneath his uniform, guard Gene Upshaw even wore a plastic bag, one he had picked up at the team's hotel. The cold froze Hayes's stickum; he had to keep knocking it off his hands in big clumps.

The wind, blowing off Lake Erie, dominated the game. Neither team scored while moving against the wind, and the wind led to the coaching decision that eventually decided the game.

With 58 seconds left and the Raiders ahead, 14–12, the Browns had moved to the Raiders 14-yard line. Normally, a field goal would have been the automatic call, but kicker Don Cockroft would have been kicking into the wind—and he had already missed two field-goal attempts into that wind. Cleveland's coach, Sam Rutigliano, decided to try a pass into the end zone instead. If that failed, he could use another down to run the ball and set up a kick. The pass play that was called was one the Browns had scored on several times in recent games.

Quarterback Brian Sipe looked first to wide receiver Dave Logan, but he was covered. He then looked to Ozzie Newsome, his tight end, which he later conceded had been a mistake. "I should have reminded myself, before the play, that if Dave wasn't open to throw the ball away," he said. Raiders safety Mike Davis had been expecting a pass, because of the Browns formation. When he saw Sipe look toward Newsome,

Davis moved in front of him and intercepted the pass, to end the day's scoring.

The Raiders were one step closer to the Super Bowl, and the following week they went from Cleveland's blustery cold to the sun of San Diego for the conference championship game. There was one constant, though—they were still the underdogs. In all three of their play-off games, even the first one at home against Houston, the Raiders were on the long end of the odds. The odds makers might have been remembering the Raiders' record in league championship games; they had won only two of eight.

"We had one of our normal shoot-outs against San Diego," Plunkett remembered. "Our teams always harassed the Chargers. We figured the way to stop Dan Fouts was to keep coming at him, and eventually we'd get enough turnovers to beat them. It was always a scoring battle." Indeed, the teams had scored 116 points in their two league games, the Chargers winning the first at San Diego in overtime, 30–24, the Raiders winning the second, 38–24, at Oakland.

This time the Raiders jumped off to a 28–7 halftime lead, but in the second half the Chargers narrowed the gap to 28–24 before the Raiders could get a first down. "I remember Ted Hendricks grabbing my jersey and saying, 'You've got to score. We can't stop them,'" Plunkett said. Plunkett took charge just enough to guide the Raiders to two field goals, and the defense held the Chargers to a field goal on their next possession. The Raiders won, 34–27, and advanced to the Super Bowl in New Orleans, where they were two-and-a-half-point underdogs to the Philadelphia Eagles, the NFC champion. In the euphoria of the win over San Diego, the odds didn't bother anyone.

Super Bowl week was a nervous time for Al Davis. He paced the sidelines frantically at practice, barking at the players, cursing at his coaches. Davis, who always wants to win, had an especially fervent desire now, because this was the Al-Davis-versus-the-world Super Bowl. He had taken on the NFL, and he didn't want the rest of the league gloating at his expense if the Eagles won. He knew, too, that he had reason for concern. This was not one of the great Raiders teams, merely one that had been able to make the big play at the right time. He spent more time than usual with his coaches, going over and over the game plan after exhaustive film sessions. He was trying to will his team to victory.

In great contrast to their boss, the Raiders players enjoyed themselves all week. New Orleans is a party town, the Raiders' kind of town. They amassed $25,000 in fines for breaking curfew during the week. The first to do it was John Matuszak, which was surprising only to those who believed him when he announced, at a Wednesday morning press conference, that he would be "the enforcer" to make sure no Raiders were out on Bourbon Street after hours. "If the boys want to go out this week," Matuszak said, "they'll just have to go through ol' Tooz. We're here to win a football game. And I'm going to see to it personally that there isn't any funny business."

That night—or, more accurately, early Thursday morning—Matuszak was restless, bothered by the insomnia that had dogged him since childhood. Wednesday night had always been a night to party, following as it did the hardest practice of the week for the defensive players. He decided to go for a stroll on Bourbon Street. The stroll lasted several hours, and Matuszak finally rolled into the Thursday morning press conference, which had started at 9:00 A.M., at 10:35. His absence was obvious, because players at these press conferences sit at tables with their names on them, so writers can interview them; Matuszak's table was conspicuously empty. As always, Matuszak had the last word. "I am the enforcer," he said. "That's why I was out on the street, to make sure no one else was."

Not all the Raiders were out there with Matuszak. "I was concentrating on my job, watching films, figuring what I had to do," Plunkett said. "By that time I was pretty banged up. I had a torn rotator cuff in my left shoulder, and I had a real bad bruise down below. I could hardly run. The only time I ran was on game day. I was pretty much a physical wreck. But

I took my cortisone shots on game day and felt pretty good for the game."

Davis wasn't bothered by the players' partying, and neither was Plunkett, who thought it kept them loose for the game. "I think it helps to be loose in a big game," he said. Plunkett added that he ran into Philadelphia's quarterback, Ron Jaworski, before the game and shook his hand, but "he looked like he didn't know what was going to happen. He didn't have that look of confidence I thought he would have—and should have."

The Raiders were certainly confident, and they were approaching the game much differently than the Eagles were. Not that they weren't working hard in practice—in fact, Gene Upshaw got into a fight with a reserve defensive lineman one day—but the tone set by Davis and coach Tom Flores was much different than that set by Dick Vermeil, the Eagles coach. Davis had always believed in allowing his players to be individuals, in dress and behavior. Vermeil, as much as any coach in the NFL, wanted his players to conform to dress and behavior codes. The Eagles arrived in New Orleans all dressed in green, the team color; the Raiders, as usual, were dressed in various styles, none of them from the pages of *Gentlemen's Quarterly*. As for breaking curfew, when Vermeil was asked what he would have done if one of his players had acted as Matuszak had, he said, "I'd have put him on the first plane back to Philadelphia."

Vermeil had done a remarkable job with the Eagles, who had been a perennial second-division team, by virtue of a work ethic that eventually drove him out of the game, a victim of coaching burnout. He worked such long hours that he had a cot put in his office, to sleep nights. That kind of drive got Vermeil and the Eagles to the Super Bowl, but once they were there it probably worked against them. "We knew that Vermeil had worked them so hard, we had an obligation to the rest of the league," Upshaw said. "They're such copycats in this league. If it had worked for Vermeil, they'd all be working the crap out of their players. For the rest of the league, we had to beat them."

There was added pressure for the Eagles because they were upholding the interests of the league. The commissioner, Pete Rozelle, would be presenting the Vince Lombardi Trophy to the owner of the winning team, and he most emphatically did not want to present it to Davis, with whom he was battling in court.

All that extracurricular baggage may have bothered the Eagles. It certainly didn't bother Davis—who would invent opponents if he didn't already have them—or his team.

Plunkett thought that the Raiders had the advantage for an odd reason: the Eagles had beaten them during the regular season. "When you've lost to a team, unless it's a real blowout, you're going to be better prepared than they are the second time you play," he told me. "Because they were successful, they weren't going to change what they did, but because we had lost, we had to find ways to defeat what they had done the first time. We were concerned after what they did to us the first time, beating us to a pulp on defense. We had a very good game plan. We got rid of the ball quicker. I'd been around the league long enough to tell my receivers to, instead of running a pattern fourteen yards, run it at twelve, so I could get rid of the ball faster. We ran some screens and quick passes, so even if the linemen missed blocks, the ball was gone. It was similar to what the 49ers do now."

"They had run stunts all over the place in that game in the regular season," Upshaw said. "When we came back home, Ollie Spencer told us, 'Until you stop those stunts, you're going to see them.' It's a rule in football that if you don't stop something you're going to see it for the next three weeks. So we had learned how to stop them."

Defensively, the Raiders felt that they could control Jaworski; they had done it in the first game, and they would do it this time. The problem was to get their offense working. "Everybody had picked Philadelphia to beat us because they'd beat us before," Upshaw said. "But we knew going into that game that we could beat them. We had a lot going for us emotionally. We wanted to stand up for Al, who had always supported us. We had worked our asses off to get there. It was Plunkett's first time, Flores's first time as a head coach."

As often happens in the Super Bowl, the game didn't live up to the pregame hype. The Raiders took a 14–0 lead in the first quarter, and the Eagles never got closer than 11 points the rest of the way, in a 27–10 Oakland win.

One of the Raiders' changes from the regular-season game with the Eagles was to go back to their original blocking scheme in the offensive line. In the earlier game, the Eagles defensive linemen had used a lot of stunts, and Raiders Art Shell and Gene Upshaw had followed them, often knocking each other out of the play and letting the Eagles through. This time they "stayed home" and blocked whatever defensive linemen came their way. Plunkett was sacked only once in the game.

Given time to throw, he had easy pickings, because the Philadelphia cornerbacks couldn't begin to cover Cliff Branch and Bob Chandler one on one. Plunkett threw three touchdown passes, two to Branch, completed 13 passes out of 21, for 261 yards, and was named the game's Most Valuable Player, to cap his comeback year. As Plunkett admitted later, he also got lucky on one play in the first quarter. "I was running around trying to get away from pressure, and I saw Kenny King about twenty yards downfield. I threw it to him, and he ran another sixty yards for our second touchdown. That could just as easily have been a sack, but it turned out right for us."

To Todd Christensen, later to become an All-Pro tight end but then a special-teams player, that one play was a microcosm of the season. "A lot of what happened to us that year was pure luck," he told me. "King would never be confused with Marcus Allen for his catching ability, but he caught that one. That was the year of stickum, and when we looked at the films later we saw that King actually caught the ball between his wrists. It never hit his hands."

Christensen remembered another part of that play. When Jerry Robinson, an Eagles outside linebacker, who later became a Raider, blitzed from the outside, Gene Upshaw "did an absolute takedown. I mean, if you were watching a football game for the first time, you'd have asked, 'Do they allow wrestling in the NFL?' But Ben Dreith was the referee that day, and he always liked us because he went back to the AFL days. Nothing was called, but I think if there'd been any other referee it would have been called. And that really changed the game. Instead of scoring, if we'd been shoved back to our ten, we might have had to punt and give the Eagles good field position, and who knows what would have happened from then?"

Not surprisingly, the much-awaited confrontation between Rozelle and Davis turned out to be a dud, too. Rozelle, who had started his career in public relations, is a smooth man in public presentations, and Davis, though always eager for a fight, doesn't like direct, one-on-one confrontations. He tends to conduct his battles through others. Upshaw had blustered before the game about the players confronting Rozelle, but that didn't happen, either. With Art Shell taking charge, the players were courteous to Rozelle, not wanting to spoil their triumph with a silly performance in the locker room.

"I think it's a great credit to you for putting this team together," Rozelle said to Davis, "and I think that Tom Flores clearly did one of the great coaching jobs in recent years—all season and particularly today." The two shook hands, and Davis said, "Thanks very much, commissioner. This was the Oakland Raiders' finest hour."

It was, of course, almost the final hour for the *Oakland* Raiders, as the fans who turned out by the thousands to greet the Raiders on their return home and watch them parade down Oakland's Broadway the next day probably knew. Many season-ticket holders finally conceded and gave up their tickets for the 1981 season. For the first time since 1968, there were empty seats in the Oakland Coliseum at Raiders games.

That last season was a poor one, too. "I hurt my thumb in the first game," Plunkett remembered, "and I couldn't throw long at all. We got shut out three games in a row, which was embarrassing as hell. Because we won the Super Bowl, we didn't make some of the changes that probably should have been made. Uppy and Art were getting older, and at some of the other positions players were getting up in age. When you win it's hard to make those changes. I thought that hurt us enormously."

The Raiders finished 7–9 for the year, and the most memorable event was a Monday-night home game on December 7. To protest the imminent move to Los Angeles, a large segment of the crowd—as much as a fourth of it—stayed out of the stadium for the first five minutes of the game. (One distraught fan brought a banner that read: WILL ROGERS NEVER MET AL DAVIS.)

The ABC-TV crew did not mention the fans' protest, nor did the cameras pan over the empty seats in the stadium.

• • •

When the jury ruled for the Raiders and the Los Angeles Coliseum on May 7, 1982, the NFL's attorneys immediately filed for a stay until the verdict could be appealed, and Judge Pregerson gave temporary relief until July 2, so that the appeal could be heard by the Ninth Circuit Court of Appeals. That court held over the appeal until the following year (when it denied a motion to overturn), and on July 7 Al Davis signed a new memorandum of agreement in Los Angeles, covering the next ten seasons.

The Raiders played their 1982 season in Los Angeles, but they still had one foot in northern California. They held their training camp in Santa Rosa again, and they still practiced in Oakland, at the facility built for them on Port of Oakland land. Except for one weekend, when they played the San Francisco 49ers at Candlestick Park, they had to take a flight for *every* game, including short flights to Los Angeles for "home" games.

"I'll never forget that season," Upshaw said. "I told the players the 49ers game would be our only 'home' game. The players didn't know what to do because, even though the franchise had been moved, there were still appeals and even one case—the eminent-domain one—still going. So they kept their homes in Oakland."

Not just the players. Davis hasn't sold his home in the Oakland area, and his wife still lives there, although she travels to the Raiders games. Davis keeps an apartment in Marina del Rey, a Los Angeles suburb. And Davis has never completely severed his ties with Oakland. His closest friends are from there: Oakland furniture dealer Sam Bercovich is always in Davis's private box at games, and Davis talks and visits frequently with Bob Albo. Jim Otto, the Hall of Fame center from the Oakland years, also is often in Davis's box at games.

Davis and Los Angeles have never been a good mix; Los Angeles is the land of illusion, and Davis is the nitty-gritty, practical guy for whom reality—the reality of winning—is everything.

"I'll never forget this," Mel Durslag said. "When he moved to L.A., CBS did a feature that opened with people getting out of Rolls-Royces in front of some posh shop on Rodeo Drive. They said, 'Now, this is Al Davis's country.' Well, nothing could be more remote from Al Davis's way of life. Then they showed some movie stars, which is far removed from him, too. He's the most antisocial guy I've ever seen. Nobody impresses him in the picture business. He's met a couple of guys along the way. He's friends with James Garner, who used to be on the sidelines, even when the team played in Oakland. I think he might have been friends with Ricardo Montalban. That's about it. Other owners are always entertaining celebrities in their boxes at the game, but you look up into Al's box and who's there? The well-known Sam Bercovich."

In Los Angeles, some say people are not big time unless they're instantly recognizable in the Polo Lounge in Beverly Hills. There's some question whether Al Davis has ever been in the Polo Lounge, and it is nowhere in his sense of priorities. He has always had his favorite restaurants, but they have been modest ones, where he knew the owner and could expect to have a table always ready for him (always with a telephone) and to have his privacy respected. His pattern has not changed in Los Angeles.

"He has a single-purpose life, and that's the football team,"

Durslag said. "He has no hobbies. He doesn't play golf. The football team is his life, literally. There's no other dimension. He reads, but he doesn't go to movies, he doesn't go to plays. He works on the football team, day and night. He goes to the office in the morning, goes to practice during the season. After practice he works out and goes to dinner, sometimes by himself, sometimes with someone else. Then he goes back to his apartment and looks at films. That's his life. That's all he seems to care about. I regard that as a form of mild lunacy, but it's his life.

"Al lives very simply. He has an apartment in the Marina, but it's not a luxurious place. It doesn't reflect his money. He's not a guy who even begins to live up to his wealth. He doesn't buy a lot of clothes, though they're good clothes. He wears Raiders stuff a lot."

• • •

Al Davis had again trusted his own judgment when he drafted USC running back Marcus Allen before the 1982 season. Although Allen had been a Heisman Trophy winner, most of the scouts doubted that he was fast enough to be a topflight running back in the pros. Many thought he would have to be shifted to wide receiver, to take advantage of his pass-catching skills, and teams find it difficult to use a number-one draft pick for a player who will have to switch positions. Two running backs, Gerald Willhite of San Jose State and Darrin Nelson of Stanford, were taken ahead of Allen, but neither has had anything like Allen's pro career. Only Clem Daniels can seriously challenge Allen's right to be called the best Raiders running back ever.

Allen fit perfectly in Davis's system. In his rookie year, which was cut to nine games because of a players' strike, Allen rushed for 697 yards, caught 38 passes for another 401 yards, and scored 14 touchdowns. Projecting those figures over the usual sixteen-game season, Allen would have had 1,239 yards rushing, 68 receptions for 713 yards, and a total of 25 touchdowns; the latter would have been an NFL record.

Allen was outstanding from the beginning, rushing for 116 yards as the Raiders opened the 1982 season with a 23–17 win over the 49ers in that one "home" game in San Francisco. The next week was even better, a 38–14 win over the Falcons in Atlanta. Then the season took a two-month hiatus because of a strike called by the NFL Players Association—a strike that would probably have been settled much more quickly, and with less acrimony, if Al Davis had been involved in the negotiations. He wasn't, of course, because of his lawsuit against the league.

The relationship between the Players Association and the owners had been a stormy one for years, marked by an earlier strike in 1974 and lawsuits in the mid-1970s. Free agency was at the center of the problem. A court ruling in 1977, in a case involving John Mackey, a former Baltimore Colts tight end, had said that the restrictive NFL player contracts were an antitrust violation. That was consistent with a 1976 ruling by an arbitrator that had granted free agency to baseball players whose contracts had expired. The NFL Players Association's executive director, Ed Garvey, however, had bargained away free agency in exchange for a requirement that players join his union. (Violations of antitrust statutes can be protected by a labor agreement.) That was where matters stood when the 1982 strike was called.

Earlier, Davis had been a member of the NFL's prestigious Competition Committee, which makes recommendations to the owners on everything from rules to playing conditions. But he had been taken off the committee and thus had far less influence than before. Even so, he attempted to intervene in this case and suggested a plan that involved bonuses for striking players, as a way to get them back to work. Davis had a more realistic view of what a team's relationship with its players should be than did many of the NFL owners. Instead of viewing the strike as a "war" that the owners had to win, he just wanted to resume the season (especially since he had his team back on track). But his fellow owners would not support his plan, and the strike went on for seven weeks. Lacking the financial resources of the owners, the players finally had to give in and return to their teams.

The Raiders resumed winning after the strike, and they ended the season with an 8-1 record, the best in the AFC and tied with the Washington Redskins for the best in the NFL. The play-offs that year included three rounds, counting the league championship game, and after beating the Cleveland Browns, 27-10, in the first round, the Raiders lost to the New York Jets, 17-14, in the second round. "Everything evens out," Todd Christensen noted philosophically. "In 1980 we didn't deserve to win. In 1982 we should have been in the Super Bowl, and I think we would have beaten the Redskins there, too."

Although the loss to the Jets was unexpected and a bitter disappointment, it had been a good season for the Raiders, and the crowd of 90,688 at the Los Angeles Coliseum for the Jets game seemed to justify Davis's decision to move the team.

Appearances were deceiving. There was already trouble in paradise.

·10·

A Third Win, but
Trouble in Paradise

When Al Davis signed his deal with Los Angeles, Scott Ostler
gave him this advice in his *Los Angeles Times* column:

"Welcome to L.A., Al Davis. Sorry there's no confetti and
banners, Al, but we used 'em all up on the Dodgers and Lakers
victory parades. This town is practically an assembly line of
world champions.

"The teams that need work, we send 'em out to the
suburbs for a season. We've got a couple of 'em called the
Angels and the Rams being tuned up in Anaheim right
now. . . .

"Al, I think it's only fair that we let you know that there
are a few things we expect of you, too. A little friendly advice:
This isn't Possum Corners, and merely showing up with a football team won't impress our sophisticated fans. We have come
to expect a certain level of, uh, entertainment, I guess you
could call it. . . ."

Davis either didn't read Ostler's column or didn't pay any
attention to it. He should have. Los Angeles is a tough market—some think the toughest in the country—and Davis did

little to accommodate it. That hurt him from the beginning, and it got worse when the team turned bad.

The Raiders immediately got involved in a ticket snafu, which was blamed on Al LoCasale. Tickets did not get out on time, and some influential people got bad seats—a category that includes about 75 percent of the seating at the Los Angeles Coliseum. It was hardly all LoCasale's fault. NFL teams usually sell most, if not all, of their tickets on a seasonal basis, three months before the Raiders could even get started in 1982. Moreover, the Raiders had long been notorious for their lack of modern technology, Davis believing that everything important should be stored in the mind, not on computers, which might be tapped by others. Finally, a certain complacency may have set in because ticket selling in Oakland had been simple, most season-ticket holders renewing year after year.

No matter. When something goes wrong, Al Davis always looks for a scapegoat, and LoCasale was elected. A man who revered Davis and had deflected heat from him in Oakland for years, LoCasale was nonetheless banished from Davis's good graces. "LoCasale never recovered from that," said Mark Heisler, the *Los Angeles Times* beat writer for the Raiders for five years. When I visited the Raiders facility in the fall of 1990, LoCasale was working as the intermediary between writers and head coach Art Shell, but he is not as deeply involved with the operation as he was before 1982.

The ticket problem was quickly rectified, but a larger problem—Davis's indifference, bordering on contempt, toward public relations—plagues the Raiders even now. In Oakland it hadn't mattered, because the combination of a relatively small stadium, a rabid fan base, and a consistently winning team had filled the stadium for thirteen years. In Los Angeles, Davis had a cavernous stadium to fill, with more than 90,000 seats, and, as Davis himself testified in the antitrust trial, it is a bad stadium, with only about 28,000 seats between the goal lines. Because of the track circling the field, the stands are set back, so that even the seats between the goal lines are not close to the field.

Moreover, Davis's team was now playing in a city whose fans are notorious for their fickleness. No California city will support a losing team for long, but Los Angeles fans will drop one almost overnight. In 1967, when pitcher Sandy Koufax retired from the Dodgers and they dropped from a pennant winner to seventh place, their attendance fell by a million. More telling, in the second game of the 1990–91 NBA season, the Lakers—a team that had won seven conference titles and five NBA championships in the 1980s—could not sell out against the Portland Trail Blazers, the team expected to battle them for the division title. Into this area, Al Davis brought a team coming off a losing season. Not surprisingly, the Raiders had only one good crowd in their four regular-season home games in 1982, 65,776 for a game against the Rams. Attendance at the other three games fell in the 52,000 to 55,000 range.

Davis made the situation worse by not even trying to ingratiate himself with the media, politicians, or other influential people. Even with Durslag he wasn't often willing to be quoted. That didn't bother Durslag, because Davis would help him in a more important way. "He would explain things if I needed it," Durslag said. "You want to write intelligently, so if you can get somebody to explain to you, you can write without looking like a horse's ass. Al would do that for me, and that was more important than being able to quote Al Davis."

Davis was unavailable to almost everyone else. In Oakland he had usually made time for the beat writers, but he no longer did that in Los Angeles. Heisler thought it might have been because of Davis's conflict with the Times, the area's major newspaper. "Davis didn't like Alan Greenberg, who was the first guy on the beat for the Times," said Heisler—who viewed his reassignment to the Lakers beat in 1990 as "being paroled" after five years—"and he didn't like my coverage, although I don't think it was personal with me. So if he'd talked to other beat writers, it would have given the Times a chance to claim that he was playing favorites because he wouldn't talk to Alan or me."

During that first year Durslag tried to get Davis to talk to the beat writers. "I said to him, 'Al, the guys like you, you talk their language. Why don't you meet with these guys every two weeks and have coffee and just talk football? They'd really like that, and you'd help yourself a lot. You've got nothing to lose.' But he wouldn't do it. First of all, he said, 'I don't like to be doing that and upstaging my coach.' Secondly, he resents encroachment on his time. But he does have guys he talks to, all over the country. He'll talk to Jim Murray, Leonard Koppett, Bob Oates, Will McDonough."

Davis's alleged concern for his coach can't be reconciled with the way he has treated his coaches over the years. He's been willing, even eager, to let the world know who's really running the Raiders, who's really in charge. He didn't worry about upstaging John Rauch or even John Madden. Tom Flores remains little more than a shadow person to most people because the Davis image was so overpowering, and nobody believes that his current coach, Art Shell, has much autonomy.

"Al decides whom he wants to talk to and the guys he doesn't want to talk to," Durslag said. "There's no way for an outsider to try to understand how he reaches these decisions, except that he's partial to more seasoned sportswriters. If he mentions old-time players like Marion Motley or Otto Graham, and the reporter's eyes flutter . . . he can't stand that. So the guys he talks to are ones who have been around for a while. He feels it's his life, and he doesn't give a damn what others think. He'd rather we all write nice things about him, of course, but he's not going to change his life so that will happen."

There is a sharp contradiction between what Davis can be when he chooses and what he actually is most of the time. "In one-on-one situations," noted Durslag, "most people find that, even if they went in disliking him, they come out liking the guy." Bill Robertson, Davis, and Ed Snider of Spectacor had a meeting in November 1991 with influential members of the community to discuss the new deal for renovating the Los Angeles Coliseum. "Al absolutely charmed them," Robertson told me. "He was very gracious, and everybody was very pleased with the way the meeting went."

That's the "good Davis," in sharp contrast to his behavior when he first came to Los Angeles.

"Before he moved here," said Durslag, "his biggest enemy was Pete Schabarum. But when he moved, Schabarum wrote him a letter. I read it. It was a very warm letter, welcoming Al and the Raiders to Los Angeles. Schabarum told him he had just the place for the Raiders to train, in Norwalk. He knew the mayor and volunteered to talk to him on behalf of the Raiders. Al didn't even answer Schabarum. Pete's a hard-nosed guy, and that started the feud.

"Al doesn't do little things involving the social graces. He doesn't write thank-you notes, and he doesn't respond to people who help him. At the same time, he thinks in his mind that he'll be there to come through for people if they need him. He embarrassed the hell out of me one time. I'd been backing the Raiders, and my publisher at the *Herald*, John McCabe, just let me run with it. And the paper took up the Raiders as an editorial campaign. McCabe, who's a great guy, was a Raiders fan, and he bought season tickets. The paper ran a nice editorial on Al when everybody was going crazy about the way the Raiders were handling ticket sales. He sent Al a copy of the editorial and a nice long note, and he gave me a blind copy of the note. When I saw it, I said to Al, 'These guys have been very supportive of me. Please write the guy a note.' He said, 'Yeah, I'll do it,' but he never did. When McCabe needed something, Al helped him. But letter writing isn't part of his makeup. He feels if he means right toward a guy, that's all that's important. I'm not sure he's right about that."

As with everything else, the Raiders' public relations reflect Davis's views. The Raiders don't even *have* a public relations director, and haven't since the mid-1970s in Oakland. In the publicity-conscious NFL, that's incredible, and it drives other teams' public relations people crazy; when their teams are playing the Raiders, they never know who to call for information, credentials for their beat writers, or interviews with players.

There's no question that has hurt the image of both Davis

and the club. "I think most people get their perception of Davis from the media, which may not always give the whole picture," said longtime Raiders announcer Bill King, an avowed admirer of Davis and close enough to him to be a regular at his pregame Saturday night dinners. "I've found him to be incredibly loyal to his friends. I just don't see that side of Al that I read about so often. I think, in a way, Al is like a gunslinger from the old West. It's like everybody is out to prove he's the one who can bring Davis down. I think that happened in Oakland, and I think it's happened in Los Angeles, with the politicians there."

It all goes back to Davis's unwillingness to take the time to explain his actions. "Al's idea of PR is winning the Super Bowl," Durslag said. In the Raiders' second year in Los Angeles, amid all the chaos and conflict, that's exactly what the team did.

• • •

"I've always admired Al's ability," King said. "He has always been able to rebuild and keep things going. The team missed the play-offs in 1971, but he picked up players like Jack Tatum and Phil Villapiano, and he was back the next year. I thought John Madden stayed a little too long with some of the veterans who had done so well for him, guys like Pete Banaszak, and fell off to a couple of 9-and-7 years. But then the next year Al puts together a team that wins the Super Bowl. Same thing after the 1981 season—two years later he's got another Super Bowl winner."

To quote Durslag: "One of Davis's real strengths is knowing what holes need to be filled and being able to put his hands on that kind of player. He knows where to go for players, not just premium players but guys who can do the job adequately. He has a very good index on talent."

Nothing proved that more than the 1983 team, which Davis put together in a variety of ways. He already had Jim Plunkett, and he had drafted Marcus Allen in 1982. To correct an obvious weakness at one cornerback, he signed All-Pro cornerback Mike Haynes, who had been holding out because of a contract dispute with the New England Patriots, during the 1983 season. Davis didn't care how much he had to pay Haynes, if Haynes could make the Raiders a winner. He did cost them their number-one draft pick in 1984 as compensation, but that was a steal—they could never have gotten a player of his ability with that draft pick.

Greg Townsend, who would become a pass-rush specialist in the defensive line, was a fourth-round draft choice; with his shaved head, he brought back memories of Otis ("University of Mars") Sistrunk. Howie Long, who had played his rookie year in Oakland, was about to develop into the most feared defensive lineman in the league.

In 1980 Davis had drafted Matt Millen, a defensive lineman from Penn State, who was a fearsome middle linebacker for the Raiders for years. Millen was a cauldron of emotion, striding up and down the sideline when he wasn't in the game, grabbing teammates or yelling at them in the course of action, thrusting a fist into the sky after a big play, arguing vehemently with coaches on the sideline.

A gentle man off the field, Millen has a short fuse when he's on it. One time he was angered because Chicago Bears guard Kurt Becker didn't listen when Millen warned him twice to stop diving at the back of his knees. "I kicked him and told him to not ever do that again," Millen said. "He does it again, and I lost my mind. On the next play I didn't even look at the ballcarrier. I went after Becker. I got up on top of him, got him by the throat, and was just pounding him. I grabbed his face mask, twisted it around, and spit right in his face. On the last play of the game, I chased him all the way up the tunnel at the Coliseum, and I'm about halfway up there when I thought, 'Man, what am I doing?' I really felt bad. I found him outside the locker room and said, 'Excuse me, Kurt, but I really feel bad that I did that. I never should have spit on you.' "

Then there was linebacker Ted Hendricks. Hendricks, who hated practice, once rode to the workout field in full uniform on a charging horse, carrying an orange traffic cone as a lance. He was known to practice with crow or ostrich feathers stuck in his helmet, and one time, just before Halloween, he wore no helmet at all, just a pumpkin. Another time he put up a table at midfield, unfolded a café umbrella, and greeted his teammates while sipping lemonade. "Al Davis is interested in what happens between the lines. Otherwise, he'll leave you alone," Hendricks said, when asked about his behavior. "As long as you are successful, no one should be able to say anything to you, except maybe pat you on the back."

With players like Millen and Hendricks already on hand, it was no surprise when Davis traded for Lyle Alzado, who fit right in. Although the Raiders were Alzado's third team, it could legitimately be said that he was born to be a Raider.

Alzado had been one of the best defensive linemen in the game when he played for the Denver Broncos and the Cleveland Browns. But the Browns thought he was at the end of his career and traded him to the Raiders on draft day in 1982— virtually giving him away for an eighth-round pick. Alzado had quite a bit left, as it happened, and he played four seasons with the Raiders. He was a throwback to the early Raiders, probably most resembling the hard-playing Ben Davidson. (In the spring of 1990 Alzado was stricken by a brain tumor, which he blamed on steroid use.)

Alzado's style wasn't a pose. He was a tough guy, who had considered a boxing career at one point. Boxing in the Police Athletic League in Brooklyn, he had a 44–1 record, and he went on to win the New York City heavyweight title in the Golden Gloves competition. Even after he turned to football, he had one more brief fling at boxing in 1979, in an eight-round exhibition against Muhammad Ali, then the world heavyweight champion. Alzado trained vigorously for the match against the overweight Ali, but whatever thoughts Alzado had of actually beating him were erased in the first few seconds of the match. At midring, Ali flicked three straight left jabs off the bridge of Alzado's nose, so fast that Alzado had no time to react. He realized then that he was badly overmatched, and he was content to protect himself and just spar with Ali for the remainder of the bout.

The Raiders made good use of Alzado's aggressive personality, and even encouraged it. Before a game someone would feed him an outrageous quote from an opposing player to psych him up. "I don't know if what they tell me is true or not," Alzado said at the time, "but I can't take a chance that they're lying to me."

Offensively, Davis moved to correct other weaknesses. When his number-one draft pick, Don Mosebar, an offensive lineman from USC, was unable to play because of a bad back, Davis traded for veteran guard Charlie Hannah of the Tampa Bay Buccaneers.

The most intriguing story on that 1983 team, though, was tight end Todd Christensen, who dramatically illustrated the tiny margin between hero and bum in pro football. An unwanted player who had been cut by two teams and rejected by five others after tryouts, Christensen went on to become an All-Pro tight end and had four straight seasons in which he caught more passes than any Raiders receiver ever had: 92, 80, 82, and 95, in 1983 through 1986.

Christensen was drafted as a running back by the Dallas Cowboys; asked to play tight end, he refused and was cut. He was picked up by the New York Giants and played one regular-season game before being cut. Then he was picked up by the Raiders, five games into the 1979 season, and played on special teams the rest of the year. Again Davis would do it his way. He had always felt that the size and ability required of tight ends and fullbacks were comparable, and he had successfully shifted Billy Cannon from fullback to tight end, Hewritt Dixon from tight end to fullback. Both had become stars. Christensen's conversion to tight end would be his most successful yet.

"In minicamp in 1980, Tom Flores asked me what position I'd like to play," said Christensen, now an analyst for NBC. "I'd told the Cowboys I wouldn't play tight end, but by 1980 I was twenty-four and finally getting smart. Do whatever it takes to make 'massa' happy. Plus I knew by then I didn't have the body to be a pro running back. So I said I wanted to play tight end. My big break came in an exhibition game in 1980, with the 49ers, when the 49ers got up on us, 33–0. We're talking real garbage time here, so I got in the game along with Jim Plunkett and caught a couple of touchdown passes. Big deal, right? Well, it was for me, because at least it proved I could do it, and that was the beginning of my rapport with Plunkett."

By 1983, Christensen was the Raiders' main receiving threat almost by default. Cliff Branch was thirty-three and had lost a step. The other wide receiver, Malcolm Barnwell, had speed but no understanding of the offense. "You'd call a play, and he'd invariably run the wrong one," Plunkett said. "You had to talk to him constantly in the huddle. He was confused out there all the time."

Barnwell was virtually the only weakness on that team, probably the best the Raiders ever fielded. "I mentioned on the first broadcast that I had a feeling this team could go all the way," Bill King recalled. "The overwhelming memory I have of that team is speed. Al has always liked speed, and this time he really had it." Davis also had players who were confident of their own, and the team's, ability. Typical of their attitude was a statement by offensive guard Mickey Marvin when he heard another player repeat a favorite coaches' cliché, "We'll take what the defense gives us." Marvin snorted and said, "Screw that. We'll take what we want to take."

"We could score on anybody," Plunkett remembered. "It was Marcus Allen's second year. He was a great running back, very explosive, and he caught the ball very well. Todd Christensen had a superb year—he really came to the forefront. Kenny King was playing fullback, and with his speed at fullback, he surprised a lot of people. Defensively, we were very, very good. We controlled the line of scrimmage."

Christensen remembered the close games. "We were 12–4 for the season, but there were games we barely won. Ted Hendricks won one game by blocking a field goal at the end" (a 21–20 win over the Kansas City Chiefs). "Against Denver, John Elway first showed the kind of skills that would make him such a great player when he took the Broncos the length of the field for a 20–19 lead. But Plunkett completed four straight passes, and then Chris Bahr kicked a field goal to win it with no time left. That game was at the L.A. Coliseum, and everybody was standing and cheering. But I had just read Bill Russell's *Second Wind*, and I remembered him saying that the same people who cheered him were the people who booed him later. In sports you should savor the moment, because there are so few of them, but all I could think of was that two weeks from now these people might be booing."

Plunkett remembered that season for the quality of the team. "We were so good, the only one who could have screwed it up was me. I always liked to take chances, put the ball up and go downfield. That got me in trouble sometimes, as I'd be the first to admit, but as often as not we'd come up with enough big plays to offset the mistakes." As a matter of fact, Plunkett *did* get into trouble and was benched midway through the season.

After a 4–0 start, the Raiders lost to the Washington Redskins and the Seattle Seahawks in high-scoring games, sandwiched around the 21–20 win over Kansas City that Hendricks had saved with his field-goal block. Against the Redskins, the Raiders played without Allen, who had a pulled hamstring, and Washington took an early 20–3 lead. Then Plunkett hit Branch on a team-record 99-yard touchdown pass, Greg Pruitt returned a punt 97 yards for a score, and the Raiders had a 35–20 lead. But Washington wasn't through. The Redskins rallied for 17 points, highlighted by a 66-yard pass from Joe Theismann to Joe Washington, to win the game, 37–35.

That loss was understandable, because the Redskins had won the 1982 Super Bowl (and would return to the Super Bowl after the 1983 season), but the Seahawks were a middle-of-the-road team, 9–7 in 1983, a team that the Raiders should have handled with relative ease. Interestingly, though, since they came into the NFL, in 1977, the Seahawks have finished ahead of the Raiders only five times—but they are the only team to have a series edge over the Raiders, 14–12 as of the beginning of the 1991 season. (The Philadelphia Eagles are 3–2 against the Raiders in the regular season but lost to them in the 1981 Super Bowl.) "They've never bought into the Raiders mystique," Christensen said.

In the loss to the Seahawks, Plunkett was intercepted three times and sacked eight times. After that game Davis ordered coach Tom Flores to use Marc Wilson at quarterback. "I felt that was unfair, because we'd put plenty of points on the board," Plunkett said. "I was benched because of my mistakes; I threw too many interceptions. But we still put a lot of points on the board."

There was more to it than that—as there usually is with Al Davis. He had drafted Wilson, an All-American from Brigham Young University, in 1980, and he was anxious to see what Wilson could do.

Wilson had a great game in his first start, throwing for 318 yards and three touchdowns against the Dallas Cowboys, though the Raiders still needed a Chris Bahr field goal at the end to win another offensive shoot-out, 40–38. But the next week, against the Seahawks again, Wilson threw three interceptions and was sacked five times. The Raiders lost, 34–21.

Unfortunately, that would be the pattern for Wilson, one of Davis's bigger mistakes and an example of how he was changing for the worse in his evaluation of players. Davis always used to go "against the numbers," searching out players who were productive rather than those who had nothing but the physical attributes of size, speed, and arm strength that the scouts focus on, sometimes to the exclusion of ability. Now Davis, too, seemed to be going for the "numbers." Wilson certainly had a lot in his favor. He was 6 feet 5, which gave him the ability to look downfield and throw over the defensive linemen, and he had the arm to throw long or short with accuracy. In practice he would appear to be a great quarterback. At times he would appear that way in games, too, but more often than not he'd have a bad game just when the Raiders needed a big one.

The Raiders season was probably salvaged when Wilson hurt his shoulder in the next game, against Kansas City, trying to make a tackle after an interception. The Raiders were trailing at the time, but Plunkett came in and guided them to a win. With Plunkett again established at quarterback, the Raiders won six of their last seven games to win their division.

In the final game of the regular season, against the San Diego Chargers, Todd Christensen caught three touchdown passes. "I had been in a race all year with Cleveland's Ozzie Newsome for the NFL receiving title. Don't ever let athletes tell you they're not aware of their statistics. I came into the huddle late in the game and said, 'Hey, Plunk, I've got a chance to win this thing, so throw me a sure thing.' We had the game won by then, so he just sent me out on a route where I was sure to get open. I caught it, and I won the receiving title."

• • •

By the time the Raiders got to the play-offs in 1983, said cornerback Lester Hayes, "we felt we were invincible. We felt we couldn't lose." Certainly they played that way. Few teams have been so overpowering in postseason play as that Raiders team, which won three games by a cumulative score of 106–33.

Even years later, the players remembered how good the team was. After the 1990 Super Bowl, in which the San Francisco 49ers crushed the Denver Broncos, 55–10, Christensen got a call from his former teammate, Matt Millen, by then an inside linebacker for the 49ers. "He called me from New Orleans," Christensen said, "and told me, 'Hey, Todd, our 1983 team beats these guys.' Well, that was pretty incredible to me, after the way the 49ers had taken the Broncos apart. Everybody was saying they were the best of all time because of their speed.

"But Matt starts going down the matchups. He says Hayes and Haynes would have shut off Jerry Rice and John Taylor. Sure, Joe Montana would complete his share, but he wouldn't kill us because we had such a great defense, with Vann McElroy and Mike Davis as the safeties, Ted Hendricks and Rod Martin as outside linebackers. Reggie Kinlaw would have sacked

Montana a couple of times. Then I said, 'But, Matt, we didn't have great wide receivers. Cliff Branch was slowing down, and Malcolm Barnwell? Forget it.' But Matt said, 'Hey, we win, 17– 10, because you wear out the safety, Chet Brooks.' I couldn't argue with that."

First to fall to the Raiders in the play-offs were the Pittsburgh Steelers, a 38–10 loser at the Coliseum. Hayes set the tone with an early interception of a Cliff Stoudt pass for a touchdown, and Allen scored twice. Next up were the Seattle Seahawks, the Raiders' nemesis, for the conference championship game.

Practice was so intense that week that Tom Flores shortened the workout on the final day—there were so many fights that he was afraid someone might get hurt. "What's wrong with fighting?" Lyle Alzado asked Flores. "I never knew a man I didn't want to fight."

"There were 93,000 people at the Coliseum," Christensen remembered, "and you didn't have to be a genius to figure this is an important game. I've always said, don't give me any speeches, and Tom wasn't much of a speech maker. But after he had said a few words to us before the game, he turned it over to Lyle Alzado. Alzado was an absolute thespian, anyway, but he really turned it on. His speech was full of *k*s—I can't say the words because I'm a Mormon, but you can fill in the blanks. He talked about how the Seahawks thought they were going to beat the Raiders at their home, and as he talked his voice kept rising to a crescendo. The thing is, the team doesn't buy into that kind of thing usually, but this time everybody did. There was so much fervor; everybody was riveted. By the time Lyle was through, you could have brought back the old Packers or Steelers, and it wouldn't have made any difference. We were ahead, 30–0, at one point, and we coasted home, 30–14."

Even after that showing, the Raiders were underdogs to the Washington Redskins in the Super Bowl. That wasn't surprising, since the Redskins had won it the year before and had beaten the Raiders in the regular season. With their huge offensive line, known as "the Hogs," they were regarded as one of the top teams in the game's history.

The Raiders possessed some advantages the odds makers hadn't counted into the balance. One was the team speed that King had noted earlier; the Raiders, overall, were a much faster team than the Redskins. That gave Davis great confidence. "I've never seen Al so relaxed as he was before that game," King remembered. "He was nothing like he was for the Super Bowl against the Eagles, when he was antsy all week. This time he was very calm. He knew he had the team to win."

The biggest edge the Raiders had was Allen, who hadn't played in the regular-season game that the Redskins won. "In the first game, with Marcus out, we didn't have much of a running game and had to throw the ball," Plunkett said. "This time we had much more balance. Plus there was no way the Redskins could prepare for Marcus because they hadn't played against him. They said after the game that they just weren't prepared for him at all. I really felt I was the key to the game. I couldn't make mistakes and give them the opportunity to get into the game. Otherwise, I knew our defense could stop them, and we could put plenty of points on the board."

The Raiders' domination of the game started with their defense, drawn up by their defensive coordinator, Charley Sumner. Sumner was not a media favorite, because he gave terrible interviews. *San Francisco Chronicle* sportswriter C. W. Nevius recalled the time he overheard a Los Angeles sportswriter's "interview" with Sumner. "Charley was answering every question with 'yep' or 'nope.' Finally the guy asked him about a defense, and Charley said, 'You saw it. Write what you think.' I came up and said, 'Gee, Charley, you were really hard on that guy.' Charley said, 'Well, I don't know him at all. I'm not going to answer his questions. Now, it's different with you. I know you. What do you want to know?' So I asked him about a defense, and he said, "You saw it. Write what you think.' "

But the man can coach and is as innovative a defensive

thinker as anyone I've known. Against the Redskins he devised a perfect defense—and he called the play that decided the game.

Sumner had decided that the great Raiders corners, Lester Hayes and Mike Haynes, could take the Redskins receivers, Art Monk and Charlie Brown, one on one. He was right. Hayes and Haynes covered the Washington receivers so tightly that the Raiders defensive line was able to pressure quarterback Joe Theismann the whole game, and to sack him six times. Then Sumner and fellow assistant Steve Ortmayer devised a punt-blocking scheme. Overloading one side to make the Redskins think they were coming from there, the Raiders left Derrick Jensen alone on the other side. He slipped in to block a punt that the Raiders recovered for the game's first touchdown, in the first quarter. A 12-yard pass from Plunkett to Cliff Branch helped the Raiders to a 14–3 lead just before the end of the first half.

Now, with the Redskins holding the ball on their own 13-yard line and just 12 seconds left in the half, Washington coach Joe Gibbs thought he could catch the Raiders by surprise and called for a screen pass to Joe Washington. Sumner spotted the formation and remembered that the Redskins had used it for a screen pass in the regular-season game. He didn't have time to change the defense, but he sent in outside linebacker Jack Squirek as a substitute for Matt Millen and told him to look for a pass to Washington. Theismann retreated to pass and lofted it over the arms of Alzado—but he didn't see Squirek, who dashed into the middle of the play, intercepted the pass, and ran into the end zone. With the Raiders up, 21–3, at halftime, there was no way the Redskins could catch them.

But there was still one big play to come. Allen, who had scored an earlier touchdown, got the ball on a play that was supposed to go over left guard. Ken Coffey, the Washington strong safety, came up to support the run. Seeing him, Allen circled back and headed in the opposite direction. That kind of play is fairly common in college football, where running backs usually can outrun defenders. It's rare in pro ball, because the defenders often have the speed to catch backs—and Allen was not exceptionally fast. This time it worked, though. Coffey reached for Allen and just brushed him—as close as any Redskins defender got. Allen headed down the right sideline and raced to a 74-yard touchdown, the longest in Super Bowl history to that point.

"I felt somebody grab at me, and then I saw an alley," said Allen, probably as instinctive a running back as any in football. Darrell Green, the Redskins quick cornerback, "didn't see me going by," Allen went on, "and I thought I could outrun the other guys. Cliff Branch gave me a good block going down the sideline." That made the final score 38−9 and helped Allen, who gained 191 yards in the game, win the Most Valuable Player trophy.

Ironically, that triumphant game may have figured in Allen's later problems with the Raiders when, at Davis's orders, he was forced to play second fiddle to Bo Jackson. "If you think about it," Christensen said, "the Raiders have had a lot of great players, but there was never anybody bigger than Al Davis. But suddenly you had Marcus Allen, who had won the Heisman Trophy while playing for USC and who was now the Super Bowl MVP while playing for the team in Los Angeles, and for the moment Davis was overshadowed."

Overshadowed or not, Davis was savoring his triumph and wasting no opportunity to rub it in with NFL commissioner Pete Rozelle. It had been a big year for Davis, who had seemingly proved he was right about his decision to move: the Raiders had had two crowds of nearly 93,000 for their two play-off games at home.

In his postgame speech and trophy presentation Rozelle referred to Flores as "one of the best coaches in the game." Later Davis told reporters that Rozelle had slighted Flores. "He's one of the best in the *history* of the game," Davis insisted. Davis also cornered some reporters from Bay Area newspapers and repeated the theme he had used so often in court—that Rozelle was against him, the league was against him, but he had showed everyone.

It was tiresome, and even Davis finally realized it, saying, "Hey, I don't want to take away from the players. It's their day."

·11·

Al Davis
Doubts Himself

The Raiders followed their Super Bowl championship with seasons of 11−5 and 12−4 in 1984 and 1985. They couldn't get past the first round of the play-offs in either year, but the club averaged better than 70,000 in attendance per game for that period. Al Davis's idea of good public relations seemed to be working.

Then the bottom fell out. For four straight years, 1986 through 1989, the Raiders missed the play-offs, and Davis started to question himself, eventually even bringing in his first coach from outside the Raiders organization. The problem with his one-man rule was that the team collapsed when that one man wasn't paying attention. Davis had shifted his focus from the football field to the courtroom, and it showed in two particular problem areas—Marc Wilson and the draft.

Davis's mistakes in pushing certain players into the starting lineup could be overcome when the player was someone like Charles Philyaw, a defensive lineman. But this time the player was Wilson, a quarterback, and that was a much more critical position.

"It was a case of the 'tender trap,' because Wilson would show just enough to make you think he could be a good quarterback," announcer Bill King said. "Every year in training camp he'd look so good throwing the ball that everybody would say, 'Who needs Plunkett?' But then he'd have one of those awful games, and Jim would be back in there. It wasn't that he lacked courage, because I saw him take some terrible hits and come back. But he wasn't the quarterback you wanted in there for the final two minutes, when you needed that touchdown to win.

"I remember one game when he was rushed hard in the first quarter. I looked down at the bench, and he was just sitting there with his mouth open, looking vacantly out at the field. How would you like to have to block for that guy for the next three quarters? Players sense that in a quarterback, that he isn't the leader they need. He had all the physical attributes, a strong, accurate arm, but I always felt he was a little slow in getting the ball out there. The receiver would be open, and then he'd crank it up—and he didn't have a quick delivery. By the time the ball got there, the defensive back would have time to recover, and he'd make what looked like a great play to knock the ball down. But if the ball had gotten there just a split second sooner, it would have been a catch. In all the years I've been broadcasting, he was the most frustrating player I've seen. I wanted to come down out of the booth and just shake him."

To me, it seemed that Wilson was on the wrong team. A quiet person, he might have fit in perfectly on a team like the San Francisco 49ers, whose coach, Bill Walsh, wanted players who did not provoke other teams with their comments and who played in a controlled, almost businesslike fashion. Under Walsh, the 49ers had a system in which the premium was on the quarterback's completion of a high percentage of his passes, with few interceptions. In contrast, Davis had installed a gambling, almost reckless style. Jim Plunkett was certainly not the wild man off the field that Ken Stabler had been, but he was more than willing to risk an interception in an attempt to make a big play. Daryle Lamonica had been the same way. Wilson didn't have that kind of nerve—but still he threw too many interceptions.

Davis's almost willful blindness to Wilson's deficiencies damaged the Raiders both present and future. They not only lost games, they also lost a chance at Dan Marino in the 1983 draft. Because he had Wilson, Davis passed on Marino (as did twenty-five other clubs, of course), and the Miami Dolphins got him on the next-to-last pick of the first round. And there may never have been a quarterback better suited to Davis's system than Dan Marino. Davis's hope that Wilson would make it big also cost Davis money, because he had to sign Marc to a big contract to keep him from Donald Trump, who wanted Wilson for his New Jersey Generals of the USFL. But Davis wasn't the only Raider who made a mistake on Wilson. On draft day in 1986, Davis was ready to trade him to the Philadelphia Eagles when coach Tom Flores talked him out of it.

Finally, just before the second game of the 1988 season, Davis traded offensive tackle Jim Lachey to the Washington Redskins for quarterback Jay Schroeder. Davis had stolen Lachey from the San Diego Chargers, giving overweight lineman John Clay in exchange, and Lachey was soon being compared to legendary Raiders linemen like Art Shell and Gene Upshaw. Even Davis wasn't sure about what he'd done. "Davis will sometimes compare Schroeder to Daryle Lamonica, saying that it took Daryle some time to learn the system," said *Los Angeles Times* writer Mark Heisler. "Other times he'll say, 'I'm not sure I did the right thing.' "

Schroeder was an unusual player, having played only two seasons at UCLA (and not as a starter) before signing a pro baseball contract with the Toronto Blue Jays. His baseball career went nowhere, so when the Redskins selected him on the third round of the 1984 draft, he joined them a year later. He looked like an excellent pick when he became the starter in 1986 and threw for twenty-two touchdowns, completing 51 percent of his passes. But the next year he lost the job to Doug

Williams, who took the Redskins to a Super Bowl championship, and it was only a matter of time before he would be traded.

In some ways Schroeder seemed to be the ideal Raiders
quarterback, big (6 feet 4 and 215 pounds) and with a powerful arm that some thought was stronger than John Elway's.
But he played mechanically, was prone to error, and didn't
always seem terribly interested in his football career. Before
having shoulder surgery in 1989 he told friends that he was
concerned over what it would do to his golf swing. "Schroeder
is the product of the way quarterbacks are developed now,"
Todd Christensen said. "They don't call plays, and they can't
be spontaneous. You still see spontaneity in a quarterback like
Joe Montana, who can make something out of nothing, but
not with Schroeder. He reminds me of that Kansas City quarterback, Steve Fuller. We used to cheer when Fuller rolled out
because we knew he'd make a bad play, and it's the same way
with Jay. He doesn't know what to do."

Part of Schroeder's problems were mental; he did not take
criticism well, was often sulky, and seemed to lack the mental
toughness a quarterback—especially a Raiders quarterback—
needs. He also had physical problems; his stride was different
from play to play, for instance, causing some throws to go into
the ground. Gene Washington, a former wide receiver with
the 49ers who worked on Raiders pregame shows, noticed
something else. "He carries the ball too low," Washington said.
"He has to bring it up too far before he can throw it, so he
has to hurry his short throws. That's one reason he's inaccurate on those throws, and it also gives the defense more time
to adjust."

Ever since he came to the Raiders, Davis had always had
an excellent quarterback. He inherited Flores, traded for Lamonica, drafted Stabler, and signed Plunkett as a free agent.
Now he was learning what happens to a team that doesn't have
a solid quarterback.

"The thing that surprises me is that Davis has always been
a guy who overcame the numbers," Christensen said. "He didn't

believe that you had to be a certain size or have the right time in the forty. Now he's got a quarterback who comes right out of the computer—Jay Schroeder has the perfect size and a great arm. But he's not a great quarterback."

Tom Keating and Marv Hubbard, Raiders players from the Oakland days, noticed that Davis and his scouts were succumbing to the same weakness with other players. "He used to be a guy who looked at what a player did, not what he looked like," Keating said. "His strength was that while everybody else was going by a guy's forty times, or his height and weight, he would pick a guy who didn't fit by the numbers but who got the job done. Like me. I was never big enough, according to the scouts. But now he seems captivated by the numbers. He'll pick a guy on the strength of his speed or his size, and a lot of these guys have been busts."

Hubbard remembered a conversation with Dan Conners, a former Raiders linebacker who now scouts for the team. "Dan told me, 'If I'm going to miss on a guy, I'd rather miss on a guy who's got the size or speed.' I told him, 'There are a lot of guys who wouldn't have been around in the old days if Al had thought like that. Fred Biletnikoff, Pete Banaszak—and you and me.' "

King thought the team's trouble began with two terrible drafts in 1985 and 1986. "There are only two players left from those two drafts," he noted. "So the team was losing players like Art Shell and Gene Upshaw and not replacing them." Sometimes Davis had bad luck. For instance, his 1988 number-one pick, Notre Dame wide receiver Tim Brown, a Heisman Trophy winner, was a good choice and had forty-three catches in his rookie year, but he tore up his knee the next year and lost virtually the whole season; he was still recuperating and of limited value in 1990. More often, though, it was simply bad judgment. Some of Davis's first-round picks were fiascoes, such as defensive end Bob Buczkowski and offensive tackle John Clay. Another first-round pick, wide receiver Jessie Hester, became noted more for the catches he missed than the ones he made, and he was gone after three years. Not until 1990 did

Davis again have the kind of successful draft that had built his earlier champions.

As the team declined, many questioned anew whether Davis had done the right thing in moving. The Los Angeles environment had changed the mental and emotional outlook of the players. "Moving to L.A. was a bad move for the team," said Lester Hayes, who played through the 1987 season. "In Oakland there was no such thing as egomaniacs, but when we got to L.A. you had Sunset Boulevard, every PR agent in the area in your jockstrap. Some individuals just can't handle that. Hat sizes went from seven to seventeen. We split into factions. The forty-five-man team we'd had in Oakland was null and void."

Matt Millen, who played in both places before his release in 1989, saw a clear difference between the cities. "The fans in Oakland were much more knowledgeable. After a game guys would come up to us and say, 'Great game, but you missed a block or tackle.' In L.A. they had different priorities. They didn't seem to care. It made a difference to the players, too. At first it didn't matter as much, because we had mostly older players whose heads couldn't be turned by the extra attention, but when the younger players came in it was different."

"The attitude didn't change initially," remembered Jim Plunkett. "We were still basically the Oakland Raiders. We just happened to be playing in Los Angeles. But as more players came in, it changed, because they didn't know what it had been like before. In Oakland, maybe four or five players got speaking engagements for grand openings or whatever. In Los Angeles it was fifteen, twenty, or twenty-five players, so it distracted more and more from your study habits and concentration.

"We had our camaraderie in Oakland. Every Thursday night we'd have twenty-five or thirty players get together. You didn't have to drink—there was soda pop there, as well as liquor, and appetizers. We'd just sit in a group and have a good time, and then go back to work the next day. By the time I left in L.A., if we got three people together on Thursday night it was a big deal. It wasn't the same as Oakland at all. L.A.'s so spread out. There are very few players who live in the same town.

They live where they can afford to live, especially the younger ones. Instead of everybody living in a fairly small area, as they did in Oakland, they're spread out all over the place."

In Oakland, despite the team's image, the majority of the players were solid enough citizens. As Plunkett noted, there were even some players who didn't drink at the team parties. In Los Angeles, the temptations were many and varied. "The drinking got out of hand," Hayes said. "Can you imagine what it is like to spend every day of your life drinking? Every strip bar in Los Angeles knew us. It was 'nightmare on Elm Street.' "

A week before the exhibition opener in 1989, defensive back Stacy Toran was killed when his car plunged off the road. Toran's blood alcohol level was reportedly far over the legal limit. That didn't surprise Hayes. "I think of the times guys would drink so much they'd drive home from training camp at a hundred miles an hour," he said. It wouldn't be until the 1990 season that Art Shell, coaching the team with which he had had so many wonderful playing years, got the team drinking under control. "He dissolved the 'happy-hour posse,' " Hayes said.

• • •

The team's on-field decline didn't become precipitous until the last part of the 1986 season. At 8–4, the Raiders were in position to win their division again when they hosted the 3–9 Philadelphia Eagles on November 30, in a game infamous in Raiders history.

It was a game of big plays. Randall Cunningham, in his second year as quarterback of the Eagles, was sacked ten times, but he also threw three touchdown passes, all to Mike Quick. Greg Garrity returned a punt 76 yards for another Philadelphia touchdown. Plunkett threw two touchdown passes to Jessie Hester, who dropped a third; a Henry Lawrence holding penalty nullified another Raiders touchdown. At the end of regulation time the score was tied, 27–27.

In overtime the Raiders went to the Eagles 12, close enough for a field goal. "But Chris Bahr didn't like to kick from the right hashmarks," Bill King remembered, "so Tom Flores called a running play just to get the ball into the center of the field. We didn't have to be any closer. But Marcus Allen, with his running-back instincts, tried to make something of the play and fumbled." Andre Waters picked up the fumble for Philadelphia and raced all the way to the Raiders 4, where he was finally tackled by Dokie Williams. Cunningham scored two plays later to win the game.

"That broke our back," Plunkett remembered. "I almost felt like quitting. It devastated everybody. We lost our next three."

The Philadelphia loss caused a dramatic tailspin in the franchise. Starting with that game, the Raiders went 13–26 until Art Shell was hired as head coach after the fourth game of the 1989 season, by far the team's worst stretch since Al Davis had come to the franchise in 1963. That loss was also a major factor in Davis's feud with his star running back, Marcus Allen.

Davis's problems with Allen, which probably had started with the Super Bowl after the 1983 season, had only intensified as time went on. In 1985, with Davis still trying to prove that Marc Wilson could be an NFL quarterback, the Raiders had an uncertain passing offense. Allen stepped into the breach with by far the best season any Raiders running back had ever had, rushing 380 times for 1,759 yards, both club records. He became the first Raiders back to lead the NFL in rushing, and he also caught 67 passes for 555 yards. He scored fourteen touchdowns and was named the league's Most Valuable Player. "But in the first round of the play-offs," Christensen remembered, "we lost to New England, 27–20, and Marc Wilson threw four interceptions. After the game, in the locker room, Davis said, "We're never again going to be so dependent on one guy. We've become one dimensional." Davis was referring to Allen. Davis also held against Allen the fumble that caused the 1986 loss to Philadelphia.

As if to underscore his dissatisfaction, Davis had selected Bo Jackson on the seventh round of the 1986 draft. Jackson, a Heisman Trophy winner in college, had originally been drafted number one by the ill-starred Tampa Bay Buccaneers in 1985, but he had signed a baseball contract with the Kansas City Royals instead. The Bucs' rights expired after one year, enabling the Raiders to draft him. Jackson then decided he could combine careers, playing with the Royals until the end of their season and then joining the Raiders while their season was well in progress.

Jackson was an extremely gifted athlete, unquestionably the fastest power runner ever to play in the NFL. He made some incredible runs for the Raiders, 91 yards in his first season, 1987, 92 in 1989, and an 89-yarder in key game late in the 1990 season. He also was sometimes a divisive factor, because he played only part of the season and because he had a tendency to come out of a game with what others regarded as minor injuries. "Marcus is, to use a Hebrew term, a real mensch," Christensen said. "I saw him catch five passes in one game when he had a broken wrist—you could see the cast on his arm. Contrast that with Bo, who won't play because he has a sore tonsil."

Allen never publicly complained, but it was obvious that Jackson's presence bothered him. For half the season Allen was the offensive leader for the Raiders; for the second half he was at best coequal with Jackson, and usually was overshadowed by Jackson's more spectacular play. By 1989, with Allen trying to renegotiate an already lucrative contract, the relationship between Davis and Allen was so rancorous that Allen and his agent, Greg Bautzer, got permission to see if they could arrange a trade with another team. When no team was willing to offer more than a second-round draft pick, Allen returned to the Raiders.

Mel Durslag thought that Davis's dispute with Allen resulted from Davis's view of the team. "I think Al just felt early that Marcus was trying to set himself apart from the team, and the team is what's important to Davis."

After the Super Bowl win in 1984, defensive coordinator Charley Sumner had left to become head coach of the Oakland Invaders of the now defunct USFL. That was another factor in the team's decline—the only one that couldn't be traced directly to Davis.

"When we lost Charley, our defense went downhill," Lester Hayes said. "You like to have a stand-up guy you can respect. Well, with Charley it went beyond respect. It was love. I loved Charley, and our entire defense loved him. Bob Zeman came in, and he taught a different style. My foundation had been attack, blitzing everyone. He taught a 'soft' defense—bend but don't break. At times we were playing tight coverage with a three-man rush. That was crazy."

Hayes wasn't alone in feeling that Sumner was something special as a defensive coach. In 1986, when the Raiders' Howie Long was named Defensive Lineman of the Year, a media conference was held in Anaheim during Super Bowl week. After the conference I talked to Long about Sumner, who had just been rehired by Davis for the third time. "He'll get us playing tough again," Long told me. "We haven't been playing like the Raiders, but he'll change that. Just watch." This time with the Raiders, though, Sumner didn't last even two seasons before he quit, unhappy because he was passed over for the head coaching job.

As the team deteriorated, some old favorites began to go, and not always happily. Hayes was kept on injured reserve for all of the 1987 season, although he insisted he could play and wanted to; he never played again for the Raiders. Hayes shared the club's interception record with Willie Brown, who had become the defensive backs' coach, and Hayes claimed that the Raiders wouldn't play him because they didn't want him to pass Brown. Some scoffed, but I didn't. Brown was always one of Davis's favorites. Of all those who have played for the Raiders, it's possible that only Jim Otto ranks ahead of Brown in Davis's affections.

"I didn't get along with Hall of Famer Willie Brown," Hayes admitted. "I like to think fast, and I need to absorb quickly and consistently. His coaching technique was strictly 'Bad News Bears.' It was boring going to meetings. He was talking outdated techniques. One day he even brought in film of him covering Caucasian Clydesdales in 1968. Well, how was that going to help me in 1988? But when a Hall of Famer and a player have a fight, it's the player who gets cut loose."

Hayes is still bitter about his departure, and he hasn't gone back to see his old team. Todd Christensen isn't bitter, but he thinks his release, in training camp before the 1989 season, was handled poorly by Davis.

"I'd hurt my knee in 1988, and then in the off-season, in May, I had my gall bladder removed," Christensen told me. "In June we had a minicamp. I was almost thirty-three, and I knew the reality of the situation. I went to Al and said, 'If you're going to cut me, let me know now so I don't have to go through all this again.' But he told me, 'No, no, you'll get your chance. Get in shape.'

"So I went through my rehab and went to camp, but I could see what was happening. When you get to a certain age in the NFL with a big salary, they just figure you're gone. Actually, the last two weeks of camp I felt I was running and catching as well as I ever had, but I was gone anyway. I was disappointed that he handled it that way. The decision was made before camp even started, and I would have liked to have him tell me then. I didn't have to come to camp and go through that rigorous training when I didn't have a chance.

"But in the final analysis, I think we're even. He gave me my chance and compensated me well for what I did, and I reciprocated by making a lot of catches and key plays for him.

"Matt Millen and I had talked about this before, that we wouldn't get the 'gratis year' that Davis gave some players, keeping them around after their usefulness was past, because we'd bargained hard. The guys he kept around like that—Gene Upshaw, Art Shell, Willie Brown, Cliff Branch—were generally guys that didn't get paid real well. Davis used to say, 'I'll take care of you,' but I felt that I'd rather get $600,000 for three years than $300,000 for five years. That's the way it comes out with the math I learned."

• • •

There was another inevitable result of the Raiders decline: coach Tom Flores resigned after the 1987 season.

The relationship between Davis and his coaches has always been the subject of much speculation. Some have accused him of pulling all the strings, of making all the coaching decisions, but that is an exaggeration. My observation of Davis in Oakland coincides with Mel Durslag's opinion of what has happened in Los Angeles: Davis works with his coach on the game plan for each week, especially the offensive strategy, and contributes a fair amount. He doesn't actually make up the game plan, but if a coach wants to do something very different from what Davis wants, he had better be prepared to argue strongly for it.

Davis will be on the practice field during the week, acting almost like an assistant coach in working with players on techniques, but the responsibility of preparing the team for a game is the coach's. Although Davis has occasionally sent messages to the sideline during a game, he normally leaves his coach alone on game day. "People say he runs the game from the press box," Durslag said. "That's a falsehood. It's the rarest occasion when Al will send down a message from the press box." I remember only one such occasion from the years I covered the club, when Davis sent down a defense during a 1968 game in Kansas City. Mark Heisler of the *Los Angeles Times* remembered that Davis had Al LoCasale call down during one game in 1987 to tell Flores to put in quarterback Rusty Hilger. "Flores later said it had been his idea," Heisler said, "which was a remarkable coincidence."

Davis haters construe his actions as unconscionable interference with a coach's job, but, as Hank Stram has pointed out, a Raiders coach knows what to expect: Davis's pattern, after all, was established twenty-five years ago. Other owners would be foolish to interfere with their coaches, because they lack the intimate knowledge of the game that Davis possesses. Davis would be foolish not to get involved.

"Al has a lot of experience," Durslag noted. "He goes back thirty years in pro football alone. When you're at it as much as he is, day and night, you've got to assimilate a certain amount of knowledge. He knows how to set up for a game. Al isn't very often outsmarted. Al is very good at seeing where a team can be attacked. He's very smart at attacking weaknesses. He'll see some flaw in a player or team."

For a time the Davis-Flores combination worked well. Flores, a soft-spoken gentleman who was highly regarded by his players, had great respect for Davis, and after Flores guided the Raiders to two Super Bowl wins Davis called him one of the best coaches in NFL history. The team's deterioration was not Flores's fault, but it is a fact of coaching life—and not just with the Raiders—that the coach gets blamed when the team goes sour. Flores wasn't fired, but he could see what was happening. "Davis has a way of showing people the door and saying, 'This might be a good time to leave,' " Heisler noted.

Flores saw the open door and resigned in January 1988. "I was frustrated," he said, "and so was Al. I knew it was going to take a major rebuilding, and I was tired. I had never been able to get away from it. The last year we won the Super Bowl, I had an apartment in L.A., and my family was living up in Lafayette, near Oakland. I took four days to be with them, and then I went back to L.A. and back to work. I couldn't take that anymore. I had to get away. Al and I talked about it at the Shrine East-West game in January, and when we got back I announced my resignation." Flores landed on his feet, eventually becoming president and general manager of the Seattle Seahawks.

Although Davis was ready for Flores to leave, the departure left a void. Davis had traditionally picked a new head coach from within the organization—John Rauch, Madden, Flores—but this time there was no assistant coach he wanted to promote. Some speculated that he might hire his personal favorite, Willie Brown, but Davis knew that Brown, though a great player, was not even a very good assistant coach. As often happens with the best players, Brown could not identify with those having lesser talent. He was not head coach material.

Defensive coordinator Charley Sumner had been a head coach briefly, before the USFL went under, but Sumner was too independent to be a Raiders head coach. Davis wasn't going to promote a man who would openly defy him.

Art Shell was the third candidate, and someone Davis thought would eventually make a good head coach. But he didn't feel that Shell, who had been a Raiders assistant since 1983, was quite ready for the head job—especially since he would have the added pressure of being the first black head coach in the NFL.

There was another factor weighing on Davis as he deliberated. For the first time he wondered if the NFL had caught up to his style of football. The most successful offensive style in the NFL then was that of Bill Walsh and the San Francisco 49ers, which ran counter to Davis's theories by emphasizing ball control instead of the big play. Walsh had been a Raiders assistant for one season, 1966, and in his 1990 book, *Building a Champion,* had credited Davis for the foundation of his own success. For his system Walsh built on the complicated Raiders blocking schemes and on their technique of using their backs as pass receivers. The 49ers, though, seldom went for the long pass that had always been a staple of the Raiders attack, preferring short passes that were sometimes little more than long pitchouts. In Walsh's system, there were few interceptions and many first downs, which had the side benefit of keeping the 49ers defense rested and strong for the late minutes of the game.

Another team using much the same style of offense was in the Raiders' division: the Denver Broncos. Their offensive coordinator, Mike Shanahan, was given credit for the development not only of their offensive system but of quarterback John Elway. In 1986 and 1987, with Shanahan running the offense, the Broncos had twice gone to the Super Bowl, and they had beaten the Raiders in all four of their games during those seasons.

Davis interviewed several coaches from outside his organization: Washington Redskins assistants Dan Henning and Joe
Bugel, 49ers assistant Dennis Green, and San Diego Chargers
offensive coordinator Jerry Rhome. He had gone through the
charade of talking to coaches from other teams before hiring
Madden and Flores—hoping to get information about the operations of the teams—but this time he was seriously looking
for a coach.

Finally he hired Shanahan, in February 1988. As usual with
Davis, he had a hidden agenda as well as the obvious one; he
thought that hiring Shanahan would disrupt the Broncos and
Elway—and it did, at least momentarily. Mostly, though, he
wanted to change the Raiders style of football. He said that to
me, incredibly enough. We were both on the program for a
"roast" of former basketball star Rick Barry in San Francisco
that April, and Davis and I chatted briefly before the dinner.
"This is such an important occasion, I'll even talk to you," he
said.

The Shanahan hiring accomplished one thing—the Raiders beat the Broncos twice the next season. Their success against
the Broncos was not matched by success against the rest of the
division, however. The Raiders finished 7–9, an improvement
over the 5–10 mark of the previous season but not enough to
get them into the play-offs, and they lost four of their last five
games.

Shanahan was a prime example of a topflight assistant who
was not ready for the wider responsibilities of a head-coaching
job. In some ways, in fact, he was a throwback to John Rauch.
He was not even accustomed to being on the sideline, because
he had called plays from the press box for Denver. Only those
who have been on the sideline know how much more difficult
that can be, with all the noise from the stands and the field
impeding thought.

In Denver, Shanahan had Elway, who probably had as much
natural ability as any quarterback has ever had. Shanahan was
able to channel that ability so that Elway finally attained his
potential. He didn't realize that his quarterbacks with the

Raiders, Steve Beuerlein and Jay Schroeder, were not as talented as Elway. He kept trying to force Beuerlein and Schroeder into the Elway mode, and it didn't take.

Most of all, he didn't realize that the Raiders were a different team than the team he had left—or than any other team in the NFL. He put in the petty disciplinary rules that Davis had always eschewed. One that riled everybody: he told the players they could no longer sit on their helmets on the sideline, as they had done for years. It was a small thing but an important one, because it showed that he simply did not understand the emotional makeup of the team.

Shanahan also didn't get along with his assistant coaches. Sumner quit after the 1988 season, disgusted at having been passed over. Willie Brown was fired, and defensive line coach Earl Leggett went to Denver. Shanahan also tried to fire offensive coaches Tom Walsh and Joe Spinella, but Davis stopped him, and then Davis fired Nick Nicoli, who had been hired by Shanahan.

Shanahan put in the short-pass offense with which the 49ers and the Broncos had been successful. Perhaps Davis would have stayed with him if the offense had worked for the Raiders, but when the team started the 1989 season with a 1–4 record, Davis fired Shanahan, eating the remainder of his three-year contract.

"He pictured Mike Shanahan disrupting the one thing in life that he cared about, the football team," Durslag said. "Shanahan was a nice guy, but he didn't know anything about coaching a football team. He was hurling guys off the coaching staff and disrupting everything. It suddenly occurred to Al that Shanahan was taking the football team away from him. So he returned things to normal by hiring Art Shell, who was an old-time Raider guy."

Even now Davis wasn't certain that Shell was ready for the head-coaching job, but he had to give Shell his chance. Shell thus became the first black head coach in the NFL. "I knew that if anybody hired a black coach, it would be my buddy, Al," Shell said. "He doesn't think in those terms. He wasn't trying to make a statement, but if I was qualified to do the job, he'd hire me, and he did."

Despite his playing success, Shell hadn't originally contemplated becoming an NFL head coach. "It was John Madden who first made me think I could be a head coach in the NFL," Shell told me. "I had thought of coaching in high school, maybe, or even college, but never on the NFL level, but John got me to thinking about it. Then, when I became an assistant, well, you always think you want to run your own show. I was determined to work as hard as I could as an assistant and learn as much as I could, so I'd be ready when I got my chance. And when the time came I think I was ready."

Shell immediately dropped all of Shanahan's rules—players again sat happily on their helmets on the sideline. He also made the Raiders feel that they could again be as tough at home as they'd been in Oakland.

The Los Angeles Coliseum had never given the Raiders much of a home-field advantage. Because of the running track surrounding the field, the stands are set back from the field, so that a noisy crowd isn't as much of a factor as it is elsewhere. The stadium, seating 93,000, has rarely been filled, and those who come aren't always Raiders fans. Ollie Spencer remembered going to a Raiders–Chicago Bears game and sitting among a large contingent of Bears fans—unthinkable in the Oakland days. "I asked one of them if he came out to other Raiders games," Spencer said, "and he said, 'No. I'm from Chicago, so I came out today. I don't care anything about the Raiders.' "

Shell made the Raiders tough at home again—they were 6–0 at the Coliseum in 1989 after he took over—in part by reminding the players of what it had been like in Oakland. "In Oakland we called the Coliseum 'Black Bottom.' We didn't ever think we should lose at 'Black Bottom.' So I started calling the L.A. Coliseum that. The thing is, we regard the Coliseum as our backyard. It's just like in your own backyard, you know where the tire iron is hidden if you get a burglar. Well, we know where everything is at the Coliseum, so we think we should always win there. If we get beat, we're going to make the other team earn it. They aren't going to just come in and win because we don't play well."

The Raiders struggled on the road, but their overall record under Shell was 7–5, which brought them to 8–8 for the 1989 season. Their improvement under Shell boded well for the future. The only question was: where would that future be? Al Davis had been shopping the team again.

·12·

Los Angeles
Is Still Home

Luxury boxes or suites were supposedly a key factor in Al Davis's decision to move his Raiders to Los Angeles. He had hoped to get more suites there than he could in Oakland, and to charge a higher rental for them. But by 1987 the Oakland Coliseum had built luxury boxes for its remaining client, the baseball A's, and Davis still did not have his suites in Los Angeles.

There had been problems about them from the beginning. USC had objected because it would be necessary to take out seats that the school sold at premium prices. And the Olympics were being held at the Coliseum in 1984, for the second time, and nothing could be done until they were over.

After the closing ceremonies of the Olympics, Davis and the Los Angeles Memorial Coliseum Commission (LAMCC) finally signed a ten-year lease, retroactive to 1982. (Until then, the Raiders and the LAMCC had been operating under the memorandum of agreement that Davis had signed in 1980.) The luxury boxes were not included in the lease, because Bill Robertson, who had negotiated the deal with Davis, was waiting to finalize that part of the agreement until the appeals on the antitrust suit against the NFL had been exhausted. By 1987 the suit had been put to rest and the Coliseum had collected its damages from the NFL owners, but a final agreement on the luxury boxes still had not been reached.

Davis had promises from Robertson and from Mike Frankovich, who followed him as president of the commission, that the boxes would be built, Robertson told me, and he said that Los Angeles mayor Tom Bradley, state senator Bill Campbell, and county supervisor Kenneth Hahn had also been committed to luxury boxes. "It would have cost about $9 million to do the work," Robertson said, "and Al would have been content. There would have been no problems at all. We got about $19.5 million from the lawsuit, plus $4 million from the Olympics, but the commission wouldn't agree to spend $9 million of that on the boxes."

The problem apparently stemmed from the new president of the Coliseum board, Alexander Haagen, though it had seemed at first that Haagen wanted to accommodate Davis. Before becoming president of the commission Haagen had asked Robertson to set up a meeting with Davis (although warned that Davis didn't like meetings), and one was arranged, at the Raiders practice facility in El Segundo. "Haagen said to Al, 'This is one of the best things that ever happened to Los Angeles. We're going to do everything we can to get this done,'" Robertson told me. "But when he became president of the commission, he got together with Pete Schabarum, who was a member of the commission, to wreck the deal. Pete even tried to get us to drop our antitrust suit. To me, that was it, so I got off the board."

Robertson felt strongly that Davis was maligned during the controversy about the boxes. "A lot of the flak Al Davis gets for being a greedy bastard came because the commission created the environment," he said. "If the commission had done what it was supposed to do, there wouldn't have been an Irwindale or a Sacramento or Oakland again. Like any businessman, Al was looking for the best deal, but he got a lot of heat for that.

"The *L.A. Times* latched onto the idea that he was out to fleece this community. I met with the editorial board, and I said, 'How can you take that position? Indianapolis took $80 million of taxpayers' money to get a team. Minneapolis spent $55 million of taxpayers' money to build a stadium. The Coliseum never spent a dime of taxpayers' money on the Raiders.' "

During the 1986 football season the Raiders started ripping out seats in preparation for the construction of the luxury boxes, but Davis ordered that stopped when the Coliseum Commission would not come up with the money for other stadium improvements. The Coliseum wanted the Raiders to replace the seats; when Davis refused, the Coliseum had to do it.

The next bombshell came from Davis. On August 20, 1987, he signed an agreement for a new stadium with the community of Irwindale, accepting $10 million in a nonreturnable upfront fee. That tiny community, about twenty miles north of the Rams' home in Anaheim, planned to build the stadium with $95 million of revenue bonds and have it ready for the 1992 season, when the Raiders' contract in Los Angeles expired.

"Nobody in L.A. even knew where Irwindale was," Mel Durslag said. In fact, the community was known mainly for its huge gravel pit, and the possibility of its building a stadium had seemed a joke even to Davis at the outset. "Al wouldn't even answer their calls at first," Durslag remembered. "He thought they were crackpots. They came after him, tugging on his arm, begging him to take their money. They're a little town, wanting to go big time." Davis soon realized that the Irwindale politicians were very serious.

Davis liked the idea of having a new, state-of-the-art stadium built to his specifications, and Irwindale would still have been in the larger Los Angeles metropolitan area, though far from the center. By this time, because of the problems he and his team had encountered, Davis had lost much of his earlier enchantment with the city of Los Angeles.

Shortly after that the Coliseum filed a $58 million lawsuit

against the Raiders for starting but then stopping work on luxury boxes. The Raiders filed a countersuit against the Coliseum for failure to fulfill verbal commitments. "The Coliseum lawsuit was a very frivolous suit, in my opinion," Robertson said. "It was a very sordid scenario."

The Irwindale deal eventually fell apart, for a variety of reasons. An environmental report caused a delay, and then climbing interest rates made it impossible to raise the money. Two city councilmen who had supported the deal were defeated for reelection, and the council members who replaced them did not favor it. Davis kept the $10 million of up-front money and looked elsewhere. The cynical asked: what did you expect? "I don't think he used Irwindale," Durslag said. "He didn't want the $10 million, he wanted the stadium. It was a beautiful stadium they had planned, all spit and polish, everything he wanted and under his control."

But Irwindale's failure left an opening for two more bidders for the Raiders: Sacramento and Oakland.

In retrospect, it's clear that Davis never took the Sacramento option seriously, except as an offer that might give him leverage in his dealings with Oakland. Sacramento, the California state capital, is a small city hungry for big-time sports. The Sacramento Kings of the NBA, a terrible team but the city's one major-league franchise, sell out every game. The Sacramento Sports Authority, headed up by land developer Gregg Lukenbill, had plans to build both a baseball and a football stadium, but the financing was shaky, and Lukenbill also wanted the right to buy 20 percent of the Raiders. It was inconceivable that Davis would yield that much of the club to an outsider. Besides, after he and Lukenbill met, Davis told his friends that he could not work with the man.

The Sacramento proposal, despite all the news stories it engendered, never got beyond the preliminary stage with Davis, but the Oakland negotiations were serious indeed. Although the Raiders had not played in Oakland since 1981, many in Oakland still thought of them as the home team. Some fans traveled to Los Angeles for games, and many more watched them faithfully on television. Raiders jackets, sweatshirts, and bumper stickers could be spotted throughout the East Bay, and there was even a publication in nearby Hayward, the *Sportspage News*, devoted to boosterish stories about the team.

Rumors that the Raiders would return started as early as the summer of 1988, when it was announced that they would meet the Houston Oilers in an exhibition game at the Oakland Coliseum the next summer. Fans and even some writers speculated that Davis was testing the waters, to see if the Oakland and East Bay fans would again support the Raiders if they returned.

In fact, Davis had had nothing to do with the scheduling of the Oilers game. George Vukasin, the president of the Oakland Coliseum Board, was trying to convince the NFL to put an expansion team in Oakland when the league finally expanded, and he wanted a sellout crowd for an exhibition game to remind the league of the city's interest in pro football. Vukasin reasoned that the two teams most likely to sell out were (1) the Super Bowl champion or (2) the Raiders. He could not know who would win the Super Bowl (it turned out to be the cross-bay 49ers), so he signed up the Raiders.

Several months later, in January 1989, Vukasin's focus changed from an expansion team to the Raiders. He had received a phone call from Ed DeSilva, a contractor and a friend of Jack Brooks, who has been a Raiders partner since 1961 and is also a close friend of Davis. Following the call, DeSilva, county supervisor Charley Santana (a sports fan and an avid follower of the Raiders), and Vukasin met in DeSilva's office to discuss what it would take to get a football team, preferably the Raiders. DeSilva then asked Brooks to talk to Davis and get his thoughts.

Brooks, a land developer who was born and raised in Oakland, is a good negotiator, a man of judgment and patience. Those traits were to be as valuable as his friendship with Davis in his new role as the negotiator and intermediary between Davis and the Oakland representatives.

The day after hearing from DeSilva, Brooks called Davis

in Los Angeles. Davis told Brooks he wasn't really interested, because the deal with Irwindale was still alive. "But we had a rambling discussion," Brooks said, "and from that I distilled eleven items." Of the eleven items, Vukasin remembered, the Oakland group saw problems with only two: fifteen acres of free land for a Raiders Hall of Fame and $50 million in moving costs. Those eleven items remained the basis for discussions, and several meetings were held between Brooks and the Oakland representatives. Brooks noted with some amusement that at one meeting there were twenty-three people on the other side of the table from him, "and I believe most of them were lawyers."

Despite Davis's disclaimer, the Oakland negotiators were thinking now in terms of the Raiders, not an expansion team, because they assumed that the Irwindale deal would fall through. The Oakland group proceeded to draft first a letter of intent and then a memorandum of agreement for Davis and the Raiders. Davis continued to be coy, insisting that Brooks say he was still not interested. As the meetings progressed and the proposals became more specific, Davis dropped that pose.

One key point was the reconstruction of the Coliseum to add luxury boxes and roughly 11,000 more seats, Brooks said, and Davis agreed to come to Oakland and look over the Coliseum. "It was not a negotiating meeting. It was at my request that he let me know what he thought of their proposed improvements and what he would like to see. We walked around together. If you're going to build a house, you go out with the architect and you say, 'I want this room bigger and this one smaller.' That's basically what we did. There were no major structural changes. He just suggested some things from his own experience that might improve it. At that point, we seemed to be fairly close to agreement on structural changes. Al said, 'Maybe I should give Oakland serious consideration. They seem to be sincere, they seem to be moving along, they seem to be ready to make a serious deal.'

"Al never attended negotiating meetings, at any time. He and I talked back and forth, and I pretty much got his thoughts on the whole thing and met with the Oakland people. After a few compromises, we got fairly close, Al conceding some things, they conceding some things. We were still dealing with the eleven original concepts—that never changed. I conveyed to the Oakland people that Al would seriously consider a deal."

It helped, too, that the August 26 exhibition game between the Raiders and the Oilers turned out to be a huge success. Within two and a half hours of the time the tickets went on sale, the game was sold out.

It was a bizarre evening. Time had inevitably worked its changes on the old Raiders fan base. Many season-ticket holders had died; others had turned bitter because Davis had moved the club; still more had grown old enough to prefer their football on television rather than at the stadium. Few of the former fans attended the game, although many of their children probably did.

It was a relatively young crowd, and I compared it in my *Chronicle* column to a crowd at a rock concert, full of energy— much of it misdirected, unfortunately—and eager to see an Event. The gates were opened in the morning, though the game didn't start until 7:30 P.M., and it was obvious that those who came early had spent the time drinking. Several fights broke out in the stands, and the police made nearly a hundred arrests. Even so, the enthusiasm of the crowd and the rapid sale of the tickets helped Oakland's cause. "Davis was very much impressed with it," Vukasin said.

There had been rumors that Davis would announce at the game that he was returning to Oakland, but those stories were extremely premature. The negotiations were continuing, but they were still far from the stage at which a decision could be made. Oakland mayor Lionel Wilson had distanced himself from the negotiations, no doubt remembering the disappointment of 1980. At an early meeting with Vukasin and Don Perata, the chairman of the Alameda County Board of Supervisors, Wilson had said he wanted the county to lead the way on the negotiations, and Perata had agreed to be the public spokesman.

About a month after the exhibition game Perata called a press conference to announce the city-county proposal that was the basis for negotiations. When I talked to Wilson beforehand, he said that he had not even wanted to speak at the meeting and could not support the package as it stood. Specifically, he wanted a fifteen-year lease, instead of the ten years in the proposal; he wanted Davis to agree to indemnify Oakland against any lawsuits brought by other communities; and he wanted Davis to agree to return any up-front money if the deal fell through.

When Wilson told Brooks he had to have those concessions before he could recommend the deal to the Oakland City Council, Brooks had no serious problem getting Davis to agree. "I talked to Al and told him it didn't make any difference whether the lease was ten years or fifteen years. The Raiders were going to build the improvements and own them. What do you do after ten years—abandon the improvements and walk away? From a practical view, it didn't make any real difference. Al said, 'Yeah, I think you're right. If they want fifteen years, give them fifteen years.' " The other concessions were a little more difficult, but Davis agreed to them. He told Brooks, "If they want it, give it to them. If I say I'm going to do something, I'm going to do it."

While the negotiations were going on Davis became more visible in the Bay Area. He attended baseball and basketball games; he was the presenter for Fred Biletnikoff at the Bay Area Sports Hall of Fame dinner; he appeared at the funeral of Andy Herrera, a former Raiders limited partner. Raiders fans in Oakland and the East Bay thought Davis wanted to "come home," which was partially true; he told friends that he was very conscious of the fact that the team's success had started in Oakland and that most of its best years had come before it left.

Davis also had another goal: admittance to the Pro Football Hall of Fame. He belongs there, especially since former Dallas Cowboys coach Tom Landry and former Cowboys general manager Tex Schramm were elected to the hall in successive years (1990 and 1991). Under Landry and Schramm, the Cowboys had a record very similar to that of the Raiders under Davis. If anything, the Raiders have been slightly better.

In twenty-nine Landry-Schramm seasons, the Cowboys were 250–162–6; counting ties as half wins, their regular-season winning percentage was 61 percent. In twenty-eight years under Davis, through the 1990 season, the Raiders were 269–130–11, for a winning percentage of 67 percent. The Cowboys had twenty winning seasons, all consecutive. The Raiders have had twenty-two winning seasons, with a consecutive streak of sixteen. The Cowboys were in nineteen play-off games, with a 20–16 record; the Raiders have been in seventeen play-offs, with a 20–13 record. The Cowboys were in five Super Bowls, the Raiders four; but the Raiders have won three of their four, the Cowboys only two of their five.

In Dallas, the Cowboys were run by a triumvirate: Landry coached the team, Schramm ran the front office, Gil Brandt gathered information for the draft. In Oakland and Los Angeles, Davis has done everything for the Raiders, coaching the team for the first three years, building it into a championship-level team, and directing every phase of its operations.

Yet Landry and Schramm are both in the Hall of Fame, and Davis is not. Clearly the animosity he created by his move to Los Angeles has kept him out. Just as clearly, he could have virtually wiped the slate clean by moving back to Oakland.

He almost succeeded in January 1991, making the list of seven Hall of Fame finalists before being rejected by the voters, a committee of football writers from every NFL city, plus Oakland and Baltimore. If his team had been heading back to Oakland, he would have gotten over the hump.

Davis in fact came excruciatingly close to moving the team back. By March 1990, the proposal had been refined enough to be voted on by the city council, the county board of supervisors, and the Coliseum Board. The question of timing was important. Wilson wouldn't put the proposal up for a council vote unless Davis, then in Florida for the NFL league meetings, announced he was going to return. Davis didn't want to make an announcement until he was sure he had a deal. Wilson and Perata said that Davis would have to make an announcement by Friday, March 8. Davis didn't, and the deadline was extended to the following Monday. It seemed as if Davis could never agree to any deadline, whatever it was.

Again the importance of having Brooks in the negotiations was paramount, because he was able to persuade Davis to go against his basic desire. Brooks told Davis, "Al, my best judgment is, you have a deal." Davis finally said, "If you think we have a deal and you think it's important that I make an announcement, I will, but I don't really want to do it."

Davis did announce on March 11 that he was returning to Oakland, and Wilson put on a Raiders cap for a press conference.

The proposed deal showed dramatically how the economics of pro football had changed. When the Raiders moved from Oakland, their average ticket price of $12.57 was the highest in the league. Under the new proposal, all tickets were to be priced at $30, and premiums would be added for the best seats. There would be eighty-seven luxury boxes available for season rental at $45,000 each. Club memberships, a new category expected to include about 6,650 seats, would be sold for $700 to $1,100 a year, including game tickets. The best field-level seats, approximately 13,000 of them, would carry a one-time fee of $2,000 to $3,000. Another 13,000 seats throughout the stadium would require premiums of $50 to $300 in addition to the basic ticket price. A final 3,170 "club loge" seats would carry premiums that would bring their yearly price to between $1,250 and $2,000.

City council hearings on the proposal had drawn a group of supporters who looked much like the Hells Angels, but the negotiators were looking neither to that group nor to the old Raiders fan base to pay the ticket prices. The type of fan who used to come to the Raiders games would be priced out of most of the seats. Only 26,000 of them (out of the proposed seating of about 65,000) would be sold for the straight $30 general-admission price. The East Bay had changed since the

Raiders left, as new money flowed into Contra Costa County, just east of Oakland and Alameda County. Contra Costa residents, many of whom lived in million-dollar homes, were not expected to balk at the high prices.

As part of the proposal, Davis and the Raiders would get $54.9 million, disguised as an "operating loan." But the most controversial section was the guarantee of ticket revenues to the Raiders in exchange for the Coliseum's taking over the marketing of tickets. The negotiators felt that provision was necessary because of Davis's total lack of marketing knowledge or skills. "Whenever we mentioned marketing," noted Vukasin, "the Raiders people would give us that blank look, like 'What's marketing?' "

The combination of the "operating loan" and the ticket guarantees came to $602 million over the fifteen-year period, and that gave opponents of the proposal a handy target. Oakland was in the midst of a mayoral race, and Wilson's two challengers in the primary, Elihu Harris and Wilson Riles, Jr., both opposed it, insisting that it would eventually cost the city money—though proponents were just as insistent that it would make money for city and county.

"We were projecting a $50 million profit for city and county," Brooks said, "and that was even if we couldn't sell all the tickets. Even if we didn't make our projections, if the city and county just made $40 million, is that so bad? If all the premiums were taken off, the city and county could still have made $20 million."

As criticism mounted, Wilson phoned Brooks and asked that the ticket guarantees be removed from the general-admission seats. "That took me about thirty seconds," Brooks said. "I didn't even have to phone Al about that." But it didn't satisfy opponents of the proposal, who mounted a petition drive to force the issue onto the June primary ballot. In the face of that opposition, the city council took back its approval of the plan. "The county supervisors and the Coliseum held firm throughout," Brooks said. "It was only the city that withdrew its support."

Wilson and the council really had no choice, because it was clear to everyone who lived in Oakland that the measure would have been defeated if it had been put on the ballot. For all the talk about the "Oakland" Raiders, most of the team's support had always come from the southern part of the county, outside the city limits. Oakland residents were split on the team's return, and many of those who were undecided were swayed by the argument that Oakland, suffering from serious budget problems, would eventually have to pay out public money.

Fighting for his political life, Wilson asked Brooks if the contract could be restructured to eliminate all ticket guarantees. It was restructured, but too late for Wilson, who ran third in the primary. The Raiders issue wasn't the only reason Wilson lost, but it was a factor.

The delay gave Los Angeles a chance to get back in the running. The Spectacor Management Company, the largest builder and operator of stadiums in the country, had been commissioned by the Los Angeles Coliseum Commission to operate the stadium and to make another deal with Davis to keep the Raiders there. That seemed impossible, because of the animosity between Davis and the Coliseum Commission, accentuated by the cross lawsuits. But then mayor Tom Bradley persuaded Bill Robertson to rejoin the commission, solely because he had Davis's confidence.

"I told Bradley I wanted to make inquiries first," Robertson told me. "I didn't want to come back on unless I thought there was a chance we could keep the Raiders. I called Al and said, 'Do you think I should go back on?' and he said, 'By all means, I think you should.' So it was obvious to me that there was a chance, or he wouldn't have said that. I talked to Ed Snider at Spectacor and Mike McGee, the athletic director at USC, and they thought I should go back on, so I did. My role in this second venture with the Raiders was merely to get the parties together so we could make a deal. I assured the principals that we would do everything feasible to put the deal together, that we would do everything possible politically to make the path easier for them."

Even with Robertson back on board, Los Angeles was play-ing catch-up, and Oakland should have been able to close a deal quickly. Yet problems kept arising, even though the newly restructured Oakland deal had gained the approval of many who had opposed it originally. "We didn't use common sense in determining deadline dates," Vukasin said. "We would meet and say it had to be done at a certain date, but we didn't think about how long it would take the attorneys. At the same time, I think people were really getting tired, because we were on call with this for eighteen months."

The Oakland A's brought in their own consultants. They wanted assurances that the changes in the stadium wouldn't hurt the baseball ambience, and they wanted some additional construction changes. They also insisted that no construction equipment remain in the stadium during the baseball season; all the work would have to be done in the brief period between football and baseball seasons.

The Oakland negotiators, on the advice of their lawyers, had not been able to give Brooks any warranties that there would be no problems with the Coliseum structure when the additions and changes were made, or that there would be no problems with the field. But the Coliseum field, already twenty-two feet below sea level, would have to be sunk another six feet because of the changes. "The original soils report was okay," Vukasin said. "Then, just to be sure, we brought in another company. They drilled a hole and got a six-foot geyser. We then had them check all over the field, and that's the only one they found, but it cost us more than $100,000 because we were working twenty-four hours a day on that for a while, and it cost us precious time. I understand Davis was prepared to make an announcement on August 28 that he was coming to Oak-land. We asked him to hold off until we got the water problem corrected."

The week before the 1990 season started, Vukasin told a meeting of the Coliseum Board and city and county officials that "the Raiders are 4–1 in the exhibition season and they're playing Denver at home. If they win the game and draw more than 40,000, we're in trouble."

The Raiders drew nearly 55,000 and won the game, and, yes, Oakland was in trouble. In fact, Davis had met with Los Angeles mayor Bradley the preceding Friday, and Bradley had promised Davis that the lawsuit against the Raiders would be dropped if he kept the team in Los Angeles. That cleared the way for a deal.

"It was a time for decision making," Brooks said. "Al asked me, 'Can you give me assurance that the Oakland deal will be completed, and we can do the construction in the time period, and the water problem will be solved?' I said, 'No, I can't give you that assurance.' At that point, I think Al really wanted to make the Oakland deal, but he had much more certainty with L.A. I think it was a very difficult decision for him to make. Before he made that decision, at two-thirty in the morning, he and I were on the phone going over these things, item by item, looking for solutions. We spent two hours on the phone."

The next afternoon, September 11, Davis announced that he would sign a new agreement in Los Angeles with Spectacor. The deal provided that the company would spend $145 million to renovate the Los Angeles Coliseum (some estimates placed the renovation cost higher, perhaps as much as $200 million) and build the luxury boxes. When the renovation was finished, Davis would sign a twenty-year lease; until then, he and Spectacor basically have an agreement to agree. In addition to having the lawsuit against the club dropped, Davis was allowed to keep the initial advance the Coliseum had given him in 1984 for stadium improvements, which had grown with interest to $10 million, and he got an additional $20 million from Spectacor, which would be his even if the deal fell through, as with the Irwindale deal.

"I told Al he can make the Forbes 500 list on the deals he doesn't make," quipped Durslag, who was skeptical that the deal would go through. In his column in the *Los Angeles Times,* he noted that "the trouble with the Raiders deals starts when the contract is signed."

In Oakland and the East Bay, sports bars took down their Raiders banners, restaurants canceled plans for dinners to celebrate the team's return, and fans vowed that their unrequited love affair was finally over. Raiders memorabilia were burned in an impromptu ceremony in front of an Oakland restaurant near my home and my wife's office. Nancy and I watched with amusement, sipping champagne. I had hoped the Raiders would return, but I no longer had any emotional ties to the team. I had long ago realized that the old Raiders fans were chasing a dream. This was not the same team that had left—Howie Long was the only player who had been on the team in Oakland—and there was no way of re-creating the feeling that had existed. We had all changed, even Davis. I had been enraged when Davis moved the team and had excoriated him in print. This time, there was only mild disappointment.

Oakland officials were shocked. Councilman Dick Spees, the spokesman during the latest negotiations, had just the day before said he was confident that the Raiders would return. Mayor Wilson, who would leave office at the end of the year, said, "Had it not been for the unfortunate fact that politics took the negotiations hostage, the original deal would still be in place, and the Raiders would once again be playing in Oakland."

Among those involved in the negotiations, there was no inclination to blame Davis this time around.

"I guess it's glamorous to focus on one guy, he's a no-good guy, a black knight," said Brooks, who was disappointed that the team would not return to his home area, "but he wanted to come back to Oakland. But it just couldn't work out."

"I don't have any trouble with Al," Vukasin said. "I get along with him fine. I think he's a guy who has a hard time making a business decision, so he delays and hopes time will take care of it. I think if he had said in August that he was coming back to Oakland, he would have forced everybody to make the deal."

It was truly the end of an era. Vukasin estimated that, because lawyers were involved every step of the way over what turned out to be an eighteen-month neogtiation, the Coliseum, the city of Oakland, and Alameda County had expended $5 million. Asked if Oakland would try again for the Raiders if the deal in Los Angeles were to fall through, Vukasin had a measured response, but the message was clear: over my dead body.

"The aura of the Raiders and the fan base made people think we should try to get the Raiders back," he said, "but that's changed now. I don't think you'll ever see the Raiders returning here."

• • •

It's difficult to know who was more disappointed by Davis's decision to stay in Los Angeles, Oaklanders or Angelenos. In Los Angeles, it was almost as if people couldn't wait for Davis and the Raiders to leave. A *Los Angeles Times* poll taken during the negotiations with Oakland showed that two-thirds of the population didn't care whether the Raiders stayed or left. When Davis announced for Oakland the *Times* ran an editorial entitled, "Good riddance, Al Davis." Even when he announced that he was staying, much of the newspaper coverage was scornful: *Los Angeles Daily News* columnist Ron Rapoport said he was working on a country-and-western song about Davis to be entitled, "It Would Be a Whole Lot Easier to Say Hello If You Weren't Always Walking Out the Door."

Until it was renovated, Davis would still be saddled with the Los Angeles Coliseum—a dilapidated, outmoded stadium. Durslag scoffed at those who talked about the Coliseum's historical value. "The real Colosseum is in Rome," he noted. "Talking about the historical value of this dump is like talking about the 'Gucci' purses you buy in Tijuana, Mexico." And the area around the Coliseum has deteriorated badly in recent years. Security has been a problem as far back as the AFC championship game against the Seattle Seahawks after the 1983 season, when the crowd poured onto the field to tear down the goalposts and the police were powerless to stop the surge.

During the third game of the 1990 season, against the Pittsburgh Steelers, some Raiders fans beat a Steelers fan so badly that he was briefly in a coma and hospitalized until he recovered. The incident inspired a debate in the city council, but *Los Angeles Times* columnist Bill Boyarsky wondered why. "The politicians knew what they were getting when they begged Al Davis to keep the Silver and Black in town," Boyarsky wrote. "Trouble. This man has encouraged an outlaw image for his team. . . . Commitment to Excellence is the team motto, but in the public's mind Commitment to Violence is more accurate. The Raiders always have viewed themselves as an outcast brigade, and their followers in the stands strive mightily to emulate. . . ."

Boyarsky's prose was overheated, but his column accurately reflected the attitude of many Angelenos toward Davis and his Raiders. The Raiders have not developed a loyal constituency, mainly because of their lack of success in the last half of the 1980s. "This town will drop you so fast if you lose," reiterates Durslag. "Al felt the fans would come back if he gave them a team that won a few games. When he finishes 8−8 or 7−9, he expects to get killed. He goes into a silence then, works on films, makes trades, tries to rectify the problem."

When in doubt, Al Davis always starts with the quarterback. When Bill Walsh decided to hold an instructional camp for NFL quarterbacks in March 1990, Davis signed up his two quarterbacks, Jay Schroeder and Steve Beuerlein, first. As it happened, the two Raiders quarterbacks were the only ones who got Walsh's coaching; after the second day, NBC, for whom Walsh was a commentator, forced him to cancel the camp because of a conflict of interest apparent only to the network hierarchy. Walsh saw enough to think that Beuerlein was the more advanced but that neither quarterback ranked with the best in the league.

Because he had traded for Schroeder, Davis did everything possible to give him a chance. Beuerlein helped, inadvertently, by holding out. Wanting Schroeder to feel that the job was his, that he would have no competition, Davis stonewalled on Beuerlein's contract negotiations. Beuerlein didn't sign until the end of training camp, and he was never put on the active roster during the season.

Then Davis signed a new assistant coach, Mike White, who had worked as an assistant for Walsh with the 49ers in between jobs as a head coach of the University of California in the 1970s and Illinois in the 1980s. White knows the passing game, and he has had some excellent quarterbacks—Steve Bartkowski, Vince Ferragamo, and the late Joe Roth at Cal, Jack Trudeau and Jeff George at Illinois. He worked with Schroeder on the consistency he would need to become a top-flight quarterback.

Finally, Davis and Shell worked out a plan to put the emphasis in the Raiders offense on the running backs, Bo Jackson and Marcus Allen. Shell said he wanted a game plan that had thirty or thirty-five runs and only twenty or twenty-five passes; in fact, there were games in which Schroeder threw fewer than twenty passes. That was a sharp deviation from the passing-oriented style of the past, but it was clearly the only way this team could function well.

Davis also came up with a strong 1990 draft. Though first-rounder Anthony Smith was injured in the exhibition season and missed the regular season, second-round pick Aaron Wallace, a linebacker, and fourth-rounder Torin Dorn, a cornerback, were solid.

The Davis-Allen feud continued, with the Los Angeles press often critical of Davis and rumors circulating that Allen might be traded. One rumored trade had him going to the San Francisco 49ers, whose star running back, Roger Craig, was injured. Allen would have been a perfect fit in the 49ers offense, which often uses backs as pass receivers. In retrospect, it's clear that Davis was just teasing Allen, because his asking price for Allen was too high. He wanted either defensive end–linebacker Charles Haley or wide receiver John Taylor from the 49ers, neither of whom the 49ers would have traded. From other teams, he was asking for a number one draft pick—for a player no team had thought worth more than a number two the year before, when he was a year younger.

"It would have been suicidal to trade Marcus, because he's a real team leader," Mark Heisler said. "The players all respect him. Some of that has been undercut when Bo returned, but even then, he's been a powerful force. The team would miss him."

Allen would become even more important when Jackson suffered a hip injury in the AFC championship game in January that threatened to end his athletic career. That injury led Davis to sign Craig as a free agent, along with another former 49er, Ronnie Lott.

The Raiders started and finished strong in 1990, winning six of their first seven games and their last five. In between they lost twice to the Kansas City Chiefs, both times because Schroeder did not play well—but, at 12–4, they finished a game ahead of the Chiefs to win the AFC West. They were in the play-offs for the first time in five years.

Their first-round game against the Cincinnati Bengals was at home. The game was played before 92,045 fans, the Raiders' largest crowd ever, but the statistic requires an asterisk. Bo Jackson and NBC combined to buy up nearly 9,000 unsold tickets so that the game would be an official sellout and could be televised in the Los Angeles area.

It took a big pass play from Schroeder to Ethan Horton, the latest of Davis's reclamation projects, to win the game. At North Carolina, Horton had been the Atlantic Coast Conference Player of the Year in 1985 as a running back and was drafted on the first round (the fifteenth pick overall) by the Kansas City Chiefs in 1986. He played little for the Chiefs, though, and was cut during the 1986 exhibition season. For two straight years the Raiders signed him and then cut him. Finally Davis called him in Chapel Hill, North Carolina, where Horton was working as an academic counselor at his alma mater, to say he wanted Horton to come back as a tight end. Horton agreed, and he got his chance to start in 1990, when starter

Mike Dyal was injured after three games. Horton, who had run the 440 in high school, had the speed Davis liked in his tight ends.

Midway through the fourth quarter, the Raiders were on the Cincinnati 41. Horton, who had already caught three passes for 36 yards, made a move to the right flat, with Bengals linebacker Leon White covering him, and then cut upfield with White trailing. At about the Cincinnati 10 a perfect Schroeder pass settled over Horton's shoulder and onto his fingertips. Horton juggled it momentarily, but pulled it in and ran untouched into the end zone. That put the Raiders up, 17 – 10, and settled the game, though they added a field goal with just 19 seconds remaining.

The Raiders' euphoria died a painful death the next week in Buffalo. The Bills scored a play-off record of 41 points in the first half and went on to win, 51 – 3. The Bills' hurry-up offense devastated the Raiders, forcing them to call two timeouts in the first half in an effort to regroup. Since their base defense wasn't working, they went to an extra defensive back, but that didn't work, either. Whatever chance the Raiders might have had evaporated on their third series of plays. Under pressure, Schroeder flipped the ball directly to Buffalo linebacker Darryl Talley, who returned it 27 yards for the touchdown that put the Bills ahead, 21 – 3—in only the first quarter! Once again, when Schroeder needed to have a big game he went into a funk, completing just 6 of 18 passes in the first half, 13 of 31 overall. He was intercepted five times, finally giving way to veteran Vince Evans late in the game.

Earlier in the year Davis had been comparing Schroeder to Daryle Lamonica, because the two were similar passers. But Lamonica, confused at the start of his first season with the Raiders, had progressed rapidly during the season and was the league's MVP by the end of it. Schroeder made no such progress, except in fits and starts. Despite all Davis had done to protect him and advance him, Schroeder was the same quarterback at season's end that he was at the start.

Certainly he was capable of some beautiful plays, such as

the pass to Horton in the play-off game against Cincinnati. He was capable of courageous plays; against the San Diego Chargers, when his receiver could not break open on a rollout pattern, he ran for the first down, hitting a tackler head on, instead of going into the quarterback slide, because that was the only way he could get the necessary yardage. He was effective, though, only when he was a part of the offense, not the main gun. He didn't come through often enough with the big plays, and he bombed in the biggest games. Davis may have refuted the critics who thought his system of one-man rule could no longer work, but he had not yet solved his quarterback problem.

• • •

In his sixties, and in good health, Davis had outfought Wayne Valley and outlived Ed McGah, his original partners, to become the sole general partner of the Raiders. His confusing title, president of the general partner, reflects that; the corporation is the general partner, and a new president will be chosen only upon Davis's death—however inconceivable it may seem that there would ever be a Raiders franchise without Al Davis. But what did it all mean?

Davis had beaten the National Football League to move to Los Angeles; he had taken his team to four Super Bowls, winning three of them, and had achieved the best winning record in sports. What was left to prove? Could he continue to focus so narrowly on the goal of winning when he had already won so much? Trying to find the answers to those questions and others, I visited the Raiders practice facility in El Segundo in midseason of 1990.

The image of Los Angeles may be glamour, but there is nothing glamorous about El Segundo, a nondescript town south of the Los Angeles airport. When I stopped for lunch at a coffee shop near the Raiders facility, I overheard a conversation between a waitress and a young woman who said she had come from England on a visit but planned to stay because she liked El Segundo. The waitress laughed. "Everybody else I know is trying to get out of here," she said.

El Segundo means "second" in Spanish, fittingly enough, since the Raiders are very much second to the Rams in Los Angeles (even though the Rams are an Anaheim team), and they are second in the pages of the city's major newspaper, the *Los Angeles Times*. Bill Robertson thought the fact that the Rams had always played in the *Times* charity game accounted for the newspaper's bias. He also felt that, because he was a labor leader, the *Times* was biased against the Raiders, with whom Robertson was linked. "The *Times* is not sympathetic to the labor movement," he noted.

It isn't just the *Times* that is indifferent to the Raiders, though. On a Monday I sat in on Art Shell's weekly meeting with sportwriters. Only three were there.

One of my questions was quickly answered: Davis is as involved as ever with the franchise, from working on the practice field to putting pressure on his coaches when things go wrong. The day before my visit the Raiders had lost to Kansas City, and tension was palpable throughout the building. Shell, who had a notably sunny disposition as a player, was almost surly in his dealings with the other reporters and even in his conversation with me, which did not deal with the frustrations of the loss. I was supposed to meet with my old friend Fred Biletnikoff, but he canceled because of an extra meeting Davis had scheduled—nobody is allowed to relax after a loss.

I had forgotten just how obsessed Davis can be with his silver-and-black color scheme. Those were the only colors used in Shell's office and throughout what I saw of the main building, as well as in the adjoining ticket complex and the building in which Raiders memorabilia are sold. Even the tractors carrying equipment to the field were painted silver. Three rows of stands that obviously dated back to the days when the facility was used by a junior high school had been painted silver, with black stanchions.

When I went out to the field, Al LoCasale was standing there, and his greeting was perfunctory, barely cordial. Lo-Casale and I have had some serious ups and downs. At one time we had been close enough to go out on the town together in New Orleans, before the fourth Super Bowl, but his loyalty to Davis later caused him to curse me many times because of my written criticisms of his boss.

As we talked, though, LoCasale relaxed, speaking first of his family in Alameda and then of the team. "Look at the size of these guys," he said, pointing out offensive tackle James FitzPatrick. "I remember when we thought Art Shell was big, but this guy goes three-thirty. And the speed. If El Segundo were a separate country, they'd have a helluva four-hundred-meter relay team for the Olympics, with Willie Gault, Sam Graddy, Tim Brown, and Mervyn Fernandez."

Our conversation ended abruptly when Davis came out on the field, LoCasale walking away before he could be accused of consorting with the enemy. As I watched Davis striding up and down, barking out commands as always, I couldn't help but reflect on my long association with the man and his team.

Our relationship had run the gamut, and I hoped I could finally view him with some objectivity. Was he an evil man? Not really. Those he had chosen to battle—Wayne Valley, Pete Rozelle, the other NFL owners—were important men with powerful resources, so he could not be accused of taking advantage of weaker men. He could be tough with his players, coaches, and employees, but they had also reaped the rewards of success because of his methods. Reluctantly, I found that I agreed with Durslag: Al Davis's actions in moving the Raiders from Oakland were no more reprehensible than those of other owners, including Bill Bidwill and Robert Irsay, who had moved their teams in the wake of Davis's move.

Once, I had scorned the man. Now, I thought he had lost his way. He had chosen a lonely path as a young man, thinking that was the way to success, but what had his success brought? He was a rich man, but his wealth seemed to afford him little pleasure. He lived alone in an apartment, his wife lived four hundred miles away, and he had scant contact with his son.

The drive that had seemed understandable and even admirable in a young man of thirty-three didn't seem fitting to a man of sixty-one. Most men grow emotionally with age, but Davis's peculiar personality traits had only deepened. If anything, his focus on a football team to the exclusion of everything else had become even more pronounced with age, and he was so insecure that people did not remain his friends if they voiced any criticism. He had a team that was, by his measurement, the most successful in professional sports, but he was living and working in an area that cared little for him or his team. Davis had always talked of "dominating" his environment, but now he was trapped in a second-class setting, and unable to devise a method to escape. A master negotiator, Davis had painted himself into a corner.

My feelings were reinforced when I saw Davis months later at the Bay Area Sports Hall of Fame banquet. Two tables of former Oakland Raiders players were there, and Davis visited with them before the dinner. His former players have an affection for him, because he created an environment in which they could have great success. But more than anything else, the occasion reminded me that the glow of the Raiders years in Oakland cannot be recaptured.

Predictably, when Davis spoke he used the opportunity to promote his own cause. As he talked of the great crowds in Oakland, and the great games, I thought, "You screwed it up, Al. You can't put the genie back in the bottle. You had it all in Oakland, a great team playing in a community that loved you and the team. It was an incomparable experience, but you wanted more, and you got less."

Always be careful what you wish for, because you may get it.

Index

(Teams are referred to by their team name, NOT by their city name [i.e., Raiders, not Oakland Raiders or Los Angeles Raiders]).